DISCERNING THE DIVINE

DISCERNING THE DIVINE
God in Christian Theology

BARRY L. CALLEN

Westminster John Knox Press
LOUISVILLE • LONDON

Book design by Sharon Adams
Cover design by Eric Walljasper, Minneapolis, MN

First edition
Published by Westminster John Knox Press
Louisville, Kentucky

This book is printed on acid-free paper that meets the American National Standards Institute Z39.48 standard. ♾

PRINTED IN THE UNITED STATES OF AMERICA

04 05 06 07 08 09 10 11 12 13 — 10 9 8 7 6 5 4 3 2 1

Library of Congress Cataloging-in-Publication Data

Callen, Barry L.
      Discerning the divine : God through the eyes of Christians / Barry L. Callen.— 1st ed.
         p. cm.
      Includes indexes.
      ISBN 0-664-22752-X (alk. paper)
         1. God. 2. Theology, Doctrinal. I. Title.

BT103.C35 2004
231—dc22

                                                                                    2004050879

Contents

Preface

*F*ew in the ancient world failed to believe in the existence of divine powers that maintained order in this world or disrupted it when and how they chose. The world was assumed to be full of gods and goddesses. Jews tended to be very different, however, because they consciously restricted their belief to one God alone (Deut. 6:4). To most outside observers, the Jews were essentially "atheists," nonbelievers who rejected so much that was commonly assumed to be true. The task that later faced the first Christians, who of course were deeply rooted in the Hebraic believing tradition, was also to address effectively a world of people who took for granted that they had many divine options from which to choose. Early Christian evangelists often were misunderstood and sometimes actively persecuted because of their stubborn "atheism," their refusal to worship the gods who presumably were the sources of the Roman Empire's legitimacy, prosperity, and military successes. Believing is crucial to human life, but determining the proper focus of one's belief is no simple or even safe matter.

This book approaches the world of Christian theology through the lens of its most basic subject, God. Does God exist? How can we know? If God does exist, and we somehow can know it, who does God turn out to be? What is God's nature, intention, and way of relating to us humans and our troubled world? Is God one or many, he or she, distant, near, or somehow both? Is the God of Abraham the same as the Father of Jesus and the Allah of Islam? On these questions hang the issues related to Christian believing, living, and mission.

More than merely posing such basic questions, this book functions as a review of the range of answers that have been offered by Christians across the centuries. Yes, inside the Christian community there are multiple answers, or at least significantly different nuances of the same answer. This book is an introduction to the world of Christian theology in general, including its history and present situation. In these pages the reader will confront the enduring issues related to belief in God, meet key Christian interpreters, be introduced to prominent sources, and be assisted with understanding the often complex ideas and language that frequently isolate Christian believers from the faith's most careful thinking and daring believing. At the heart of it all is belief in the one God who is said to be known best in Jesus Christ. Rooted in the singularity of this God as proclaimed in the Hebrew tradition, Christians also have affirmed vigorously a marvelous and even mystifying multiplicity in relation to the divine singularity (Trinity)—and their affirmation has undergone a long struggle to clarify itself to new generations of believers in ever changing cultural and philosophical settings.

The story of this struggle to understand and proclaim God to the world is told here with a modest level of detail so that it is accessible to those who are not scholars. The hope is that minds will be opened, hearts warmed, and issues clarified, and that God will be known more fully, loved more deeply, and served more faithfully. The challenge always faced, of course, is that we are talking about none other than *God*. Surely, if God really is God, the divine being and life lie beyond the comprehension of our finite minds. Dogmatic arrogance is suspect by definition. On the other hand, as Roger Olson has well said,

> [W]e must avoid using God's incomprehensibility as an excuse for refusing to trace the clues of divine revelation as far as they will take us in understanding God. God is not honored or glorified by lazy thinking about him. He revealed himself so that his human creatures might know him and be transformed by knowing him.[1]

Many theological voices are allowed to speak here, ancient and contemporary, conservative and innovative. While fairness and balance are sought, the author clings to biblical foundations and upholds the enduring significance of the orthodox believing tradition of Christians. Finally, the core of this orthodox tradition is the one God, known best in Jesus Christ, via the Bible, by the Spirit, in the midst of the present. The intent of these pages is to enable a substantial step into Christian theology without saturating the reader with esoteric theory and incomprehensible language. It is hoped that this quest for wisdom concerning God, and thus Christian theology in general, will prove to be devotionally rich and of practical value for the everyday lives of the faithful. Seeing God through Christian eyes is intended to transform life into the image of Jesus for the sake of the redemption of a lost world.

---

1. Roger E. Olson, *The Mosaic of Christian Belief: Twenty Centuries of Unity and Diversity* (Downers Grove, Ill.: InterVarsity Press, 2002), 151.

Chapter 1

Launching the Journey

A right conception of God is basic not only to systematic theology but to practical Christian living as well. It is to worship what the foundation is to the temple; where it is inadequate or out of plumb the whole structure must sooner or later collapse.
—A. W. Tozer, The Knowledge of God

Everything else remains insecure in theology before one has made up one's mind on the doctrine of God.
—quoted in Philip Clayton and Carl E. Braaten,
The Theology of Wolfhart Pannenberg

*T*he above two quotations set the stage quite well. The goal of Christian life is stated simply in Ephesians 3:19: being changed through being filled with the fullness of God. But being filled by and with God requires knowing God and then responding appropriately. Rightly knowing and relating rightly to God is basic to all else, although the challenge of knowing God appears to surpass human ability. Thus, we are faced with the apparent dilemma of needing to know the One who by definition is beyond the feeble reach of unaided human knowing. Who can fully fathom the mystery of God's being or the amazing love of the Divine as seen in Jesus? The human quest and theological task, in short, are to discern the Divine and to be filled and transformed by receiving the fullness of God. Pursuit of this discerning, filling, and transforming is both essential and complex, difficult but not optional for the serious Christian believer.

Until our minds are made up on the question of God, the many other aspects of Christian theology remain insecure and fluid. Our way of thinking and living as Christians reflects directly our conception of and actual relationship to God—even they are not near the surface of our awareness and have not been carefully examined. The theological journey of Christians is influenced significantly by the way the God question is approached, the way God is thought about, and how it is presumed that God relates to the immediate world that the presuming person knows best. In short, what we think it means to be "spiritual" depends on how we think about the "Spirit." Despite the complex theory and specialized language often involved, the journey of theology is a practical one, for "clarity concerning Being (ontology) helps us understand not only who God is but who we are and what kind of world we inhabit."[1] Here is a journey really worth taking.

The Complex God Question

Discerning the Divine adequately is a challenging task, but such discerning is what theology is all about. *Theos* is Greek for "god." *Logos* is Greek for "order, reason, word." Therefore, "theology" (*theos-logos*) is an ordered reasoning about the nature of divinity. Surely God, if really God, is rightly known by humans only as God wishes to be known and enables the knowing. Christians believe that God intentionally, out of love, reveals the divine self. The God who self-reveals, however, is still the One who remains veiled in mystery. In some sense, God is always unseen by humans. The circumstance is much like God's kingdom. We are unable to say exactly where or when it is (Luke 17:21), although it is everywhere at all times. According to the Christian tradition, God, while wonderfully and revealingly present and knowable especially in Jesus, nevertheless is always out of sight and beyond full human comprehension (Job 23:8–9; Ps. 97:2).

Is God the ultimate cause of all that is (Genesis), the ultimate symptom of all that is wrong (Freud), and/or the ultimate cure for the human dilemma (Jung)? Whichever is correct, we regularly hear the dire warning that there is a tragic loss of the centrality of God in today's upbeat churches, a loss that encourages people to transform worship into entertainment, preaching into marketing, believing into technique, being good into feeling good about ourselves, and faithfulness into success. By contrast, it surely is the case that "God does not exist to satisfy human ambitions, cravings, the appetite for consumption, or our own private spiritual interests. . . . God is sovereign in worship; we are not. Our concern must be for God's kingdom, not our own empires, popularity or success."[2] Ironically, with this expression of the loss

---

1. Clark H. Pinnock, *Flame of Love: A Theology of the Holy Spirit* (Downers Grove, Ill.: InterVarsity Press, 1996), 22.

2. From the "Cambridge Declaration," the Alliance of Confessing Evangelicals, Cambridge, Mass., April 20, 1996.

of God comes an assertion of renewed divine "popularity." According to a recent front-page feature in the *Boston Globe*, "From Books to TV, the Lord is Hot!" Hot? Is God the infinite Creator or just a momentary cultural craze fueled by baby boomers now fearful of their own mortality? How easy it is to create a "god" in our own image and use our believing for our own benefit!

Who is the "God" under so much current discussion? Joseph Joubert once said, "It is easy to know God so long as you do not tax yourself with defining Him." Samuel Butler added, "I know not which is more childish—to deny God or to define Him." A key question faces us all. Assuming that God exists, is God to remain relatively undefined and thus left to be whatever one's intuition or imagination or logic or need creates? Or is there a way to approach the gaining of an appropriate "apprehension" (not comprehension) of God, an apprehension adequate at least for the basic demands of our human existence—redemption from sin, right relationships, meaning for life, and a sense of destiny?

Today there clearly is a fresh openness in the public arena to the quest for knowing whatever is real beyond oneself, one's immediate circumstances, and this material and fragile existence of ours. Attitudes toward things "spiritual" have changed considerably in recent generations. Increasingly left behind are the arid and antagonistic religion-science debates. People are open again to the mysterious, paranormal, suprarational, spiritual dimensions of human life. "Holistic" thinking is in vogue. The "God question" is alive and well. Even so, there is real danger afoot, at least from the view of traditional, orthodox Christian believers.[3] The consumer mentality of acquisition-oriented individualism easily capitalizes on honest spiritual questing. The frequent result is a popularity of what is novel and a focusing on what is merely relaxing, fun, and personally satisfying. The assumption too often is that the spiritual quest is about *us*, *our* needs, *our* fulfillment, *our* happiness. But, in fact, according to the Judeo-Christian tradition, a true finding of God

> begins with the act of *God,* continues through the wooing of *God's Spirit,* and issues in the willing submission . . . of the human spirit *to him.* . . . We can understand our human spirituality only in the light of our creatureliness . . . and that of *God's* initiative on our behalf.[4]

So the crucial subject for us humans is God, and the challenge for us is to know the real God and to respond appropriately in light of divine initiative

---

3. See Barry L. Callen, *Authentic Spirituality: Moving Beyond Mere Religion* (Grand Rapids: Baker Academic, 2001).

4. Edith Humphrey, "It's Not about Us," *Christianity Today,* April 2, 2001, 69. Emphasis added.

and for the purpose of our own and the world's renewal as God intends and is willing to enable.

The very word *theology* suggests a "discourse about God." The issue of issues is God. The possibility of enlightened conversation about God rests on the classic Christian affirmations that God *is* and that God graciously chooses *to be present with* and thus to some degree *can be known by* us limited and wayward humans. Accordingly, there is only one arena of questions that is so substantive that it impacts all others. It concerns the existence, nature, and purposes of God. Does God exist? If so, what is God like and what is God up to? How can we know? From the answers given here, one tends to presuppose the essential answers to most other questions related to Christian believing and living. The good news is that God wants to be known! In fact, God "spares no pains to help us understand what he is like and how we may enter into a relationship with him."[5] Encouraged by this truly good news, we can proceed with the theological journey.

Geoffrey Wainwright has said that "where doctrinal differences exist among Christians, it is ultimately the conception of God which is at stake."[6] For example, it has been suggested that the Roman Catholic understanding of the church implies a view of God as irreversibly, exhaustively, and corporeally present in the world; by contrast, the Protestant understanding presumes that God retains sovereignty, mystery, and eternity, revealing and hiding, speaking and being silent, never being dissolved into human words, rituals, or institutions. Whether or not such a suggestion is accurate, clearly there are multiple understandings of God inside the Christian community—let alone outside. For instance, Delwin Brown identifies four ways of "locating" God, each prominent among some Christian theologians of the twentieth century. Each way leads to its own distinctive type of spirituality and style of theological reflection.

> Views of God that focus on [1] God as *Source* move the Christian toward a spirituality of *gratitude,* a mode of life rooted in joyous celebration of the mysterious givenness of life itself. Theology undertaken within this perspective will be mystically inclined. . . . Views of God that emphasize [2] God as *Agent* lend themselves to a spirituality of *guidance.* God's [revealed] will as guide, and obedience to that will, are primary. Theology is an explication of God's will as it pertains to all of life. . . . Where primacy

5. Allan Coppedge, *Portraits of God: A Biblical Theology of Holiness* (Downers Grove, Ill.: InterVarsity Press, 2001), 11.
6. Geoffrey Wainwright, *Doxology: The Praise of God in Worship, Doctrine, and Life* (London: Epworth Press, 1980), 287.

is given to [3] God as *Incarnate*, the form of Christian life that follows may
be called a spirituality of *presence*. . . . Theology will be a tentative exploration of the presence of a deity who is at one with the manifold creation.
Locating [4] God as *Goal* of all things . . . gives rise to a spirituality of *hope*.
. . . Thus, theology will try to be attentive to every discernible movement
toward that future.[7]

Langdon Gilkey was correct in insisting that "questions of the reality of
God and the possibility of language about him are still our most pressing theological problems, prior to all other theological issues."[8] So what is the answer
to the God question? This much is clear. The answer will not come easily or
be lacking in some complexity and controversy. The answer must deal with
the circumstance that, if reflective of the biblical tradition, God is the most
fundamental reality, a reality that cannot finally be reduced to the objective
sentences, abstract ideas, and religious institutions of mere humans. Christian
theology, whatever else it manages to be, always should have an element of
the *apophatic* (see glossary). For instance, as Robert Barron reviews the theistic vision of Thomas Aquinas (1225–1274), God is said to be "simple,"

The Known God Who Is beyond Human Knowing

This inherent, overwhelming hiddenness of God must not be forgotten
as we stand in wonder before his self-disclosure. Only as we remember the depth and darkness of the mystery shall we with sufficient awe
and gratitude receive the revelation. Only thus shall we be possessed
by that fear of the Lord which is the beginning of wisdom. However
well known, the one God, when truly encountered, is confronted as the
mysterium and *tremendum*, never as one comprehensible, clearly
definable, and comfortably familiar.

The wonderful truth is that the God who surpasses our understanding has revealed himself to us, even to our understanding, in many
ways. The "unknown God" is the self-revealed God who can be proclaimed with confidence to all men (cf. Acts 17:23).

—L. Harold DeWolf, *The Case for Theology in Liberal Perspective*

---

7. Delwin Brown, "Locating God for the Twenty-First Century," *Quarterly Review: A Journal of
Theological Resources for Ministry* 22, no. 2 (Summer 2002), 122–23.
8. Langdon Gilkey, *Naming the Whirlwind* (Indianapolis: Bobbs-Merrill, 1969), 104.

"strange" (ever surprising and yet always the same), the One who cannot be fully understood or selfishly controlled.

> The God who comes to us in Jesus Christ, who lifts us up beyond ourselves and moves us to salvation, the God of ecstatic self-offering, the God whose outreach of love is greater than we can think or imagine, is very strange. . . . God is uncanny. Whatever you can say or think or assert concerning God falls infinitely short of who God actually is. Indeed, the best and finally the only response to the divine power is silence, the silence of awe and reverence and hope.[9]

The known God is also the hidden God. All theological affirmations should be couched in sincere humility.

Pursuing questions about God (i.e., doing theology) tends to be a journey tinged with the awareness of the magnitude and ongoing nature of the task. In one sense we are seeking knowledge of the Unknowable One. Augustine is often quoted as once saying, "God is not what you imagine or what you think you understand. If you understand you have failed." He added in his *De Trinitate,* "God is more truly imagined than expressed, and he exists more truly than he is imagined." Granting this difficulty of understanding and expressing in regard to the divine, Christian faith nonetheless affirms a genuine knowledge of the divine, a knowledge based on an intentionally *self-revealing* God. Thus, the Nicene Creed, a classic fourth-century Christian attempt to speak appropriately about God, begins confidently with this:

> We believe in one God,
> the Father, the Almighty,
> maker of heaven and earth,
> of all that is, seen and unseen.

This creed, respected in the Christian community worldwide, dates from long ago. Should its age disqualify it from current use? Is it too old, dating from a time and culture far distant from the "advances" of our own? Or is it too new, since it is removed from the foundations of the earlier biblical revelation by about three centuries? How is this creed surviving as an ancient affirmation when it now is being heard in a time that values the new and is regularly replacing much that is presumed antiquated? Here is a limerick worth pondering, since often there is little distance between the whimsical and the wise:

> Whitehead says God turns over a page,
> And each moment begins a new stage,
>   Grows wiser and older!

---

9. Robert Barron, *Thomas Aquinas: Spiritual Master* (New York: Crossroad, 1996), 61.

> But we need His shoulder,
> And we hope He won't die of old age![10]

The Christian study of God raises many difficult questions. With reference to this limerick, many will ask: Who is Whitehead and what does his or any other philosophy have to do with a Christian understanding of God? How human-like is God? Is the Divine to be associated with certain concepts of growth, aging, and even death (see chapter 7)? Such questions are numerous. Up or down? In or out? Dead or alive? He or she? Free or bound? Determining or risking an "open" future? One or triune—or both? These and other crucial questions about God have dominated the complex world of Christian theology across the generations and certainly are doing so today. All theology is finally rooted in some concept of the God with whom humans have to deal and from whom our perspectives on all else are shaped. But who is God? And how should Christian believers go about determining the answer to this most central of all questions?

The testimonies of prominent Christian theologians in recent generations have been passionate about the subject of God. They also have been all over the map in their theistic perspectives! Assuming that God does not change, at least not in existence and essential nature, it is clear that at least those who think seriously about God have themselves been in considerable motion. This theological changeableness has been confusing and sometimes even alarming to many Christian believers. Malcolm Muggeridge once asked, somewhat cynically, "Could God pass an examination in Theology?" Even more cynically, Ambrose Bierce has defined the noun *religion* this way in his *Devil's Dictionary*: "A daughter of Hope and Fear, explaining to Ignorance the nature of the Unknowable." Is belief in God really that fickle, self-serving, and finally impossible? Does Christian theology become so sophisticated an endeavor that even God might fail an exam on the subject?

We begin with such potential negatives in mind, but nonetheless on a much more positive note. There is a series of connected affirmations that can open humans to the possibility that God really is—and is the God who is biblically revealed. Philosopher-theologian David Elton Trueblood writes wisely:

> If God really is and if we can know it, that is wonderful news indeed! It means that we are not alone; that there is power beyond ourselves waiting to back us up; that the earth's decay is not the end of the story; that the running

10. Credited to Rob L. Staples, a longtime professor at Nazarene Theological Seminary in Kansas City, Missouri. See his book *The Church out on a Limerick* (Kansas City, Mo.: Beacon Hill Press of Kansas City, 2000). "Whitehead" refers to Alfred North Whitehead, who had great impact on contemporary Christian theology, especially process theology.

down of the universe is not final. It means that what is highest in value is deepest in nature, that the things which matter most are not at the mercy of those which matter least.[11]

The Jewish-Christian believing tradition affirms that there is such wonderful news about a God who is prior to all else, foundational to all of value, and eternal beyond all that decays and finally dies. Theology is a discipline that seeks to probe the past and present meanings and implications of this really good news that roots in Abraham, flowers in Jesus the Christ, and flows by the Spirit of Christ to every person and present moment.

The Task of Christian Theology

If theology is centered in disciplined thoughts about God or the considered results of the pursuit of wisdom concerning God, it is obvious that such a discipline engages in a most crucial and difficult task. Humans are so ill-equipped for such an enterprise. There is clear need for divine self-disclosure—that is, revelation. To gain any adequate wisdom about the Divine, surely God must enable humans to know through some initiative that encounters and enlightens our quest for knowing. We can make true statements about God—especially about the distinctive complexity of what Christians affirm as the *triune* God—only on the basis of an actual presence with us of the self-revealing and redeeming God who is reflected in the person of Jesus and made understandably and practically alive for us in the ongoing work of the Holy Spirit. God is revealed only as God reveals. The divine Spirit is known only as the Spirit enables such knowing.

But even with the revealed divine presence believed by Christians to be narrated primarily through the biblical witness to God in Christ, theology remains a work largely of human construction. We who do the building are only pilgrims whose views are never beyond the need of some reform. We proclaim truth and at the same time search for it. We doubt even while we believe. Comprehension of God is beyond us humans; an adequate apprehension, however, is believed to be possible because of divine grace, especially when we choose to participate in the life of that which we pursue.[12] As Catherine Mowry LaCugna summarizes:

---

11. David Elton Trueblood, *Philosophy of Religion* (New York: Harper & Row, 1957), 84.

12. Kierkegaard, for example, insisted that religious truth cannot be engaged effectively from the posture of a presumed disinterested neutrality. Truth yields to passion and commitment, not to passivity and

Theological statements are possible, not because we have some independent insight into God or can speak from the standpoint of God, but because God has freely revealed and communicated God's self, God's personal existence, God's infinite mystery. Christians believe that God bestows the fullness of divine life in the person of Jesus Christ, and that through the person of Christ and the action of the Holy Spirit we are made intimate partakers of the living God.[13]

Christian theology, then, involves the encountered reality of God that is available to us by divine initiative, especially in Jesus. It seeks to translate this living reality into concepts and language that are both fair to the inexpressible, unmanageable reality of God and meaningful to those who now receive and consider such witnessing, thinking, and speaking.

Translating revealed divine reality into effective contemporary communication is demanding and hazardous work, but it is not optional (if one takes mission seriously) and never completed (missional settings are always dynamic and changing). Doing theology necessarily proceeds in a given cultural context, so language is a perennial challenge in expressing insights about God. As one theologian put it, "The unfathomable mystery of God is always mediated through shifting historical discourse. . . . Words about God are cultural creatures, entwined with the mores and adventures of the faith community that uses them. As cultures shift, so too does the specificity of God-talk."[14]

In light of the divine mystery and cultural reality of human language, Clark Pinnock's advice is well taken: "It would be helpful if we discussed matters as seekers after truth rather than as gatekeepers obsessed by who is in and who is out of the evangelical movement."[15] Humility is always appropriate. The theological process should proceed in a spirit of love. In 2002 a group of Christian leaders, myself included, issued a statement called "The Word Made Fresh: A Call for Renewal of the Evangelical Spirit." One of its key sentences read, "To be evangelical entails being characterized by an irenic, Christlike spirit of love toward those with whom we disagree and a cautious openness to the reform of tradition as the Spirit leads us to fresh understandings of the Word that are even more faithful to the entirety of God's revelation."

---

rational abstraction. See Barry L. Callen, *Radical Christianity: The Believers Church Tradition in Christianity's History and Future* (Nappanee, Ind.: Evangel Publishing House, 1999).

13. Catherine Mowry LaCugna, *God for Us: The Trinity and Christian Life* (San Francisco: HarperSanFrancisco, 1991), 3.

14. Elizabeth A. Johnson, *She Who Is* (New York: Crossroad, 1993), 6.

15. Clark H. Pinnock, *Most Moved Mover* (Grand Rapids: Baker Academic, 2001), xii.

What is the current culture of at least most of Europe and North America? It is, of course, complex, debatable, and always changing in particulars. Even so, the following tries to point to key elements of what is being called the "postmodern" sensibilities of most contemporary people. These are perspectives and issues that are impacting greatly the doing of Christian theology in our time. They include:

> a greater appreciation of nature, linked with a chastened admiration for technology; the recognition of the importance of language . . . in human existence; the acceptance of the challenge that other religious options present to the Judeo-Christian tradition; a sense of the displacement of the white, Western male and the rise of those dispossessed because of gender, race, or class; an apocalyptic sensibility, fueled in part by the awareness that we exist between two holocausts, the Jewish and the nuclear; and . . . a growing appreciation of the thoroughgoing, radical interdependence of life at all levels and in every imaginable way.[16]

Effective thinking and speaking about God today requires deep biblical roots and creative interaction with such cultural realities. We will begin in these pages by entering the conversation in the contemporary context (chapter 2). Then we will review the biblical foundations that the conversation partners claim as basic but read differently (chapter 3).

Here are some of the pressing questions today. Are these postmodern issues the ones that should be informing our current theistic quest and tempering our language about God? If not, which ones should be? What about the One who *is* eternally, the One *truly other* than ourselves? Is there such a One? If so, how can we know? If there is such a One who can be known, is this One primarily *other* and distant or also *truly present,* actually in real relationship with our human experience or standing substantially apart from it? If God has drawn near, how can we understand and participate in this nearness without presuming to be able to fully comprehend or selfishly manage the Divine? If God is near, is the nearness equally available to all people (even those who have never heard of Jesus) and is the nearness a "risk" to God—that is, does God actually *suffer* and somehow *change* because of interacting with the contingencies of human existence? How do we respond to the criticisms which claim that Christian theism (God belief) is primarily projective in nature (critics: Feuerbach, Freud),[17] patriarchal and sexist in function (critics: feminists), static (critics: process thought), and/or arid, ideological, and socially irrele-

---

16. Sallie McFague, *Models of God* (Philadelphia: Fortress Press, 1987), x.
17. The little book by J. B. Phillips titled *Your God Is Too Small* explores and explodes many common

vant (critics: liberation theology)? How "locked in" are we to the particular perspectives of our given times and places? Can we be both rooted biblically and relevant socially?

Some of the common questions now being faced by serious Christian believers sound more like subtle accusations than mere questions. Does traditional Christian believing about God inhibit the full development of healthy human beings, predetermine the fate of individuals, fail in its maleness to save women, justify the powerful at the expense of the oppressed, and lose credibility altogether after the horrors of the Nazi Holocaust? In response, Catherine LaCugna makes an important point. All such criticisms and probing questions call for renewed focus on the *saving story* that lies at the root of Christian theism. Rather than metaphysical speculations about the eternal being of God being carried on in isolation from the saving work of God among us (a frequently suggested weakness of "classical" Christian theism), Christian theology should "start afresh from its original basis in *the experience* of being saved by God through Christ in the power of the Holy Spirit." This suggests that all authentic Christian theology is to be Trinitarian (see chapter 10). So "Christian theology must begin from the premise that, because the mystery of God is revealed in the mystery of salvation, statements about the nature of God must be rooted in the reality of salvation history."[18] The mystery of God and the mystery of salvation are inseparable. The doctrine of the Trinity (see glossary) seeks to hold them in careful balance.

Sometimes wisdom is conveyed effectively in what appears on the surface as lighthearted jest. For example, I once saw a cartoon featuring a young boy asking an older man, "How did the Israelites cross the Red Sea and escape Pharaoh's army?" The man's cynical but serious answer was, "Son, Moses was smart enough to know where the sandbars were!" While I do not share this man's antimiracle cynicism, I find his imagery suggestive for picturing the task of this book. As Christian believers today seek to cross the turbulent Red Seas of the theological enterprise, how are we going to get across safely? Is it a matter of the special knowledge of a charismatic leader (the latest theological Moses)? Dare we risk the depths beyond ourselves where only the mystery of God can part the waters? Are there "tricks" to the theological trade that secretly help along the privileged few?

How can we mere humans distinguish between real progress and a deceptive fad (sandbar) on which some theologians walk momentarily? How can

---

projections of God in an attempt to address the big problem, namely, that many people have not yet found a God big enough for their modern needs.

18. LaCugna, *God for Us,* 3–4. Emphasis added.

Christians think about God rightly and meaningfully in the context of our times without God being limited to the issues and agendas of these times? Who is God and what is God's relationship to creeds of the distant past, to present social and intellectual crises, and to future destiny? Looking at the long tradition of Christian teaching, we now can see that what have functioned as solid and saving foundations for some (orthodoxy) have for others been judged pools of quicksand to be avoided before it is too late (heresy). While the subject of God is of ultimate importance, the way through the theological wilderness sometimes seems blurred by shifting and even sinking sand. Whatever the difficulties, however, this is a journey of ultimate importance that needs to be taken.

The Paths Being Followed

The task of this book is to discern the Divine through the eyes of Christians. We will (1) follow the paths of Christian theology as they seek to recall the biblical witness about God, (2) reconsider the various emphases about God affirmed by Christians in the distant and recent past, and then (3) affirm saving knowledge of God in appropriate and relevant language. On the one hand, God has been self-revealing and graciously self-giving. On the other hand, Christians have sought in various ways and with different results to understand and respond appropriately to this divine revealing and giving. The biblical story has been consistently affirmed as basic, but in changing times the Bible has been read and applied in widely divergent ways. Has God changed, or have the biblical readers changed, or both? In what sense is God on a journey, and in what sense are we? Are definitive maps available for the adventure of faith?

In the changing Christian theologies of the past, God has taken quite a ride! Put more properly, our human understandings of God have seemed at times to be all over the map of possibilities. We may have been off track at times, but surely God has not gotten lost! God is faithful and patient, venturing with those whom he has chosen to be a special treasure, a royal priesthood, a holy nation (Exod. 19:6; 1 Pet. 2:9). From the perspective of those selected by divine grace, the challenge is to know God rightly and follow God faithfully. Such knowing and following are the interrelated tasks now at hand.

Admittedly, there are dangers on every hand. Rationalism reduces God to an axiom of logic, almost an object for the exploration of reason. At the other extreme, mysticism sees God as absolute mystery before whom we humans can only stand in awe and wonder—our reason being of little value. The study of God, to be in careful balance, appears to require a manner of understanding that goes beyond data gathering, logical deduction, and careful organization of relevant biblical texts. Required also is a knowing from the heart that seeks to make the knower "wise unto salvation" (2 Tim. 3:15 KJV).[19] Reasoning is important, but finally it is inadequate in reference to knowing God. Revelation is essential for any adequate knowing. In turn, knowing based on revelation is dependent in significant part on faithful discipleship. To not love is to not know (1 John 4:8).

Solid ground and sinking sand sometimes look much the same on the surface. Despite any and all difficulties, these pages affirm that God is and is available to be approached, glimpsed, enjoyed, and joined. A. W. Tozer and Wolfhart Pannenberg surely are right (see their quotations heading this chapter). A right conception of God is crucial for the whole range of Christian believing and living. But how do Christians dependably distinguish between reality and illusion when it comes to who God really is? Theology seeks to identify an answer as it approaches discerning the Divine, understanding the God who finally is beyond complete human understanding.

A wise saying among the church fathers of long ago was *Deus semper maior* ("God is always greater"). Only God can define God. Even in the light of divine revelation, God remains awesome and mysterious. Meaning, however, does shine through the mystery as believers remember in faith, are guided by Scripture, and live faithfully, nurtured by God's love (Gal. 5:6). The incarnation of God in Christ means that the ineffable God has exposed the face of the divine, a gripping face with a firm and loving smile. Knowing this God must be from "the inside" and be characterized with the humor of humility.

In this book, we will trace a series of Christian theological attempts to accomplish the difficult task of truly knowing God, always seeking to honor the cautions inherent in studying God. Because theological language is not readily known to many readers, at the end of the book there is a glossary of concepts and terms related to Christian theism. Recognizing that one of the major developments in Christian theology in the last hundred years is the resurgence of Trinitarian thought about God,[20] and because such thought is so basic to the distinctively Christian understanding of God, this thought is given appropriate attention (chapter 10).

To seek knowledge about God is to set out on quite an adventure, a critical

---

19. See Callen, *Authentic Spirituality*, chapter 5, "Truly Knowing: The Spirit's Eyes."

20. See Stanley J. Grenz, *The Social God and the Relational Self: A Trinitarian Theology of the Imago Dei* (Louisville, Ky.: Westminster John Knox Press, 2001), chapter 1.

Theological Rules for the Road

Pursuing knowledge of God is aided by following the unusual "rules" of seeing, dancing, *and* smiling.

Seeing from the Inside

Anyone who seeks to understand the living God celebrated in Christian worship must be willing to enter into the sphere in which praise, intercession, and supplication are taken seriously. One cannot merely stand outside the vestibule and expect to know what is happening inside from reading about it. If the Christian life can only be known from within, then the study of God is a subject that requires entry, engagement, and concrete participation in the worshiping community.

Dancing with the Church

Learning to study God is like learning to dance; it cannot be done merely by reading books. One cannot dance without practice, without allowing the muscles to move and the neural synapses to respond. To learn to dance one must dance, even if badly. Good theology is more than a tome or a string of good sentences. It is a way of dancing, an embodied activity of the human spirit in a community embodying life in Christ.

Smiling While You Study

The healthier the study of God, the more candid it remains about its own finitude, the stubborn limits of its own knowing, its own charades, Band-Aids, closets, masks, and broken windows. That is why the study of God is best understood from within a caring community that laughs a little at its own somber efforts.

—Thomas Oden, *The Living God*

journey that in Christian church history often has been volatile and controversial, to say the least. Assumed here is the simple thesis that God is who God is quite apart from our fragile human perceptions of divinity. Further, retracing the meandering route followed by Christian believers over the centuries in their search for God is surely to gain wisdom for the journey still ahead. There are no more important or difficult questions facing humans than: Who is God? How do we know? What are the implications of God-knowledge for life today and for the future yet to be? We begin the adventure by listening to the theistic discussion now in progress (chapter 2). Then we will be better positioned to remember how we got to this point (chapters 3–9) and where the long theological path had led and still leads (chapter 10).

Chapter 2

Related but Not Diminished

Scripture does not use abstract, non-relational and negative terms such as "infinite" (not finite), "impassible" (not emotional) or even "immutable" (not changeable) to reveal God's nature. These words are not only nonbiblical, but they easily distract us from the personal, positive and relational terms central in Scripture.
—C. Leonard Allen and Danny Gray Swick,
Participating in God's Life

"Openness" theologians, please take as full an account of the biblical language about God's foreknowledge and immutability as of the Greek philosophical influences that shaped classical theism. . . . "Classical" theists, please return to a more robustly biblical approach to talking about God. . . . The biblical revelation, and not a suspect theological traditionalism, must be the starting point for fresh theological reflection in every generation.
—*Editorial*, Christianity Today, *February 7, 2000*[1]

*T*his chapter's title and the two quotations above introduce the reader to key and vigorously contested issues of contemporary Christian theism. A vital term often at issue is "related." As biblically revealed, God chooses to relate actively to creation, in fact, is known primarily through the fact of and character of this relating. Therefore, God is described by use of select metaphors reflecting such involvement (see the first quote above). Through divine activity in the fallen creation, people are said to be contacted by God, and thus

1. This prominent evangelical periodical has given considerable attention to "openness theology." For example, see the issues of May 21 and June 11, 2001, for a two-part "debate" on the subject by Christopher A. Hall and John Sanders, presented under the title "Does God Know Our Next Move?" More recently, the exchanges between these two theologians have appeared in book form as *Does God Have a Future?* (Grand Rapids: Baker Academic, 2003).

God can become known—at least to the extent that mere humans can ever know God.

Christian tradition has proclaimed that God is known first and foremost as an agent, who is intentionally and self-revealingly active in the creation. But how does God relate? Why is there divine relating? What is revealed? How "risky" to God is such relating (if at all)? What resulting picture of God's nature and will emerges? Why are some prominent Christians today more theologically comfortable singing "Immortal, Invisible, God Only Wise" than the more relational "Sweet Hour of Prayer" or "In the Garden"? Is there an inherent problem in affirming both God's absolute sovereignty and God's loving-kindness, God's powerful distance and tender nearness? Responding to these and similar relational questions opens wide the field of Christian theism, especially as it has been pursued recently. In fact, "openness" is a key issue. How "open" is God to the creation? Is God vulnerable to suffering because of chosen involvement with the evil of our world? Is God open to the possibility of humans choosing against the divine will, or are all human choices predetermined and carefully controlled by God? Can God relate lovingly to the world and not be diminished in the process? If God was really in Jesus, did the crucifixion of Jesus not represent genuine loss to God? If God is diminished in any way, is God still really God?

Theological Renewal and Nervousness

While humans surely are in no position to diminish God, *we* certainly can be diminished by our inadequate views of God and our improper responses to the divine relating. Traditional Christian teaching has insisted that a proper understanding of God is intended by God to impact in particular ways who we are, what we understand, and what we do as humans. John Wesley, for instance, devoted more attention to the subject of God's nature than to God's existence. His key concern was that distorted views of the Divine inevitably contaminate the formation of Christian believers. Thus, Wesley's theology may be called "practical" in the sense that its primary intention is "nurturing and shaping the worldview that frames the temperament and practice of believers' lives in the world."[2] Christian theism is not to be merely an arid study of metaphysical abstractions, although careful thought and well-chosen language will make an important difference; it also and essentially is to be a

---

2. Randy L. Maddox, *Responsible Grace: John Wesley's Practical Theology* (Nashville: Kingswood Books, 1994), 17.

life participation in the presence and ongoing work of God. Somehow, participating and knowing are necessarily and intimately linked when it comes to knowing God.

The Christian doctrine of God is a dynamic and sometimes vigorously contested theological arena today. The current debate often focuses around "open" theism and touches on subjects crucial in the quest to *know* and *be* as true Christians. At issue is nothing less than our human understanding of the nature and working of God, and thus of who we as humans are expected to be. This debate "has everything to do with the God whom we trust, follow, honor, and obey. It has everything to do with whether he is worthy of our uncontested reliance, our unqualified devotion, and our unreserved worship. It affects the whole picture of who God is and what life in his presence is all about."[3] Assuming that to be worthy of human worship God must be infinitely great, immeasurable in majesty, glory, and power, do all such descriptions of the Divine eliminate understanding God as also near, involved, self-limiting, caring, sacrificing, even suffering? Unlimited greatness seems to imply self-sufficiency and independence, while loving compassion seems to imply a God-creation relationship, a reciprocity, a real interdependence. Often this tension is broken in ways that violate the Christian consensus over the centuries that somehow God is at once *transcendent* and *immanent* (see glossary).

If God is intensely and even vulnerably related to the human scene, as

---

The Biblical View of a Beautiful God

Christian theology has to do less with *whether* God is and more with *who* God is. Theology "ought to be beautiful because its subject is so beautiful." Atheism is partly the outcome of bad theology. Good theology focuses on the biblically revealed God with whom one can fall in love. This God is "social Trinity," God known as "beautiful and supremely lovable," the Trinity who is "not static or standoffish but a loving relationality and sheer liveliness . . . who does not alienate but fulfills us. . . . What we see most centrally in God is the shining radiance of love. . . . Augustine exclaimed, 'Too late did I love thee, O Fairness, so ancient yet so new'" (*Confessions* 10.27).

—Quotations from Clark Pinnock, *Flame of Love*

---

3. Bruce A. Ware, *God's Lesser Glory: The Diminished God of Open Theism* (Wheaton, Ill.: Crossway Books, 2000), 9–10.

"open" theists affirm as the biblical view, is God thereby enhanced or diminished as the God worthy of unreserved worship? If, on the other hand, God is viewed primarily as sovereign and majestic in ways that include God being unchanging and in full control of all things, are we dealing with a suspect theological traditionalism that reduces God to less than the relating, loving, and self-giving One revealed in Scripture, and thus One who is hardly worthy of our unreserved worship? The theistic questions are basic, vitally important, and are currently undergoing careful and sometimes contentious review.

There is much theological energy and nervousness among evangelical Christian theologians these days. Some perspective is necessary in order to understand the source of the nervousness. Help comes from an awareness of the recent history of the doctrine of God as handled quite differently by a range of Christian theologians. Particularly chapters 5 through 9 of this book seek to offer this historical review. But first come chapters 3 and 4, which explore the biblical base of Hebrew/Christian theism, the base typically appealed to by most theologians, and the "classical" formulation of theistic doctrine that developed in the first centuries of Christian church history. This formulation is now vigorously defended by some Christian leaders, while aspects of it are criticized sharply by others.

Are biblical theism and classical Christian theism essentially the same thing, with the latter only formalizing the former in creedal terms? Or are the classical formulations of the fourth century burdened with cultural accommodations to an ancient philosophy that is at odds with important biblical assumptions and not compatible with contemporary philosophical views held by Christians and non-Christians alike? Is the traditional Christian claim that God is *impassible* (see glossary) a reflection of basic biblical teaching, or more an echo of ancient Platonic thought? Is it more appropriate to refer to God and God's work in the world in formal, legal, courtroom terms (as Anselm and John Calvin did), or in family metaphors such as the creative-love theism that sees God as the interrelating Trinity who overflows in love (1 John 4:8; Eph. 3:17–18)?[4] Evangelical theology is still dominated by Calvinists who are suspicious of dynamic and relational descriptions of God, but in recent years they have lost control over the terms and boundaries of the discussion, sometimes having to yield the floor to others "who want to make their tradition less deterministic, less forensic, more open to pluralism and spiritual experience, and, especially, more open to the biblical picture of God

---

4. See Clark H. Pinnock and Robert C. Brow, *Unbounded Love: A Good News Theology for the 21st Century* (Downers Grove, Ill.: InterVarsity Press, 1994).

as relational, vulnerable, and personally affected by the world."[5] Of course, truth does not necessarily lie with who is controlling the current discussion, but any shift in control newly focuses the issues.

As the following chapters of historical review seek to make clear, there have been many dramatic shifts in Christian thought about God in recent generations. Evangelicals today are understandably anxious to reanchor this most foundational of all Christian doctrines. One approach is called "open theism," aspects of which have become a theological lightning rod for "the most heated controversy to hit evangelicalism since the inerrancy debate of the 1970s."[6] The Bible is commonly accepted as foundational, but how it is read varies significantly when it comes to the doctrine of God.

Vigorous opposition to open theism (sometimes critiqued as "neo-theism") has come from several prominent evangelicals, including Robert Morey, who refers to the "open" view of God as "finite godism."[7] Norman Geisler says that it is a "serious mutation in the direction of panentheism (all in God) or process theology" (see glossary). Rather than a wise correction of classic theism resulting from a more balanced reading of Scripture, he says it is the "dangerous trend within evangelical circles of creating God in man's image. . . . If the logical consequences of neo-theists' unorthodox beliefs about God are drawn out, they will be pushed more and more in the direction of process theology and the liberal beliefs entailed therein."[8] The "disastrous" consequence for evangelical Christianity presumably will be this: "Neotheism leads logically to a form of process theology in which God has two poles, is changing, limited, and not in sovereign control of the world."[9] Such a doctrinal domino effect is genuinely feared as both likely and very wrong. Open theists recognize this danger and have sought to clarify the lines of distinction.

Fear abounds in some Christian quarters that Christian open theists are teaching an intolerable limitation of divine sovereignty. One prominent evangelical

5. Gary Dorrien, *The Remaking of Evangelical Theology* (Louisville, Ky.: Westminster John Knox Press, 1998), 182.

6. James Beilby and Paul Eddy, eds., *Divine Foreknowledge: Four Views* (Downers Grove, Ill.: InterVarsity Press, 2001), 9. A particular lightning rod is the discussion about divine "foreknowledge." If God is all-knowing, does that knowing include all aspects of the future, even decisions of "free-will" humans that have not yet been made? Are humans really free to choose? If God knows in advance, does that necessarily mean that God determines the choices—thus, meaning that there is no real freedom? These are a few of the frequent questions at the heart of the current debate.

7. Robert Morey, *Battle of the Gods: The Gathering Storm in Modern Evangelicalism* (Southbridge, Mass.: Crown, 1989).

8. Norman Geisler, *Creating God in the Image of Man?* (Minneapolis: Bethany House, 1997), 11–12, 47, 145. He says that *panentheism* means "all in God." It is "the result of a mixed marriage between theism (God created all) and pantheism (all is God)" (47).

9. Ibid., 145.

theologian cautions that (1) biblical undergirding for such theism is questionable, (2) the critique of classical theism based on its presumed unfortunate subservience to Greek (nonbiblical) thinking may well be overdrawn, and (3) such theism may itself be more subservient to a contemporary (nonbiblical) mindset than its proponents admit or realize.[10] D. A. Carson sees in too many contemporary writers the desire "to emphasize God's personhood while dismissing his absoluteness." He is convinced that stressing divine relatedness leads to divine diminishment. Process theology, for example, argues that "God may be personal, but is certainly mutable and changing, himself (or itself) in process."[11] Carson identifies Clark Pinnock as a "traditional evangelical" who is being tempted into similar process views of God, although Carson recognizes rightly that Pinnock carefully distinguishes himself from many process theologians. Pinnock's strong biblical commitment leads him to insist that God created the universe and remains sovereignly free in relation to it. As an act of this freedom, God chooses certain relationships that are natural expressions of the divine essence.[12] God relates lovingly, sovereignly, but openly and dynamically, even vulnerably, and is *not* diminished in the process, since such relating is a natural reflection of who God eternally is.

Today there is an active and influential critique by some committed Christians of elements of classic Christian theism. It comes from Clark Pinnock, John Sanders, Clark Williamson, and numerous others. There also is strong resistance to this critique. It comes from Robert Morey, Millard Erickson, and numerous others. Clarity is crucial here. The search is on for what constitutes biblical faithfulness in regard to the doctrine of God. Open theists are both affirming and critiquing various elements of both orthodox Christian theism and contemporary process theology. With reference to Christian process thinkers, Pinnock observes approvingly that they put high priority on the love of God, hold a dynamic understanding of the world and God's interactions with it, and reject the notion that God is an "absolute" being in the sense that the Divine is unaffected by the world. On the negative side, he and other open theists

> repudiate the [process] view that God does not exist apart from a world. . . .
> They have great difficulty accepting a source of creaturely power other than
> God, with the implication that God cannot override it, even if God chooses.
> For God not to be able to do so . . . creates problems in the realm of miracles

10. Millard J. Erickson, *The Evangelical Left* (Grand Rapids: Baker Books, 1997), 104–7. A counter to Erickson's view is Gregory A. Boyd, *God of the Possible: A Biblical Introduction to the Open View of God* (Grand Rapids: Baker Books, 2000).

11. D. A. Carson, *The Gagging of God: Christianity Confronts Pluralism* (Grand Rapids: Zondervan Publishing House, 1996), 225.

12. For a good study of the tension between process and evangelical views of God, see John B. Cobb Jr. and Clark H. Pinnock, eds., *Searching for an Adequate God* (Grand Rapids: Eerdmans, 2000).

such as incarnation and resurrection and raises difficulties for the understanding of petitionary prayer. They [open theists] think that, if God were tied in a metaphysical way to influencing the world and being influenced by the world in the uniform ways process dictates, this would diminish the freedom of God.[13]

Despite such clear distinctions by Pinnock and his biblical-conservative instincts, the March 5, 2001, issue of *Christianity Today* ran an interview with Royce Gruenler titled "God at Risk" in which Gruenler expressed significant concern that "openness" theologians such as Clark Pinnock, John Sanders, and Gregory Boyd are really "Pelagian," hold only an "aesthetic" view of atonement, deny that there is real biblical prophecy, bypass the "biblical" definition of human freedom, and affirm a God who is not able to be "very helpful." Six of these openness theologians responded in the April 23, 2001, issue of the same periodical under the title "Truth at Risk." They insisted that Gruenler had seriously misrepresented their views and were distressed "to see these misconceptions disseminated in the Christian community." Is God so diminished by the "open" view that really being able to help us fallen humans now lies outside divine ability? No, not at all, they insisted: "God has all the wisdom and power necessary to help us—God can heal, guide, teach, and love us. . . . Gruenler's criticism presupposes that only a God who controls every detail—including our own decisions—can help us."

So the issues of Christian theism are very basic to the practical life of faith and very much contested today. What can and should we humans know about God's being and ways of working? After all these centuries of the Christian believing tradition, why is there still so much division on that which is most basic to the faith—that is, exactly who God is and how God relates to us humans? Part of the answer lies in different readings of the biblical revelation (see chapter 3). It often is said that such different readings are stimulated by the impact on Christian Bible readers of differing philosophical traditions and social circumstances (see chapters 4 through 9). Whatever the case, clarity is needed for the well-being of individual faith and church mission. The search continues for how best to be properly "traditional" and adequately "open."

The "Deeply Moved First Mover"

To enter the arena of Christian theistic exploration through the contemporary door is to encounter the issue of the nature and extent of divine relatedness to

---

13. Pinnock, in Cobb and Pinnock, *Searching for an Adequate God*, x.

The "Classical" and "Open" Options

	Classical Theism	Open Theism
1. Essential nature of God and central metaphors used for God	Fully sovereign over creation; emphasis on unchangeability; divine plans unaffected by the creation, including by people. *The Creator, Judge, King.*	Fully sovereign over creation; emphasis on relationality; divine plans dynamic in relation to the decisions of the creation, especially people. *The Lover, Savior, Responsive Friend.*
2. Nature of the human freedom granted by God and the nature of divine-human interaction	Compatibilistic freedom—humans are free only to do as God determines; thus, human actions are always compatible with the divine will. God predestines, controls, and takes no "risks."	Incompatibilistic or libertarian freedom—humans are given a freedom of choice that allows the frustration of even the divine will (at least within the range of the granted freedom). God's love requires "risks" of human rejection of the divine will.
3. Foreknowledge, salvation, and prayer	The future is completely definite and fully known in advance by God. Humans are saved only as God has determined. Human prayer never changes God, but is a means of bringing about what has been previously ordained.	Except for a few things that God has determined definitely will be, the future is open. God chooses to partner with humans to implement the divine will. Prayer may influence God—some divine actions, by divine choice, depend on human prayer.

creation. Clark Pinnock's phrase "deeply moved first mover" is a deliberate juxtaposing of typically opposite streams of Christian thought, each reflecting a different philosophical environment. One tradition, represented by Augustine and reflecting Aristotle, thinks of God as the "first mover," with God himself impacting but not being impacted by relationship with the creation. Another and currently emphasized tradition—represented by Pinnock and reflecting aspects of current process thought—gladly affirms the firstness of God's relating action but also views God as compassionate in a way that finds God himself deeply and continuously moved in the midst of the divine moving.[14]

If God is now very present to humanity and is present with us and known by us particularly in our suffering and experiences of marginalization (as chapters 8 and 9 explore), is God still really God in the fullest sense? Do actual presence on the human scene, intense divine empathy with sinners, and suffering over our sin not somehow diminish the transcendent creator God or even lead to God's "death" (see chapter 7)? Clark Pinnock, Gregory Boyd, John Sanders, and others sometimes are accused of encouraging a diminished concept of the Divine with their critique of classical Christian theism (described in chapter 4), but Pinnock insists that the real diminishment comes from elsewhere. Speaking of his own "free-will theism" as a careful middle position between the ancient "classical" and the current "process" positions, he explains:

> It means that we affirm God as creator of the world as classical theism does and process thought does not, and also affirm the openness of God as process theology does and classical theism does not sufficiently. This leaves us with a model of the divine which sees God as transcendent over the world and yet existing in an open and mutually affecting relationship with the world. It is a doctrine of God which maintains mutuality and reciprocity within the framework of divine transcendence.[15]

Remaining a biblically oriented evangelical theologian, Pinnock does not want to be so extreme in his critique of classical Christian theism that he falls into the even more significant errors of radical liberal (see chapters 5 through 7) or popular process views of God.

The process view of God is judged by evangelicals like Pinnock to be an extreme correction to classical theism that so honors the freedom instinct of modernity that God's very being is fundamentally compromised. This reduction is said to lead to an intolerably feeble theism clearly inferior to the God of biblical witness and evangelical experience.[16] Although God is viewed as loving, responsive, and vulnerable to the grief caused by human sin, Pinnock readily agrees with the classical insistence that the first Christian affirmation should be that God *is* even if the world is not, and God *will be* even when eventually the world ceases to be. The divine "vulnerability" is to be seen as God's love-motivated free choice, not in any way a "limitation" of God's sovereign being.

Thomas F. Torrance of Scotland affirms that God, in his greatness and out of his goodness, freely chooses to be God for the world in such a way that he allows himself to be affected by the world. Here is the hard question. Does it detract from God's greatness for God to be thought of as voluntarily undergoing change, change of the kind that does not affect God's existence or essence? I think it does not, agreeing with the Dutch theologian Hendrikus Berkhof, who speaks of God's "changeable faithfulness" in the midst of God's covenant partnership with humanity.

This emphasis of God's ability for free choice is crucial. God, if truly God, surely is constant in both his existence and essence while never being captive to anything other than his own nature—which is really not captivity but freedom itself. Since the 1970s, the debate has raged over whether or not conservative Christian theology has itself inadvertently bound God inside a set of philosophically conceived "perfections" that diminish a proper biblical understanding of the God who freely, lovingly, and vulnerably relates, interacts, and responds. In the 1970s Pinnock first took up the task of renewing evangelical theology, in part by reconceiving the doctrine of God, "liberating" it from certain rationalistic strictures judged nonbiblical in their scholasticized or "hard" forms.[17] He and an increasing number of others have been on a theological journey that has led them to a more open understanding of God.[18] Often they have received sharp criticism for their efforts.[19]

What do these current reformers say is the cause of the need for such theistic renewal? The powerful influence of the sixteenth-century Protestant Reformation and much that followed, they explain, resulted in theologians being "strongly influenced by a model of God who manipulates his crea-

16. Ibid., 317.
17. See Barry L. Callen, *Clark H. Pinnock: Journey Toward Renewal* (Nappanee, Ind.: Evangel Publishing House, 2000).
18. See especially Pinnock, *Most Moved Mover;* Pinnock et al., *The Openness of God* (Downers Grove, Ill.: InterVarsity Press, 1994); John Sanders, *The God Who Risks* (Downers Grove, Ill.: InterVarsity Press, 1998); and Boyd, *God of the Possible.*
19. For instance, Paul Helm insists that the real issue is how one understands the human plight and the

tures." Today it is important that we "challenge this root metaphor and liber-ate evangelical understanding in the direction of a free-will theism."[20] Many now join this general assessment and judge that classical Christian theism inappropriately focuses on God's absolute and inflexible sovereignty at the expense of biblical revelation and human freedom. Although truly omnipo-tent, God surely can and in fact has decided to limit the exercise of divine power in most relationships with the fallen world. Divine power remains unlimited, of course, but it is usually restrained by divine choice—at least for now. God is meaningfully related without thereby being diminished. Divine actions are directed by God's nature and are intended to help us humans know the relational God whose nature is loving grace.[21]

Proclaimed by this theistic renewal movement is a distinctive Christian theism that sees God as simultaneously sovereign over all creation and yet relating to it by choice with an intense and self-giving compassion that fea-tures reciprocating responses to human choices. God is neither immune to the evils and suffering of our world nor trapped in an ongoing codependence with this world. God relates as God's eternal and compassionate nature directs,

> fundamentally in terms of *empowerment,* rather than control or *overpower-ment.* This is not to weaken God's power, but to determine its character! As Wesley was fond of saying, God works "strongly and sweetly." That is, God's grace works powerfully, but not irresistibly, in matters of human life and salvation, thereby empowering our *response-ability,* without overrid-ing our *responsibility.*[22]

Avoiding the path of overpowerment, the current renewal emphasis insists that God chooses to "risk" active and even temporarily successful resistance to the divine will. Did Jesus not say that God's reign was near but *not yet in full effect,* since the powers of this world still persist? Paul said that God's Spirit waits and groans with us on the way to final redemption (Rom. 8:23).

As I will argue in chapters 3 and 10, God exists as a Trinitarian communion

---

needed grace of a truly sovereign God. Open theists are thought to be virtually reversing the genius of the sixteenth-century Protestant Reformation by suggesting that salvation rests in part on the free exercise of human choice (a "works" salvation?). But, counters Helm, "for God's grace to be efficacious, God needs to be able to work all things after the counsel of his own will. And in order to do that, he has to be the God of classical theism" (in Beilby and Eddy, eds., *Divine Foreknowledge,* 64).

20. Clark H. Pinnock, in Pinnock and Delwin Brown, *Theological Crossfire: An Evangelical/Liberal Dialogue* (Grand Rapids: Zondervan, 1990), 67.

21. For a full development of this view, see Barry L. Callen, *God as Loving Grace* (Nappanee, Ind.: Evangel Publishing House), 1996.

22. Maddox, *Responsible Grace,* 93.

of love and freedom. Although wholly self-sufficient in this eternal existence, God delights in what he has chosen to create, with which he interacts, and for which his love can overflow. With love as a reigning divine attribute (see chapter 3), God chooses to make room for others and seeks mutually responsible relationships with them. Randy Maddox, for instance, structures his understanding of the theology of John Wesley around the concept of "responsible grace."[23] Here lies the tension between two truths viewed as codefinitive for adequately understanding Christian theism and human salvation: (1) Without God's grace we humans *cannot* be saved; (2) without human participation (grace empowered, but free and not coerced), God's grace *will not* save. God is a grace giver; humans are to be grateful grace receivers. God is essentially a relational and loving-grace reality. Recalling the Christian doctrine of Trinity (see chapters 4 and 10), we might say that *Father* is the source of, *Christ* the initiative of, and *Spirit* the continuing presence of responsible and potentially saving grace.

This open focus and some of its implications are now being countered vigorously by many conservative Christians who fail to see adequate biblical support for them and fear that mostly they are subtle expressions of human arrogance and a diminishment of the true God. These conservatives do affirm the meaningfulness of human responsibility and divine-human reciprocity, but in ways that see God remaining in full control of all things, things that are "predestined" by God. Human freedom and divine predestination appear contradictory, but often are defended as fully complementary. An example is a popular little devotional book on prayer by Bruce Wilkinson. Here we are told that "if you don't ask for His [God's] blessing, you forfeit those that come to you only when you ask. . . . God's bounty is limited only by us, not by His resources, power, or willingness to give. . . . Your loyal heart is the only part of His expansion plan that He will not provide."[24] Apparently God grants freedom for human response, "risking" no response or the wrong response, to the detriment of believers who choose to live below their privileges. But is the response wholly a free human choice, or something predestined? How God works says much about who God is.

The Theistic Quest

Something significant obviously is happening among evangelical Christian theologians. It is liberating and enriching for some and troubling and threat-

23. Ibid.
24. Bruce Wilkinson, *The Prayer of Jabez* (Sisters, Ore.: Multnomah Publishers, 2000), 27, 29, 60.

ening for others. What is the nature and extent of human freedom? Has God limited himself in the divine relationships with humans? Does God know all things, including the decisions of free humans that are not yet made? What is involved in claiming that God is truly sovereign? These and similar theistic questions are basic and common today. How open and involved is God in human affairs? Does the sovereignty of God rule out God's being truly relational and responsive? What does "perfect" mean when applied to God—or should it be applied at all? What does the Bible actually reveal about who God is and how God works providentially in the ongoing life of the creation? Did the early centuries of Christian theologizing stray from their biblical roots in subtle but important ways that got hardened into an inflexible orthodoxy? Does God know everything in advance of its happening—and, if so, does God fully control all that happens? If God does predestine and control all, are humans more mechanical robots than gratefully responsive disciples?

If consensus answers are desired, there will be only frustration, since the jury is still out and likely hung concerning these questions. In fact, in November 2001, the Evangelical Theological Society voted on this statement: "We believe the Bible clearly teaches that God has complete, accurate, and infallible knowledge of all events past, present, and future, including all future decisions and actions of free moral agents." The result was 253 in favor, 66 opposed, and 41 others abstaining from expressing a judgment.[25] The politics of theology can be obvious but not necessarily decisive in determining actual truth.

John Wesley was convinced, as many evangelicals still are today, that God does know all (Acts 15:18), but he did not find acceptable the apparent inconsistency between such comprehensive divine knowledge and meaningful human freedom. Nor do many others. The current free-will or open theism movement joins Wesley in hesitating and is bold to venture some new assertions that it insists are as old as the Bible itself. One scholar suggests that if Wesley "had possessed a more nuanced hermeneutic for dealing with such passages [Acts 15:18], he might have decided that a 'self-limiting God' *was* consistent with his general convictions about how God works."[26] Pinnock asks:

How long do theologians intend to permit the Hellenic-biblical synthesis to influence exegesis? It is not the open view of God that suffers from a lack of biblical support. The problem lies in the conventional view that treats the Bible loosely and forces it onto a Procrustian bed and pre-established

25. See the report by David Neff, "Scholars Vote: God Knows Future," *Christianity Today,* January 7, 2002, 21.
26. Ibid., 53.

system. We do not have the right to dispose of inconvenient metaphors [about God] that do not fit our presuppositions. We must not use alien categories to critically re-interpret and eliminate what the Bible itself says.[27]

Another evangelical scholar counters that the open view thinks that it has captured the best insights from the ancient classical and contemporary process traditions. Some fresh mediation between these traditions is needed, but not of the open view kind. So John Feinberg sets out "not to bury God, but to reconstruct him—at least to refashion the idea of God from an evangelical perspective." The result? The God he describes at length is "absolutely sovereign, but he is no tyrant, nor is he the remote and unrelated God of classical theism. He is instead the king who cares!"[28] This quest for the truly related and also truly undiminished God is now shared by many Christian leaders— with numerous "classical" Christian theists claiming that, despite all the bad press to the contrary, that is precisely where they have been all along.

There is yet another position being taken today by process Christian theists such as John Cobb Jr. They doubt seriously that John Feinberg, Thomas Oden, and others have found the solution by claiming that the classic Christian tradition, when properly understood, has been in the right position all along. They also are fearful that the open model of free-will theism is too closely tied to classical theism and is in an unstable middle place between classical and process, "with just too much coercive power left to God, too much power that allows God to intervene intrusively into human affairs. A God who reserves the right to control everything, who is only self-limited for an unspecified time, and at any time could choose to be unlimited, is much too 'classical' a view of God."[29] Process theologians thus think of themselves as the true and stable free-will theists, since they see freedom as an essential characteristic of the creature. God never overrides and always acts in love.

In short, the current theistic debate raises the most basic theological questions and presents at least three broad options. The Christian understanding of providence, predestination, prayer, freedom, evil, and most other theological subjects hangs in the balance for believers. This is illustrated by the results of a written assignment I gave to a seminary class in 2001. Concerned that studying the history of Christian theism, including its complex arguments and obscure terminology, should have practical implications for Christian life and ministry, at the end of the course I asked each student to write about his

---

27. Pinnock, *Most Moved Mover,* 63–64.

28. John S. Feinberg, *No One Like Him: The Doctrine of God* (Wheaton, Ill.: Crossway Books, 2001), 32.

29. See Cobb and Pinnock, eds., *Searching for an Adequate God,* xi.

or her growing understanding of Christian theism, using the following as an organizing principle: "Because God is . . . therefore I . . ." A compilation of their observations appears below. Note the constant realization that how one understands God has immediate and practical impact. Note also the wide range of theistic perceptions—God is sovereign, constant, unchanging, dependable, and/or God is dynamic interactive, risks, suffers, and so forth. Herein is the substance and diversity of Christian reflection. In this wide range lies either the genius of complex adequacy or the germ of creeping heresy.

The following chapters offer a natural path for exploring the options, facing the issues, and approaching a thoughtful theological view of the nature and work of God as understood by Christians. They provide historical perspective and the competing views. They also instruct believers to be cautious about changing theological fashion, and they lead finally to the last chapter, which reaffirms the ancient Trinitarian view of God as an enduring and biblically faithful way to present the distinctive Christian vision of God.

This book's title, *Discerning the Divine,* intends to convey that God both is truly divine and yet can be known by humans because of God's grace-full revelation. The "beyond knowing" dimension of the theistic quest is rooted in the biblical portrayal of the darkness that God claims. It is the obscurity that Moses encountered high on Mount Sinai when he came into the dense darkness where God awaited him (Exod. 20:21). God's presence is concealed from ordinary human perception, hidden from the effort of the intellect to grasp knowledge and control the Divine. This is like the "darkness of unknowing" described by the great Christian mystics who bowed before the transcendent mystery of God and claimed to apprehend God only by the grace of imageless contemplation through the inner eye of paradox. But there also is the "being known" dimension of the quest. The Bible goes beyond the concealed mystery of God to the gracious self-revelation of the divine nature and intention. Thus, the following chapter focuses in detail on the biblical record of such divine self-revelation.

Affirmed here are the assumptions that God is self-revealing and that the biblical narrative is the foundational source for access to and proper understanding of this revelation. Being theologically sound necessarily implies being true to the biblical witness to God, in Jesus Christ, through the Spirit. Recognized here also is the critical importance of biblical interpretation. The more one insists on the Bible being the central authority for Christian faith, the more important becomes a careful interpretation of the sacred text. Open Christian theists see the Bible clearly presenting God as a personal agent who creates and acts, wills and plans, loves and values, risks and suffers, all in relation to covenant partners who are granted meaningful freedom to choose

Because God Is . . . Therefore I . . . [30]

Christian beliefs about God have very practical implications, including:

1. Because God is, I am.
2. Because God is Creator, I am creature.
3. Because God is Creator, God can be known through the creation.
4. Because God had no need to create, creation is the fruit of over-flowing divine love.
5. Because God is Creator, I am to be a reflection of the divine in my being and life.
6. Because God is holy, I—in some sense by God's grace—must also be holy.
7. Because God is self-revealing, I am a seeker.
8. Because God is mysterious, I have the need and responsibility to question.
9. Because God is mysterious and paradoxical to the human mind, I must avoid despair and yield to worship.
10. Because God is an infinite "Person," I cannot know God "objectively" and "scientifically." God is not another "object" to be studied by human standards.
11. Because God is infinite, my human language about God is fragile at best.
12. Because God is one, I must serve God and God alone.
13. Because God exists independently of creation, I will not be so arrogant as to think that the divine intentions finally depend on me.
14. Because words such as *omnipotent, omniscient,* and *omnipresent* have meaning, I know that God is fully—or at least finally—in control.
15. Because God is fully—or at least finally—in control, I must be obedient and patient.
16. Because God "risks" by granting real freedom to humans, I enjoy the possibility of a loving and reciprocal relationship with God.
17. Because God is transcendent, I will not fear; because God is immanent, I can experience life with the divine and engage in ministry as an agent of God.

---

30. These statements were compiled from the summation course papers of my class "The Christian Understanding of God" at Anderson University School of Theology, semester one, 2001–2002.

18. Because God is involved in the creation's life, I am understood and never abandoned.
19. Because God knows me, I am significant.
20. Because God willingly suffers in the face of human sin, I must willingly carry my own cross—significance and servanthood are intimately related.
21. Because God works by persuasion rather than coercion, I am free to choose obedience to the divine will (or the opposite).
22. Because God's purpose is redemptive and constant, I can rely on the divine plan.
23. Because God is relational and personal, I have the wonderful opportunity to know God intimately.
24. Because God is compassionate and responsive, I have the privilege of meaningful prayer, mutual conversation with the God who listens and answers.
25. Because God is loving grace, I can celebrate as a new creation.
26. Because God is triune, loving community is the nature and goal of the creation.
27. Because God loves, I too must be loving.
28. Because God keeps promises, I can be assured about the future.
29. Because God is and will be victorious, I am full of hope!

their own ways. More "conventional" Christian theists vigorously counter various aspects of this line of thought, also relying on the Bible to bolster their arguments.

Since the Bible is commonly appealed to as the authority source, and in order to explore this current interpretation impasse and hopefully find a way beyond it, we now turn to a consideration of the Bible's witness to the being and work of God. The Hebrew heritage presents nothing less than the Lord who is "God of gods and Lord of lords, the great God, mighty and awesome, who is not partial and takes no bribe. . . . You shall fear the LORD your God; him alone shall you worship" (Deut. 10:17, 20a). This is the Divine whom we seek to discern.

Chapter 3

Biblical Appearances

It is necessary that we be able to know God in His essence through a gift which transcends all the possibilities of our natural forces. It is necessary that this knowledge, impossible to nature alone, to which nature inevitably aspires, be possible through a gratuitous gift.
—*Jacques Maritain,* Approaches to God

Revelation is an act of God in history. . . . The supreme act of revelation and redemption is the resurrection of Jesus Christ, but this is itself the culmination and confirmation of a much larger pattern of divine revelation. The God who is revealed—the biblical God—is shown to be both independent from and yet deeply and livingly involved with creation.
—*Henry H. Knight III,*
A Future for Truth: Evangelical Theology in a Postmodern World

*T*he above quotations set the scene for placing the Bible in the center of the discussion of God as understood by Christians. We humans need and want to know God. Such knowledge is available to us only as a gracious gift of God—as "revelation." Divine revelation centers in Jesus Christ, the supreme gift, but this gift is accessible to us only—or at least primarily—through the medium of another gift, the biblical record. To know the story of God in Jesus is first to know the faithful literary carrier of the story.

The Bible is a common beginning point for most Christians. It is "the literary location where God continues to speak to us for the purpose of bringing us to faith and offering us newness of life."[1] To know God is necessarily to be closely acquainted with the biblical revelation. The believer who quests for knowledge of God's nature and intentions should read the Bible expectantly

---

1. Gilbert W. Stafford, *Theology for Disciples* (Anderson, Ind.: Warner Press, 1996), 62.

and carefully. In its text there is to be heard the sure word from God concerning God and the things of God. To probe the text properly, it must be read in the context of personal relationship to God; the Spirit who originally inspired the text is the same Spirit who now must illumine its historic meaning and current application for the reader.

The Bible may be affirmed as foundational, but there is a significant complication. We humans tend to approach the Bible with a preformed vision of God and some interpretive principles already in mind. Consequently, it is all too easy to "find" in the reading what we bring to the reading. For instance, the classical and open models of God previewed in chapter 2 each are seen by their advocates as clearly emerging from the biblical text, and each set of advocates accuses the other of having its biblical insight blurred because of something alien that was brought to the sacred text (usually an ancient or current philosophy that is said to be antibiblical). This present chapter, while trying to be authentically biblical and not captured by anything alien to the sacred text, obviously runs the risk of all textual readings. Nonetheless, we proceed because we must. If God is to be known rightly, the Bible must be engaged and well heard. We begin with a few biblical observations about God that enjoy general agreement among Christians.

God Known as God Acts

Whether God exists or not cannot be reduced to a simple matter of scientific search based solely on empirical fact since, by definition, God does not yield to the frailties of human measurability. Scripture speaks of God as dwelling "in unapproachable light," as the One whom "no one has ever seen or can see" (1 Tim. 6:16). Clinical testing and abstract reasoning are inadequate to determine the question of deity since the Bible presents God as infinite spirit, not finite object. Even so, the stubborn question of whether God *is* persists. Does God actually exist or is "God" only an idea in our human minds and hearts?

Christian theologians have developed extensive "proofs" for the existence of God. These are rational lines of thought that appear to argue in favor of God actually existing. When faith in God is seeking credibility in the public and academic marketplaces, there is a felt need to set forth the best case possible. The resulting arguments on behalf of God's existence certainly have enhanced the credibility of believing over the centuries. They are significant, cumulative, and do tend to confirm faith, although they hardly are capable of producing or finally establishing faith as unquestionably justified. Given this caution, five types of argument nonetheless have been common and widely convincing,

> **Classical Arguments for God's Existence**
> 1. From order and design (teleological).
> 2. From humanity—mind, human nature (anthropological).
> 3. From change, causality, contingency (cosmological).
> 4. From conscience, beauty, results, congruity (moral, aesthetic, pragmatic).
> 5. From the idea of perfect Being (ontological).

especially when taken together. Thomas Oden identifies them and explores extensively the reasoning of each, concluding that there is "a cumulative pattern of reasoning that in its totality is sufficient to support the claim that God exists, and exists in the way that Christian teaching has said God exists."[2]

However much logical "proofs" for God's existence are reassuring for believers and potentially persuasive for those still testing the faith option, it is intriguing to note that the Bible does not offer anything even approaching rationalized proofs for God's existence. The various biblical authors across the centuries just assumed that God is. The psalmist affirmed the inescapability of the Divine: "Where can I go from your spirit? Or where can I flee from your presence?" (Ps. 139:7). The biblical mind did not stand outside the experience of God and pose the disinterested rational question about whether or not God exists. Such existence was a beginning assumption: "In the beginning, God . . ." (Gen. 1:1). People in the ancient world rarely doubted the existence of divine powers, so the Bible does not answer directly modern doubts about the existence of God. It was taken as axiomatic that only "fools say in their hearts 'there is no God' " (Ps. 14:1).

Humans search for God, speculate about God, and often stoop to creating "gods" in their own images and for their own purposes. Then comes the prophet Isaiah, who dramatically announces, "Here is your God!" (Isa. 40:9). Who is this God who is proclaimed with such sudden confidence? The biblical answer is in sharp contrast to all fragile and fickle "idols" (40:18–20), the many divine pretenders. God is said to be the everlasting Creator who spreads the heavens like a tent and now comes with might, feeds his flock, gently leads, weighs the mountains in scales, and renders the nations mere drops in

---

2. Thomas C. Oden, *The Living God*, vol. 1 of *Systematic Theology* (Peabody. Mass.: Prince Press, 1998), 180. He explores the five categories of arguments on pages 142–79.

a leaking bucket (40:15). Have you not heard? Humans are used to seeing grass wither and flowers fade, as they themselves always do, but creation has been encountered by the only One who never wearies or dies and whose understanding is unsearchable (40:28). Knowing this God would be truly humbling and life changing, but because God is God, knowledge of God comes only if there is divine self-revelation. Humans, unaided, cannot comprehend such things. The good news from the prophet, however, extends beyond the assumption that God *is* to the dramatic affirmation that God *self-reveals*. God does come—and comes to save! God, while other than the creation itself (transcendence), chooses to be present with the creation (immanence) for self-revelation and redemptive reasons.

The God revealed in the Bible is not an evolving God whose being and nature are changing, but the eternal God whose self-revelation is increasingly clarified and understood by committed believers. A central Christian claim is that the God named "I AM" (Exod. 3) is also the God revealed most fully in Jesus Christ. The God known in Jesus is the same one who once spoke to Moses out of the burning bush and later encountered the young church at Pentecost as the Spirit. There is only one God; this God was active in the original creation (Gen. 1) and was very present in the manger in Bethlehem (Luke 2). There clearly is within the Bible an evolving understanding of the Divine, but it is not taught that God himself is progressively becoming. Instead, God is Alpha and Omega, from everlasting to everlasting the same.

The biblical teaching about God is much more practical than abstract in nature. It avoids philosophical speculation about the qualities of God's essence, focusing instead on what can be known by faith through God's self-revealing action in human history. The elements of the biblical picture of God arise in the midst of divinely assisted human observations about God's chosen ways of being with us and for us in our human need. In our living and especially in our pain, the Bible affirms that we frail and fallen people have been chosen to receive grace and revelation and thus are enabled to know God as Father, Mother,[3] Shepherd, Judge, Savior, and Friend. C. Leonard Allen and Danny Gray Swick note:

> God clearly is not the rational set of principles to which He has been reduced by many moderns. Throughout the Old Testament God is never

---

3. The "Mother" image of God, while deemphasized in much of biblical literature and Christian church history, certainly is appropriate and not lacking in biblical rootage. God is reported to be the One who has writhed in labor to give birth (Deut. 32:18), the midwife who takes from the womb and keeps safe at the mother's breasts (Ps. 22:9), and the One who "mothers" by providing suck, carrying on her hip, and dandling on her knees (Isa. 66:12). For more on the issue of gender and God, see chapter 8.

conceived of as an object to be studied, scrutinized or proved. Instead, He is the God of covenant, the One who makes promises to people and receives in return their faithfulness. He rarely calls Himself "God," but usually reveals Himself either as "the Lord"—which implies a relationship with His subjects—or as "the God of Abraham, Isaac and Jacob." In other words, He is the God who is identified and known through His relationships, not a God known in isolation.[4]

There is a strong historical focus and a vital connection between what God is as eternal being and how we come to know God through the revealing

---

The Neo-Orthodox Critique of Liberalism

The Bible does not have any philosophical doctrine about the relationship of God to the world, but it teaches both his transcendence and his immanence [see glossary]. . . . God is not . . . to be identified with any aspect of the world; he is its creator. Furthermore, God does not create, as did Plato's God, from the pre-existing matter and ideas. . . . God is the Lord and sovereign over all that is; he is in complete control. If man has freedom to defy God's will, it is a freedom that he has only by God's willingness to grant it. . . . God's transcendence is expressed in the biblical attack upon idolatry. . . .

"Neo-orthodoxy" is often defined in terms of its revolt against the immanence of the liberals. . . . The liberals had lost sight of the distance between God and man. . . . The liberals tended to find God within the self. Because God was seen as working in and through history, liberals came to identify the Kingdom of God with a historical system that man, with God's help, could build on earth. The immanent God was so close to nature that liberalism came to believe that God could be discovered as the laws of nature are discovered through patient research. Thus the uniqueness of the biblical religion, with God's search for man, was lost, and the Bible was seen as an interesting page in the ongoing search of man for God.

—William Hordern, *The Case for a New Reformation Theology*

---

4. C. Leonard Allen and Danny Gray Swick, *Participating in God's Life* (Orange, Calif.: New Leaf Books, 2001), 151.

specifics of divine action.[5] Exodus 20:2–3 reads, "I am the LORD your God, who brought you out of the land of Egypt, out of the house of slavery. [*Therefore*] you shall have no other gods before me." Human awareness of God and the motivation for faithfulness to God, and to God alone, arise out of God's prior action of redemption. God's action reveals One who is holy, quite other than us—as highlighted in the inset on the neo-orthodox critique of liberalism in the Christian tradition. Thus, we never can know God *fully*. Even so, we are enabled through the unfolding plot of the biblical story to know God *truly*. The intended purpose of this knowing is practical, enabling the present integrity and relevancy of faith. The primary focus is not on "God's being in itself, for that is not what the [biblical] text is about, but on how life is to be lived and reality construed in the light of God's character as an agent as this is depicted in the stories of Israel and of Jesus."[6] We mere humans cannot *comprehend* God, but the potential of our *apprehension* has been made possible, giving us authentic glimpses of God's nature and intent. These glimpses help us see the creation as God sees it and live the way God intends.

Like other Pharisees, Paul might have summarized the essence of his faith in the words of Deuteronomy 6:4: "Hear, O Israel, the LORD is our God, the LORD alone." Jewish and Christian belief begins with the affirmation of this "Shema" and its particular understanding of God's nature. Lives of authentic faith grow out of the implications of this divine nature. God is present, self-revealing, good, holy, and loving. The call is for humanity to listen and hear, recalling with reverence who God is through what God has done. Key commentary on the Shema is found in Deuteronomy 6:4–9, emphasizing the importance of every person reverencing and loving the one God; in Deuteronomy 11:13–22, emphasizing the urgency of obedience to the Lord with all that one is and has; and in Numbers 15:37–41, emphasizing the necessary remembrance of God's mighty act of redemption that liberated the people of Israel from slavery and made them God's own special treasure. To affirm God's oneness is to recognize reality. To obey divine expectations is to respond naturally to who God is. To remember God's self-revealing actions on the human scene is to keep faith on a firm footing, since God comes to be known primarily by memory of what he has done.

Jews hold that God called them into being as a people and provided a relationship with the Divine, with the One called "Creator of the world (*bore olam*), Master of the world (*ribono shel olam*), Almighty (*el shadai*), Holy

---

5. See Marvin Wilson, *Our Father Abraham: Jewish Roots of Christian Faith* (Grand Rapids: Eerdmans, 1989), chapter 9, "Contours of Hebrew Thought."

6. George Lindbeck, *The Nature of Doctrine* (Philadelphia: Westminster Press, 1984), 121.

One, blessed be He (*ha-kadosh baruch hu*), the Place (*ha-makom*), the Presence (*ha-shechina*), Merciful—or 'womb-like'—Father (*av ha-rachamim*), the name YHVH who cannot be spoken, our God (*elohenu*)."[7] Christians vigorously affirm this basic Jewish believing heritage and go on to affirm that this holy "I AM" is understood to be the One further revealed in Jesus, who said of himself, "Whoever has seen me has seen the Father" (John 14:9). Jesus Christ is "the image of the invisible God" (Col. 1:15) in whom "all the fullness of God was pleased to dwell" (Col. 1:19). In other words, the incarnation of the Divine in Jesus makes available a fully adequate understanding of the very essence of the true selfhood of God (see figure 2 in chapter 4, which highlights the Christian affirmation of Trinity in relation to Israel's Yahweh). Expressing such understanding, however, is difficult since human language is so earthbound. We reach for motifs, parables, metaphors, adjectives, poetry, forms of speech about God that are meaningful in the midst of their inadequacy (see *anthropomorphism* in the glossary).

Motifs and Appropriate Adjectives

The atheist (see glossary) understandably criticizes the popular "god" who readily meets all human needs, solves all problems, and satisfies all desires. Atheists typically critiqued the human tendency to religious neurosis and wish fantasy. Harry Emerson Fosdick insisted that "God is not a cosmic bellboy for whom we can press a button to get things done."[8] By dramatic contrast, the biblical God is characterized under the great categories of truth, justice, mercy, and holiness. The prominent element of divine judgment and the persistent prophetic call for believers to be self-sacrificing and socially just addresses the atheist's criticism directly. A biblical keynote of divine self-revelation is the event and then continuing motif of exodus (Exod. 6:5–7). God hears, promises, and liberates. God is the one who takes up the cause of the oppressed. Therefore, "biblical thinking is *liberated* thought, i.e., thinking that is not entrapped by social categories of the dominant culture"[9] (see more on this in chapter 8).

Two theistic motifs found throughout the Bible are rather clear, although sometimes they appear to conflict. The first celebrates God's knowledge and

7. Peter Ochs, "The God of Jews and Christians," in Tikva Frymer-Kensky et al., eds., *Christianity in Jewish Terms* (Boulder, Colo.: Westview Press, 2000), 49.

8. The range of such "bellhop" perversions of God is explored by J. B. Phillips in his classic little book *Your God Is Too Small*.

9. James H. Cone, *God of the Oppressed,* rev. ed. (Maryknoll, N.Y.: Orbis Books, 1997), 88–89.

control of the creation, present and future. God is the sovereign Lord of history (Isa. 46:9–11; 48:3–5). God both initiated and will culminate the whole process of creation. God maintains a controlling relationship with the world so that everything works out in detail just as divinely desired. God is the kingly potter and we are clay in his hands (Isa. 29:16; Jer. 18:1–6; Rom. 9:21). The second motif is an extensive array of references celebrating "God's creative flexibility in responding to open aspects of his creation."[10] God designed the world in a way that makes possible a questioning of the divine wisdom and a countering of the divine will—at least in the short term. We hear God asking questions and speaking in conditional terms about the future, regretting the outcome of certain divine decisions, and changing the divine stances in response to changing circumstances. Apparently the God who is ever sovereign is also ever present, engaged, and interactive with the creation. It appears that God seeks the highest good of all creation in a way that solicits the love of us humans in a context of our relative freedom, even to the point of God truly suffering because of human sin.

Overemphasizing one of these two motifs at the expense of the other lies at the heart of the "classic" versus "openness" theistic dispute noted in chapter 2. A key challenge before the biblical interpreter is not choosing one or the other of these motifs exclusively, a choice that would lessen this rich—even paradoxical—witness of Scripture itself. Both motifs are very present biblically, and surely they are complementary and not contradictory if read properly. As Gregory Boyd puts it, "[T]he future is settled to the extent that Scripture suggests it is settled and open to the extent that Scripture suggests it is open."[11]

Reviewing the Hebrew Scriptures, we see that God had become known within the ancient Jewish community as the One who is *living, holy, jealous, righteous, gracious,* and *purposeful.* Granted, all of these descriptions are limited human understandings of the Divine. If any one is separated from the others, it is thereby perverted. They are analogies employed to describe what is finally indescribable. Nonetheless, "they are *meaningful* metaphors which carry within them crucial, albeit not exhaustive, cognitive implications."[12] They speak of the One who really is in these particular ways, and they point to the ways we who believe are to be God's people in today's world. Taken

---

10. Gregory A. Boyd, in James Beilby and Paul Eddy, eds., *Divine Foreknowledge: Four Views* (Downers Grove, Ill.: InterVarsity Press, 2001), 23. Boyd argues that the second motif often is dismissed as unbiblical by the "classical" view because of extrabiblical philosophical considerations that lead to reading many texts as merely anthropomorphic or phenomenological expressions not really descriptive of God.

11. Ibid., 23–24.

12. Gabriel Fackre, *The Christian Story*, rev. ed. (Grand Rapids: Eerdmans, 1984), 252–53.

together in their largest biblical contexts, these six adjectives are believed by biblical writers to constitute a basic and balanced understanding of the divine being. God, especially as understood through Jesus Christ, also features *gracious and holy love* as a culminating self-definition.[13] Following, then, is a brief exploration of the seven adjectives, including loving, that together appear to constitute an appropriate understanding of God as biblically revealed.

1. Living. God is known in the biblical story to be present and active in our world. Who is God? "I am the LORD your God, who brought you out of the land of Egypt" (Exod. 20:2). God is the One who acted historically on Israel's behalf, made a people from those who had been no people. God is the alive One, the One who is and who acts to deliver, who manifests power directed by purpose. In contrast to dead idols, "the LORD is the true God; he is the living God and the everlasting King" (Jer. 10:10). God is a living reality, not an inert idea. God now is and always will be vitally present; "and they shall name him Emmanuel, which means 'God is with us'" (Matt. 1:23b). As known biblically, God is a subject, not an object. God is an initiator and thus a self-revealer who is known primarily by the nature of divine actions.

Jeremiah 10 speaks of the true and living God in sharp contrast to the "gods" conceived and even physically manufactured by mortals. The biblical God is free, aware, self-directing, a chooser, and a purposer. God is living, a willing Spirit, a personal God (Exod. 3:14; Eph. 1:9, 11), and the creative power in the universe. God is the life-giving wind that originally swept over the face of the watery chaos (Gen. 1:2; Isa. 40:12–14). For each of us humans, God is the agent of conception (Ps. 139:7, 13ff.; Luke 1:35) and the sustainer of the breath of life in our bodies (Job 27:3; 33:4). God is active and to be known especially by divine action on behalf of the chosen people, Israel. Rather than the fruit of speculation, God was the speaker, the initiator, the reality before Israel's awareness of the reality. Humans are to receive humbly the revealing and liberating word of God. The Spirit of God later would raise Jesus from the dead and one day will "give life to our mortal bodies" (Rom. 8:11).

The popular process theology of our day emphasizes the *dynamism* of God. God is relational in character and persuasive in presence. But, at least in the

---

13. This list of adjectives for the divine and the brief explanations of each appear in essentially the same form in Barry L. Callen, *God as Loving Grace* (Nappanee, Ind.: Evangel Publishing House, 1996), 85–92. They tend toward a "relational" view of God. Clark Pinnock says, "What we find in Scripture is a range of images designed to disclose something of God's nature. They seem to tell us that creation is a dynamic project and that God is personal and relational. . . . The open view of God proposes to take biblical metaphors more seriously [than 'classic' interpreters] and thereby recover the dynamic and relational God of the gospel" (*Most Moved Mover* [Grand Rapids: Baker Academic, 2001], 60–61).

view of many process thinkers, God is not always recognized clearly as the Creator, the fully sovereign One who is truly transcendent from the creation, the Alpha and Omega, the source and end of all things. The primary deficiency of some process thought is "its failure to direct its adherents back to Scripture's story of God—to the Lord of the prophets and the Father of Jesus, to the risen Lord Jesus Christ, and to the Lord the Spirit, who gathers believers in pentecostal power."[14] Biblically speaking, God lives, transcends sovereignly, creates life, and initiates saving actions on behalf of life's redemption.

2. Holy. God also is known in the biblical story to be apart from us humans, different from us. As God is immanent (see glossary), living and presently engaged in redemptive activity among us, God also is transcendent (see glossary) in otherness from us. As Peter Toon puts it, "YHWH is supremely alone outside space and time in his transcendence and wonderfully present within space and time in his immanence."[15] God is singular. There is none like God and no other than God. God's being is without comparison and stands alone. The golden text of Hebrew faith affirms God's aloneness (Deut. 6:4). This Lord is called "the Holy One" (Isa. 40:25; Prov. 9:10). The holiness of God speaks of divine mystery, glory, purity, all that fills humans with awe, wonder, and reverence. In fact, God's name is reported to be "holy and awesome" (Ps. 111:9).[16]

Isaiah saw the Lord "sitting upon a throne, high and lifted up." The seraphim cried out, "Holy, holy, holy is the LORD of hosts" (Isa. 6:1–4). The Hebrew word for holy is *qadosh,* meaning something withdrawn from common use. So God is separate from all else—holy. God is different from all else, pure and good, unstained but deeply grieved by the evil that has come to spoil creation. God expects that those who accept new life at his gracious hand will become God-like, holy as God is holy, separated from common to divine use (Lev. 11:44–45; Matt. 5:48; 2 Cor. 6:14–7:1; Eph. 5:27). For our guidance in the quest for holiness, the New Testament narrates for us a model and resource. There we are privileged to learn of the glory of God's holiness in the face of Jesus Christ (2 Cor. 4:6). The location of such glory soon spawned Trinitarian thinking among Christians who were loyal both to their Hebrew heritage and to their experience of God in Jesus Christ by the Spirit (see chapters 4 and 10). The Holy One freely chose to create, not out of need

14. James Wm. McClendon Jr., *Systematic Theology: Doctrine* (Nashville: Abingdon Press, 1994), 314.

15. Peter Toon, *Our Triune God: A Biblical Portrayal of the Trinity* (Wheaton, Ill: Victor Books, 1996), 74.

16. See the video lecture by Dwight A. Pryor, "The Holy One of Israel" (Dayton, Ohio: Center for Judaic-Christian Studies).

but love, and then chose to redeem in the person of the Son. As Christopher Hall says well:

> Part of the wonder of God is that he does not need anything outside himself to complete or satisfy himself (Job 22:2–3; 35:6–7; Ps. 50:10–12). God as Father, Son, and Holy Spirit has always enjoyed an ineffable relationship of exquisite love. No aspect of the divine nature is insufficient or wanting. In a manner of speaking, God does not need us but freely invites us into the family—for our sakes, not his.[17]

3. Jealous. The living and holy God is known in the biblical story to be intolerant of false alternatives to the divine being: "You shall not make for yourself an idol. . . . [F]or I the LORD your God am a jealous God" (Exod. 20:4–5). If God really is God, any supposed alternative is in fact a perversion of reality, falsehood, loss of true perspective, defective religion, and aborted life. Elijah cried out to the people: "How long will you go limping with two different opinions? If the LORD is God, follow him; but if Baal, then follow him" (1 Kgs. 18:21). Baal, which means "lord," and his consort, Astarte, were area fertility gods. To the Canaanites they represented security for the good life. They were treasured idols, personalized images of human desires that in fact had only whatever reality and power the creating humans granted them. Little has changed except the names. The "good life" still is projected as the favorite "god" of many. Automated industrialism and advertising, which Norman Kraus says "have given birth to a favorite daughter, consumerism," still rule the highly developed nations.[18] Self-seeking societies act like these are lords. We grant them what considerable power they now have. We bow daily, but in greed instead of humility.

The biblical prophets insist on a stark contrast between idols and the living God. Idolatry, which often comes in the form of seeking security through political alliances and military hardware, is pictured in the Hebrew Scriptures as covenant faithlessness. It also is said to be practical stupidity (Hab. 2:18–20). There is no sure hope except in the living God who creates rather than being created. "Not by might, nor by power, but by my spirit, says the LORD of hosts" (Zech. 4:6). Shared allegiance is no allegiance at all. The vigorous biblical witness is that serving God should include repudiating all idolatrous alternatives, "be they the philosopher's deifying of the elemental forces of the cosmos (Gal. 4:8ff.), the political tyrant's imposition of obligations that God disallows (Acts

17. Christopher A. Hall, in Hall and John Sanders, *Does God Have a Future?* (Grand Rapids: Baker Academic, 2003), 61.
18. Norman Kraus, *God Our Saviour* (Scottdale, Pa.: Herald Press, 1991), 71.

4:19; 5:29), the secularist's idolatry of mammon (Matt. 6:24), the glutton's capitulation to appetite (Phil. 3:19), or even the Western tourists' tolerant curiosity about ancient temple idols (2 Cor. 6:16; 1 Thess. 1:9)."[19]

4. Righteous. God is known further in the biblical story to exhibit, define, reveal, and expect what is right and to assist with bringing about what is good and just. God is righteous because God is the living source of what is good and is always faithful in fulfilling promises made to a covenant people. All people are called to be righteous as God is righteous. Since, however, we are failures, sinners, unrighteous, God also is known to be the One who renders judgment whenever deserved. The righteous God is even wrathful in judgment when necessary, but fortunately there is more. In the Hebrew Scriptures covenant theology includes unmerited promises of grace even for those who have been unfaithful.

No divine promises are to be separated from God's commitment to justice. Justice and salvation are interlocked (Isa. 46:12–13). Human beings are to "do justice" because God is just. God's throne stands on justice and judgment (Ps. 89:14; 97:2), with particular concern expressed for the poor (see chapter 8). To do what is right is more pleasing to the Lord than sacrifice (Hos. 6:6). The prophets of Israel were preoccupied with social justice because of their understanding of the nature and agenda of God.[20] This concern is seen in Nathan's rebuke of David for his lack of pity and his theft of Bathsheba from Uriah (2 Sam. 12:1–15). On the other hand, given divine grace, there came a day when David as king administered justice to the people (2 Sam. 8:15). He became the ideal of true kingship after God's own heart (Ps. 45:4; 72:1–3). Divine grace had really been at work.

5. Gracious. God is known to be active in the crises of life, often bringing good where evil otherwise abounds. God is grace-full, exhibiting a redemptive kindness wholly unmerited. Grace precedes law.[21] Divine intervention on our behalf comes before any final judgment that is based on our violation of the divine expectations of us. The confession about the Lord in Exodus 34:6 points to the very heart of God: "The LORD, the LORD, a God merciful and gracious, slow to anger, and abounding in steadfast love and faithfulness." While God always is holy, other than us, the prophets of Israel make clear that God also is "the Holy One *in your midst*" (Hos. 11:9; Isa. 12:6; Ezek. 20:41).

---

19. Carl F. H. Henry, *God, Revelation, and Authority* (Waco, Tex.: Word, 1982), 5:79.

20. See Alan Kreider, *Journey towards Holiness: A Way of Living for God's Nation* (Scottdale, Pa.: Herald Press, 1987). For review of the social justice tradition in Christian spirituality, see Barry L. Callen, *Authentic Spirituality* (Grand Rapids: Baker Academic, 2002), 195–99.

21. Contrary to the assumption of many Christians, this is true in the Hebrew Scriptures as well as in New Testament teaching.

The Holy One is graciously present with loving and saving intention. Jewish monotheism is creational, providential, and covenantal—God originated the world, guides and preserves it, and seeks to restore it, in part through partnership with a chosen and commissioned people.

God comes vulnerably near to the chosen people, loving them, longing for them in their waywardness, hurting with them, seeking renewed relationship with them and ministry through them, all because of an intense love for them and for all others. God, the Almighty Creator, comes to rescue Israel from slavery and to form a new people. Throughout its history this people of the covenant came to know God as its gracious Redeemer (Isa. 43:1–7). There was an emerging realization that those graciously chosen by God were chosen not for privilege but for a mission, to be a light to the nations. God's redemptive intention knows no ethnic or geographic boundaries (Isa. 49:6).

The story of the healing of Naaman through the ministry of the prophet Elisha (2 Kgs. 5) is a narrative presentation of the activity of God beyond the boundaries of Israel. It is a story rich in irony. The request for healing is inspired by a nobody, an Israelite prisoner of war working as a slave girl. The request is handled through the official channels of power, from king to king—even though both were powerless to act in this case. The king of Israel, assuming that God acts only within the boundaries of Israel, wrongly interprets the request as a political ruse. The healing is blocked at first by Naaman's ethnic arrogance—his home rivers are better than a muddy one in Israel. After the healing, Naaman appears to have accepted a quasi-magical view of God's actions. Since he assumed that God's healing power probably was restricted to God's geographic territory, he takes home a quantity of Israelite soil and with it, he thinks, the effective presence of Israel's God. This account both highlights the power of God to act in the face of a most dreaded disease and the freedom of God from humanly imposed particularities such as political pride, national boundaries, ethnic prejudice, and the premature exclusivity even of the chosen people of God. God embraces and relieves the pain of the fallen without being limited by or legitimating their human narrowness. God's graciousness knows no such bounds.

6. Purposeful. God is known in the biblical story as the One with a purpose. This purpose moves through and beyond the Jews to all people and all creation. God called Abraham and promised to bless his descendants. The Hebrew Scriptures begin with Adam and not Abraham. Yahweh, the God of Israel, is no petty tribal god, no local lord of an ethnic enclave, but Lord of the nations, "the God of the spirits of all flesh" (Num. 16:22; 27:16). Why did God call Abraham? The divine purpose was that "all the families of the earth shall be blessed through you" (Gen. 12:1–4). Paul later wrote, "If you belong to Christ, then you are Abraham's offspring, heirs according to the promise" (Gal. 3:29). The God of Israel is a missionary God with a redeeming purpose for all the earth. The *standing* God (transcendence) is also the *stooping* God (immanence), reaching for the lost, first through Israel, finally in Christ, and always with the full creation in view.

The story of Jonah (3:1–10) makes the point of God's universal caring, a caring that balances divine judgment with the divine purpose of redemption for all people. In this dramatic narrative the king of Nineveh becomes a better theologian of Yahweh than God's reluctant prophet! He was unwilling to accept as God's last word Jonah's ominous message of impending judgment. Instead, he entertained the daring theological option that God might relent in the face of true repentance (even if Yahweh's prophet was himself more judgmental and rigid than that). Maybe human action can influence God, potentially causing God, in light of God's sovereign freedom and redemptive purpose, to abandon the terrible decree of coming destruction. The king of Nineveh assumed that God is no prisoner of the initial divine decree of judgment. There is potential repentance. God's purpose is to restore, not destroy. There is divine compassion and restoring love that activates when there is proper human response to God's redeeming initiatives.

Does God sometimes actually change his mind, alter strategy in light of changed circumstances? There are numerous biblical texts that say he does; nonetheless, John Calvin and many others insist otherwise. God can no more change his mind than be sad or sorrowful.[22] Why? The basic reason offered is finally a philosophical one, an extrabiblical criterion for reading Scripture. Calvin grounds knowledge of God on a philosophical principle, namely, Plato's view of perfection that argues that any change in God would necessarily be for the worse. Attempts are made to locate such a principle in Scripture itself. Is there a clear way to distinguish references to God's presumed mind-changing that should be taken literally from those that are to be understood only as metaphor? In an excellent discussion of this subject, John Sanders concludes that there is no such clear way, except by recourse to an outside philosophical stance like Plato's.[23] It may be better to affirm with Scripture that God's nature and saving purpose are unchanging, but that his strategies can be and often are flexible. God chooses to be responsive in his relations with us humans. The divine purpose is tempered by the dynamic warmth of divine love.

---

22. John Calvin, *Institutes of the Christian Religion*, 1.17.12–14.
23. John Sanders, *The God Who Risks: A Theology of Providence* (Downers Grove, Ill.: InterVarsity Press, 1998), 66–75.

7. Loving. The central Christian affirmation about God gathers up all of the above qualities, attributes, adjectives, and metaphors rooted in the Hebrew Scriptures and caps them with the affirmation that God is *holy love.* Love, wrote John Wesley, is God's "reigning attribute, the attribute that sheds an amiable glory on all his other perfections."[24] Similarly, writes Dale Moody, "as holiness is the starting point, so love is the high point in the biblical unfolding of the nature of God."[25] This unfolding is reported from the very first chapters of Genesis. Throughout this picture of primeval history, one finds that for each act of God's judgment on human rebellion there is a corresponding act of unmerited divine mercy. Finally, about the eighteenth century before Christ, God actively entered human history by calling a man named Abraham. From the garden of Eden to the Tower of Babel, humankind is pictured as running away from God. God responded by launching a pattern of actions, loving-grace actions, to bring creation home again. It was the beginning of the long historical drama of God's amazing love. It was a process of divine self-revelation.

The Johannine statement is definitive: "God is love" (1 John 4:8). Love is defined properly as active concern for the highest well-being of others. The whole Bible is a dramatic narrative revealing the history of God's active concern for the well-being of the whole human family and of all creation. This view of God is based on the New Testament assumption that the character of God is defined decisively by the life and work of Jesus Christ, who is "the image of the invisible God" (Col. 1:15). This life and work pulls together, lives out, and dramatizes in self-giving love all the attributes of God. In particular, writes Craig A. Carter, "the actual character of God is revealed in Jesus' renunciation of violence and willingness to go to the cross in order to defeat evil by means of love. This is who God is."[26]

What would happen if, in the midst of our troubled world, all the attributes of this biblically revealed God were focused in one place at one time? Note the words of Psalm 85:10: "Mercy and truth are met together; righteousness and peace have kissed each other" (KJV). When they met and kissed, there was the cross of Christ. There, in that tragic and glorious event on a hill outside Jerusalem, we see best the *living* God, so present in our world; the *holy* and

---

24. John Wesley, commenting on 1 John 4:8 in *Explanatory Notes on the New Testament* (London: Epworth Press, 1950), 914.

25. Dale Moody, *The Word of Truth* (Grand Rapids: Eerdmans, 1981), 104.

26. Craig A. Carter, *The Politics of the Cross* (Grand Rapids: Brazos Press, 2001), 239. Richard Rice argues that a biblically faithful doctrine of God must show that all of the divine characteristics derive from love, because love "is the very essence of the divine nature" (in Clark H. Pinnock et al., *The Openness of God* [Downers Grove: Ill.: InterVarsity Press, 1994], 19).

jealous God, so singular and different from us; the *righteous* God, so committed to what is right and just despite the high cost; and especially the *gracious* God with a clear *purpose* being realized by a *redeeming love* beyond compare. The death of the godly for the ungodly "reveals the source of love in the subject rather than the object. God loved us not because of what we are but because of what he is."[27]

Augustine long ago stated well the wonderful simplicity and yet delicate complexity of our human understanding of God as conveyed through the biblical account:

> You, my God, are supreme, utmost in goodness, mightiest and all-powerful, most merciful and most just. You are the most hidden from us and yet the most present amongst us, the most beautiful and yet the most strong, ever enduring and yet we cannot comprehend you. You are unchangeable and yet you change all things. You are never new, never old, and yet all things have new life from you. You are the unseen power that brings decline upon the proud. You are ever active, yet always at rest. You gather all things to yourself, though you suffer no need.[28]

Herein is the holy God of love and redeeming grace. The biblical revelation yields this about God: "At the heart of it are two manifest qualities, inseparably joined: holiness and love. God *is* holy love."[29]

Paradigm and Name

The Hebrew Bible (i.e., the Old Testament) is best understood by Christians through an understanding of its theological foundation that feeds directly into the New Testament. Central to this foundation is an overarching paradigm that is appropriated with particular nuances in four different streams or trajectories of Hebrew belief.[30] Central to all is the controlling assumption that there is *one* God who is for *all* people. All that exists should be recognized as God's creation. All people are intended to live in harmony with God and each other. The whole history recounted biblically is the story of God searching for renewed shalom in all creation. Israel's life is to be a reflection of this one God

---

27. Carter, *Politics of the Cross,* 114.

28. Augustine, *Confessions* 1.4 (London: Penguin Books, 1961), 23.

29. Gabriel Fackre, *Ecumenical Faith in Evangelical Perspective* (Grand Rapids: Eerdmans, 1993), 119.

30. See Ronald Allen and John Holbert, *Holy Root, Holy Branches* (Nashville: Abingdon Press, 1995), chapter 2.

who lives eternally and for the sake of all. The four trajectories of perspective that stream from this basic God assumption are (1) the Deuteronomic (the loving God who chooses in love), (2) the Priestly (the holy God who calls to holy life), (3) the Wisdom (the orderly God who entertains all questions and holds all together), and (4) the Apocalyptic (the yet-coming God who provides hope in all circumstances). God is, loves, chooses, calls, orders, judges, and stands before us as well as above, within, and behind us.

The God who is the loving, creating, all-wise, and hope-producing One surely needs a name. In the Hebrew tradition, names represented essential nature and usually carried great significance. What is God's name? It came to be known as "YHWH" (no known vowels). So sacred was the name that often it was not spoken at all.[31] A key passage is Exodus 3:13–15, where Moses is looking for clarity and assurance so that he can face the challenge of going back to Egypt to represent God on behalf of the enslaved Hebrew people. His understandable question posed to the Divine is: "If I come to the Israelites and say to them, 'The God of your ancestors has sent me to you,' and they ask me, 'What is his name?' what shall I say to them?" (v. 13). The request for a name is a way of asking, "Exactly *what kind* of God is the God of our ancestors?" The divine answer is that God is to be called "I AM" or "I AM WHO I AM." With the verb in the future tense, the likely meaning of this "name" reported for the comfort of Moses is that the God of the ancestors is the One who promises to go with and be with Moses in his difficult assignment in Egypt. God's

---

Purification of the Divine Sanctuary

In the end, the contemplative suffers the anguish of realizing that he *no longer knows what God is* . . . because "God is not a *what*," not a "thing." . . . There is "no such thing" as God because God is neither a "what" nor a "thing" but a pure "Who." He is the "Thou" before whom our inmost "I" springs into awareness. He is the "I Am" before whom, with our own most personal and inalienable voice, we echo, "I am."

—Thomas Merton, *New Seeds of Contemplation*

---

31. When the ancient Israelites needed to say *Yahweh*, they substituted the word *Adonai*, meaning "Lord." If the name needed to be written, the scribes are said to have taken a bath before they wrote it and then destroyed the writing instrument afterward. Around A.D. 200, Christian scholars began writing the vowels for *Adonai* beneath the Tetragrammaton (YHWH), reminding the reader to say "Adonai." In the nineteenth century, German scholars inserted the vowels of *Adonai* between the *YHWH* consonants, creating the name *Jehovah*.

self-identification is "I will be with you" (Exod. 3:12), "I will be with your mouth" (4:12, 15), and "I will be your God" (6:7). God is the ever present One, the enabling adequacy who delivers in times of need and suffering. What a name!

God might be said to be evasive about the divine name. After all, many people in the time of Moses believed that knowing the name of a god brought that god under the knower's control. The God with whom Moses was involved could be apprehended only because of divine self-revelation, but could never be comprehended or controlled. God would be known primarily by what would happen. The name "I AM" seems closely related to the Hebrew verb *havah* ("to be"). It could be a combination of the present tense form (I am) and the causative tense (I cause to be). If so, Yahweh is self-identified as the One who is, creates, and causes, and the One who is uncreated and uncaused. No wonder the psalmist proclaimed, "Before the mountains were brought forth, or ever you had formed the earth and the world, from everlasting to everlasting you are God" (Ps. 90:2).

When Lloyd Douglas, author of *The Robe,* was attending college, he lived in the boardinghouse where a retired music professor also resided. Each morning Douglas would greet this man with the same question, "Well, what's the good news?" The old man would regularly respond by tapping his tuning fork on the side of his wheelchair and saying, "That's middle C! It was middle C yesterday; it will be middle C tomorrow; it will be middle C a thousand years from now. The tenor upstairs sings flat. The piano across the hall is out of tune, but, my friend, that is middle C."[32] So it is with the discerning, unchanging, and perfectly tuned God.

Here is a perennial question of theological method. Is knowledge of the Divine essentially a projection into the metaphysical realm of human thoughts, hopes, fears, language, culture, and so forth? Or has God provided humans with specific awareness of and proper orientation to the Divine so that, because they are divinely revealed, they are transcultural, timeless, and nonnegotiable? Regarding the "name" of God, Peter Toon and many other Christians insist that God has spoken progressively across both Testaments, resulting in God's name being "the Father, the Son, and the Holy Spirit."[33] These ancient words of divine definition can be problematic (e.g., the gender language debate), but we should be cautious about changing biblical language about God to avoid merely accommodating current social concerns. We humans

---

32. Donald W. McCullough, *The Trivialization of God: The Dangerous Illusion of a Manageable Deity* (Colorado Springs, Colo.: NavPress, 1995), 66.
33. Toon, *Our Triune God,* 239. See chapter 10 of this present volume for discussion of the Trinity.

are not free to name God whatever we choose. Feminist theologians, however, counter that the biblical language about God is male dominated and sexist, less divine revelation and more an outgrowth of a patriarchal culture in which the Bible evolved and by which women have been oppressed ever since. They insist that changing this old language is urgently needed to honor freshly the God who loves all people and expects justice and not more Egyptian-like oppression in the name of religious tradition.[34] This concern, while commendable, needs to stay carefully within the full picture of God as biblically revealed—especially avoiding the trap of pantheism (see glossary).

Language is always problematic when trying to speak meaningfully about God. The choice of language should be sensitive to the theological implications conveyed in relation to key biblical concerns. Regarding feminine language for God, which does occur on a few occasions in the Bible, it should be recalled that the Hebrews vigorously affirmed the utter transcendence of God against the goddess spiritualities of the Canaanites and other of their neighbors who blurred the line between God and nature. For the Bible's part, God stands infinitely above the categories of human sexuality and so has no peers, gender, or consorts. Masculine terminology for the Hebrew God indicated an affirmation of divine *transcendence* as much or more than any gender-discriminating *patriarchy*. Rather than a nature god who participates in the fertility rites essential for successful agriculture, a sexual pantheism typically identified among Israel's neighbors by feminine terms, the Yahweh God of biblical revelation is said to have created and thus was different from the natural world and was not to be confused with pantheistic goddess imagery. In principle, using exclusive male language to refer to God is not necessary or always wise. What is necessary theologically is a retaining of the distinctive understanding of God as known in Israel and then especially in Jesus Christ. Embodied in Christ is the view that among believers there is no such thing as male or female (Gal. 3:28) because God transcends human divisions, categories, and imperialisms.

Two parables of Jesus bring important clarity about God as biblically conceived. One, the story of the laborers in the vineyard (Matt. 20:1–16), is clear about the Jewish view of God as loving grace. Is God like an employer who pays a wage under a contracted set of inflexible rules? Is God like someone who holds a gun to a person's head, demanding certain actions or else? The parable beautifully portrays the grace of God, a concept so integral to Jewish thought during the time of Jesus and yet very difficult to grasp, then and now. The other parable is about the compassionate father and his two lost sons

---

34. See chapter 8 for more on gender language and references to God.

(Luke 15:11–32). The father allows an arrogant son to take premature advantage of his inheritance, victimizing the father, who nonetheless allows the son's freedom of choice. Jesus is drawing a vivid story picture of God. God also loves, risks, suffers, sacrifices, and finally welcomes home with loving grace those who are wholly undeserving. The loving God enables and desires freely chosen loving relationships with us humans. God "is *not* a pillar around which everything else moves (Thomas Aquinas) or an all-controlling despot who can tolerate no resistance (Calvin)."[35] Instead, God is the infinite subject reaching lovingly toward all created subjects. God reaches toward us even as we try feebly to reach out for God.[36] We come to know God only because God wants to be known by us and takes the initiative to make knowing possible!

The fullness of knowing God is not for humans, at least not for now. What is known by revelation is truly wonderful, and also still mysterious and only partially comprehensible by us humans. There is a strong biblical strand prohibiting humanity from fabricating any likeness to God. The second commandment and the story of the golden calf in Exodus 32 serve as permanent warnings. Nothing in creation can depict God as he truly is in his transcendence over creation. But there also is the strong biblical strand announcing divine revelation. God chooses to "draw back the veil" for at least partial glimpses. Paul says that God's very handiwork in creation discloses at least the power of divinity (Rom. 1:20). Moses is granted a glimpse of God's back (Exod. 33:23), Isaiah sees through the smoke of the temple the high and exalted God (Isa. 6), and the prophet sees the judgment of the Lord concerning Israel (Amos 1:1; 7:1, 7; 8:1).

Prominent evidence of the mystery is the doctrine of the Trinity of God, a central teaching of orthodox Christians since the early centuries of the faith (see chapter 10). Is such a triune concept really biblical? "Yes and no" is the only adequate response, with the "yes" basic and the "no" carefully qualified. I concur with Karl Barth that this doctrine, as such, is not found in the Bible. What is found there is revelation about God that implies the fact, content, and centrality of what is embodied in Trinitarian teaching. Soon after the time of Jesus, Christian thought would evolve the formal Trinity doctrine as the best available means of articulating the significance of God's redeeming action in human history and how this action faithfully mirrors the being and inner life

---

35. Pinnock, *Most Moved Mover*, 4. He adds, "God's perfection is not to be all-controlling or to exist in majestic solitude or to be infinitely egocentric. On the contrary, God's fair beauty according to Scripture is his own relationality as a triune community. It is God's gracious interactivity, not his hypertranscendence and/or immobility, which makes him so glorious" (6).

36. See Rufus M. Jones, *The Double Search: Studies in Atonement and Prayer* (Richmond, Ind.: Friends United Press, [1975]).

of God. Early biblical glimpses of Trinitarianism are found in the baptism of Jesus (Mark 1:9–11), the words of Jesus (John 14:16–17, 26), the commission of the disciples by Jesus (Matt. 28:19), the exhortation of Paul (Rom. 15:30), among other places.

The Trinity doctrine itself, while biblically based, would have to wait on this measured time of apostolic reflection. As a culmination of the biblical witness about the nature and activity of God, it soon would be formalized by the "fathers" of the early church.[37] Despite the multiplicity inherent in the doctrine, the Christian understanding of Trinity does not contradict the staunch monotheism of the Hebrew tradition, but affirms and enriches it. Christians readily join in the key biblical confession about God, the Hebrew Shema. It is a mixture of creed, praise, and prayer—addressing the one true God "with all your heart." But Christians join this confession in light of the Christ event and the continuing presence and power of the Spirit. This continuing Christ-presence and Christ-power is precisely God the Spirit who originally created all things and reflects God's nature, intent, and dynamism in the ongoing process of redemption and recreation. Spirit is the "power of creativity which flings out a world in ecstasy and simulates within it an echo of the inner divine relationships, ever seeking to move God's plans forward."[38] In creation, God seeks on the finite level to produce beings who can and choose to share in God's Trinitarian life—that of the Father, with the Son, by the Spirit.

Much can be learned about the biblical understanding of the nature and will of God by reflecting on the fact that God summons forth and enables the prayerful response of humans. God clearly is personal, accessible, and relational. Prayer, including petitionary prayer, has real meaning. With reference to God's covenant with Israel, Samuel E. Balentine affirms that "God does not choose to act in a unilateral fashion as the enforcer of a contractual fidelity. Humanity has a voice and a participatory role in this relationship."[39] In fact, the divine-human relationship functions as a "relationship of reciprocity,"[40]

---

37. Emil Brunner regarded the teaching of Trinity as a defensive doctrine that, while not forming a part of the original New Testament witness and message, is nonetheless appropriate and valuable in preserving the church's self-identity (*The Christian Doctrine of God* [1950; reprint, Philadelphia: Westminster Press, 1974], 205–40).

38. Clark H. Pinnock, *Flame of Love: A Theology of the Holy Spirit* (Downers Grove, Ill.: InterVarsity Press, 1996), 21. Pinnock adds, "From the Trinity we learn that the Creator is not static or standoffish, but a loving relationality and sheer liveliness. . . . There is only one God, but this one God is not solitary, but a loving communion that is distinguished by overflowing life" (23, 31).

39. Samuel E. Balentine, *Prayer in the Hebrew Bible* (Minneapolis: Fortress Press, 1993), 269. He adds, "Hebraic prayer is not a static activity that merely reflects a fixed world and a settled relationship with the Creator. Rather, it is a dynamic act of faith that brings into existence new possibilities for both divine and human fidelity" (271).

40. Abraham Heschel, *The Prophets* (New York: Harper & Row, 1962), 2:9.

to use Abraham Heschel's phrase. Prayer is the fundamental religious act and presupposes a responsiveness in the reality that transcends the human. The church's later creedal decision would be that Trinitarian thinking is the only adequate way to do *biblical* thinking about God. Timothy George gives the bottom line of such thinking:

> The God and Father of our Lord Jesus Christ is not a monad, a sterile one-thing that exists apart from a relationship, but has a dynamic relationship of love and reciprocity within his own being—and that as a relational being he has reached out to us in love. . . . The God of the Bible is a God of utter graciousness and love, who chooses to come into our world and to experience what we have experienced—our alienation and estrangement—and do everything necessary to redeem and love that world back to himself.[41]

In light of the theologically rich Hebrew heritage, it appears that what the monotheistic Gospel writers and Paul were doing in the New Testament was "to say a *logos,* a word, about what God has done in Jesus of Nazareth. . . . Their 'theologies' . . . are not primarily rational, philosophical investigations of the nature of God, but instead efforts in the direction of life transformation, re-presentations of the energy of the original Word."[42] Paul in his Corinthian letters notes a series of statements about God that he considered in full accord with Jewish beliefs. They are:

> God created all things and is at work throughout the creation (1 Cor. 8:6; 10:26; 11:12, etc.).
> God is one; there are no others (1 Cor. 8:4, 6; 10:20).
> God is the source of peace and blessing for believers (1 Cor. 1:3; 7:15; 14:33; 2 Cor. 1:2; 13:11, 13).
> God should be praised and thanked by the people (1 Cor. 1:4; 14:18; 2 Cor. 1:3; 2:14a; 4:15, etc.).
> God is faithful (1 Cor. 1:9).
> God's wisdom and power are beyond human conception (1 Cor. 1:19–21; 3:19).
> God will judge all humanity (1 Cor. 5:13; 2 Cor. 4:2).
> God opposes all immorality and injustice (1 Cor. 6:9; 2 Cor. 6:4, 7, 16).
> God's commands are to be kept (1 Cor. 7:19).
> God cannot be deceived (1 Cor. 14:25; 2 Cor. 11:11, 31).

41. Timothy George, "Is the God of Muhammad the Father of Jesus?" *Christianity Today,* February 4, 2002, 33–34.

42. Robert Barron, *And Now I See: A Theology of Transformation* (New York: Crossroad, 1998), 10.

Christian theology, from the beginning of the Jesus movement, "had an unmistakably 'evangelical,' missionary, practical flavor."[43] Soon, however, the commitment to evangelism would lead succeeding generations of Christians to extensive and diverse efforts at rethinking and freshly expressing Christian theism in non-Hebrew cultures, languages, and philosophical environments. One result was the emergence of the Bible itself as an "official" and clearly identified "canon" of Christian authority. Another result was the emergence over the centuries of interpretative traditions in the church; for various reasons the Bible came to be read in various ways. The question inevitably arose concerning the relation of church tradition to the Bible itself. The next chapter considers this key tension in the earliest Christian centuries.

43. Ibid.

Chapter 4

The "Classical" Portrait

We must avoid the Charybdis of deism and the Scylla of pantheism and panentheism by affirming a dynamic biblical theism that does justice to both God's otherness and his personalness. God is present to us but not inherent in us. He upholds us but is not identical with us. God is both the Wholly Other and the Infinitely Near. He is both God transcendent and God with us and for us.
                      —*Donald G. Bloesch,* God the Almighty

The inevitable encounter between biblical and classical thought in the early church generated many significant insights and helped Christianity evangelize pagan thought and culture. Along with the good, however, came a theological virus that infected the Christian doctrine of God, making it ill. . . . The virus so permeates Christian theology that some have come to take the illness for granted, attributing it to divine mystery.
                      —*Clark H. Pinnock et al.,* The Openness of God

*T*he first of the above quotations states that there is a delicate and vital paradox that lies at the heart of the Christian understanding of God. In chapter 2 the paradox is identified in the context of current theological debate ("classic" versus "open" emphases). In chapter 3 the paradox is seen again in the biblical materials themselves (two motifs and complementary adjectives for the divine). Now Donald Bloesch points toward the necessity of a critical balance, a "dynamic theism" that relates properly the "otherness" and the "personalness" of the divine.

The early Greek and Latin theologians who shaped the central or "orthodox" Christian tradition insisted on the paradox that God is both *transcendently great* and *immanently good*. This critical *both/and* may be as difficult to maintain as it is crucial to affirm. The history of Christian theology (as seen in brief in the following chapters) has witnessed the pendulum swinging from emphasis on God's greatness, from the truly transcendent One, the wholly other and unchanging being, to the vulnerably immanent One, personally involved in the history of fallen creation, relational, even risking, suffering, and in some sense changing.[1]

The second quote above moves historically from biblical times into the early centuries of Christian theologizing and judges that the needed balance called for by Bloesch was not well handled. By contrast is the significant work of theologian Thomas Oden that relies heavily on the classical formulations of those early centuries as foundational wisdom for current Christian thinking.[2] Did the early Christian theologians, the "church fathers," whose thought has become "standard" for many in the Christian tradition, formalize with care the biblically based paradox about God, or did they subtly yield to cultural accommodation and thus twist the biblical witness with nonbiblical perspectives prominent in the new times and settings? This is a very important and often debated question.

The original apostles of Jesus soon died, leaving a significant authority vacuum in the early church that came to be filled largely by Scripture, a body of sacred material judged by the general Christian community as a faithful reporting of the works of God. Added to the Hebrew Scriptures was a "New Testament." Scripture itself, however, even when commonly affirmed as authoritative, had to be interpreted by new generations in new circumstances and then shared understandably with mostly non-Hebrew peoples. How does one interpret the Bible rightly? How should the tradition (the biblically narrated story of God with us in Israel and Jesus) be related to the various reading traditions of the faith that soon arose and keep arising? Believers tend to read the Bible within their own interpretive traditions, bringing to bear their faith with the aids of their own reason and experience. Thus, with the Bible as foundation, the meaning and implications of divine revelation are sought in a way that is faithful to the Bible and relevant to the peoples being addressed.

---

1. See Stanley J. Grenz and Roger E. Olson, *20th Century Theology: God and the World in a Transitional Age* (Downers Grove, Ill.: InterVarsity Press, 1992), who speak extensively about the theological instability introduced when transcendence and immanence are out of balance. "Twentieth-century theology illustrates how a lopsided emphasis on one or the other eventually engenders an opposing movement that in its attempt to redress the imbalance actually moves too far in the opposite direction" (12).

2. Note, for example, Thomas Oden's *The Living God*, vol. 1 of *Systematic Theology* (Peabody, Mass.: Prince Press, 1998). Oden elaborates what Roger Olson calls the "Great Tradition" of the church's core and unifying teachings "stretching from the second century into the twentieth century (but especially formulated in the crucial stages of the first few centuries and the sixteenth century when the reformations took place). [These teachings] help us determine which beliefs matter the most and which are secondary or even further removed from the heart of Christian faith itself" (Roger E. Olson, *The Mosaic of Christian Belief: Twenty Centuries of Unity and Diversity* [Downers Grove, Ill.: InterVarsity Press, 2002], 33).

Figure 1
The Wesleyan Quadrilateral
An Interactive Pattern of Authority in Christian Faith

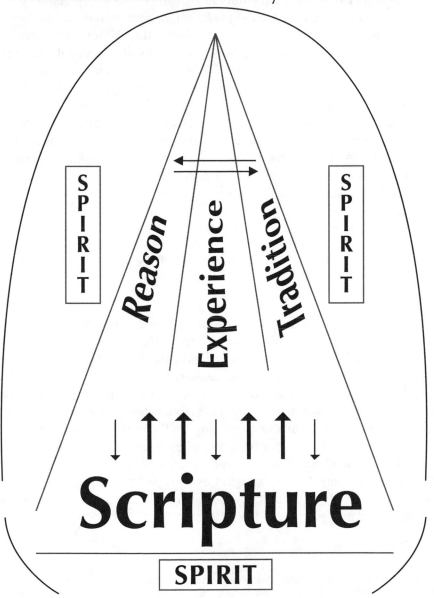

There is an interactive pattern of authority that highlights the usual elements involved in this seeking. It is called the "Wesleyan Quadrilateral" (see figure 1). The Bible is assumed to be the preeminent norm for Christian faith. This norm, however, necessarily interfaces with tradition, reason, and Christian experience, three interactive aids in the interpretation of the Word of God in Scripture. God's revelation, to be received and interpreted properly, necessarily includes a written witness (the Bible), a remembering and reading community (the traditions), a process of existential appropriation (experience), and a way to test for internal consistency (reason). Surrounding the process at all points is God's Spirit, who enables all right interpretation, past and present. This "quadrilateral" of theological interpretation, now carrying the name of John Wesley, may be described best as "a unilateral *rule* of Scripture within a trilateral *hermeneutic* of reason, tradition, and experience."[3] The point is to allow the Bible to shape our understanding of God's being and working. As the theological work of John Howard Yoder sought to make clear:

> [W]e must be sure that when we use the word *God* we are speaking of the God of Abraham, Isaac, and Jacob, the God and father of our Lord Jesus Christ, the Triune God worshipped by the church for twenty centuries, the living God and not the god of the philosophers or a projection of our own imaginations.[4]

An early interpretive tradition arose among some of the church fathers and came to be viewed by many as "classic" for all future generations of Christians. At its heart is the quest to understand exactly who Jesus was and continues to be in relation to God. The issue is a clarification of the Christian theism provided by biblical revelation as this revelation was pondered over time and expressed variously in changing circumstances. Here emerges a key question. Is the result of this pondering and expressing—especially as it became orthodoxy by the fourth century after Jesus—fundamental and fixed for Christians of all times, or is it significantly dated and in need of considerable updating again? We now turn to this early and "classical" Christian tradition, an especially significant tradition of Bible reading in the whole history of Christian theology.

---

3. Randy Maddox, *Responsible Grace: John Wesley's Practical Theology* (Nashville: Kingswood Books, 1994), 46. Howard Snyder and others speak of a "pentalateral" by adding *creation* as a key interpretative source and context in light of the actual theological work of John Wesley.
    4. Craig A. Carter, *The Politics of the Cross* (Grand Rapids: Brazos Press, 2001), 238.

The High-Water Mark of Theology?

Beyond the biblical witness itself, engaging in church mission in the wider non-Hebrew world rapidly raised the issues of culture and language in relation to Christian theology. The Christian doctrine of God attempts to distill what is understood to be God's self-revelation. Typically this revelation is believed to be centered in Jesus Christ and found primarily in the biblical narrative. Although the Bible does not offer systematic teaching about God, certainly not teaching set forth in formal and detailed doctrinal terms, it does provide essential building blocks for such a doctrine and makes clear that there is no more important subject to be addressed (see chapter 3).

Knowing God is demanding business. Beyond honoring the Bible as a basic source, such knowing comes to involve handling the issues of human experience, wisdom, and language, sometimes in dramatically changing circumstances. James H. Evans Jr. notes:

> It is one of the ironies of theological discourse that God is the one reality for which we have no referent outside human experience, but the doctrine of God in systematic theology is most prone to abstraction and speculative conceptualization. . . . In the long run, however, the only meaningful language about God is experiential, metaphorical, analogical, and functional. . . . Theologians have been more concerned about the philosophical legitimacy of their work than about its own integrity.[5]

Evans is right. Christian theology "grows out of the need to proclaim with authority and commitment the identity and mission of the church in the world."[6] This need is basic—and also prone to problems.

In the earliest centuries of the Christian heritage such issues certainly were prominent. Theologians reached for fresh theological formulation with some new language and at a new level of precision. They were highly motivated to clarify Christian identity, to legitimate it in reference to the prevailing wisdom of the world, and to conceive and articulate it in ways that would help the gospel of Christ be persuasive to people at large (people now often having no Hebrew background). The relationship between Greek philosophy and early Christian theology became very real and quite complex. A range of

---

5. James H. Evans Jr., *We Have Been Believers: An African-American Systematic Theology* (Minneapolis: Fortress Press, 1992), 53.
6. Ibid., 1. Evans elaborates: "The inadequacy of our language about God cannot obscure its corresponding necessity. The experience of God is as compelling as it is ineffable. In the Christian faith the experiential encounter with God demands both public and private expression" (54).

correlations were made between the Bible and the philosophical wisdom of that early time. Aspects of these correlations are positive, historically understandable, and still valuable—virtually baselines for the Christian believing tradition. Other aspects raise significant theological concern for many theologians today who are committed to the primacy of biblical authority.[7]

The patristic period (ca. 310–451 after Christ) is often regarded as a high-water mark in the history of Christian theology. This was the "classic" period when there evolved a significant degree of formalization of key aspects of the Christian understanding of God. The path followed was generally from the *economic* to the *immanent* Trinity (see glossary). The point of beginning, in good Hebrew fashion, had been much more that of historical reflection than metaphysical speculation. God is to be known by what God has done. The initial focus was on God's "economy," the divine process of creation and redemption narrated primarily in Scripture. Since we humans perceive God as we experience God with us and for us, emphasis was on the story of Jesus and the life of the earliest church as enabled by the Spirit of Jesus. As James McClendon Jr. puts it, "The God Christians know is the God of Jesus Christ, that is, the God known to them as they know the risen Christ and share the fellowship called church."[8] However, in the course of the church's mission and subsequent reflective thought there arose many related questions, including whether or not God's very self is Trinitarian like it appeared to be in the context of the salvation process (Father, Son, and Spirit). In particular, who was/is Jesus in relation to the eternal God, even prior to creation, and who is the Holy Spirit?

The resulting theistic understanding of Christians, couched in some extrabiblical categories, was enshrined in ecumenical creeds that are still in use and commonly accepted as Christian theological milestones (e.g., the Nicene Creed). They seek to capture the essence of biblical teaching in the context of those early centuries following the earthly life of Jesus. The distinctive thrust of Christian theistic thought came to be Trinitarian—judged to be the best way to express the fullness of the biblical witness about God. Although this formalization of thought clearly was a postbiblical development in specific political and philosophical contexts, it was firmly believed to be appropriate and biblically compatible, even biblically necessitated (see chapter 10).

In short, the historic conclusion of the patristic church was that "the God

---

7. For a recounting of the points of special awkwardness, see Clark H. Pinnock, *Most Moved Mover* (Grand Rapids: Baker Academic, 2001), especially chapter 2, "Overcoming a Pagan Inheritance."

8. James Wm. McClendon Jr., *Systematic Theology: Doctrine* (Nashville: Abingdon Press, 1994), 293.

revealed incarnationally in Christ (i.e., the Son) is also the mysterious personal ground, source, and fountain of divine life (i.e., Father) as well as the everywhere-present divine minister (i.e., Spirit). . . . The mysterious Father, manifested Son, and ministering Spirit are the three-personed God."[9] It should be noted, however, that many distinctive themes of the doctrine of the Spirit found in the New Testament faded in emphasis by the second century after Christ. While the divinity of the Spirit was clearly affirmed,[10] the classic Nicene-Constantinople creed of 381 includes "its implicit subordination of the work of the Spirit and its elevation of the importance of that of the Son."[11] The Western church came to insist that the Spirit proceeds from the Father *and the Son* (the *filioque* phrase addition),[12] affirming that the Son and Father are of one "substance," but leaving the Spirit's status somewhat unclear by comparison. The Eastern tradition of Christianity has considered the *filioque* as tending toward a subordination and depersonalization of the Spirit. This concern helped lead to a major division between Christians from the East and West (the Great Schism of 1054) that is yet to be healed, although some Western theologians today have come to significant agreement with the general stance of the Eastern tradition. For example, Wolfhart Pannenberg sees the secondary adding of the Spirit to the primary Father-Son relationship as a wrong subordination of the Spirit.[13]

In summary, this patristic period was one of the more creative times in all of Christian church history. Mainstream Christian bodies, including Eastern Orthodoxy, Roman Catholicism, Anglicanism, and the Lutheran and Reformed traditions of Protestantism regard this period as a critical landmark in the development of Christian doctrine. What had evolved was a classical synthesis that justifies this judgment: "[S]o far as the western world is concerned, [Christian] theism has a double origin: the Bible and Greek philosophy."[14] There is a strong case often made in favor of this synthesis "in which the ontological categories of Greco-Roman philosophy have been united with the personal-dramatic categories of biblical faith."[15] This synthesis evolved

9. Gilbert W. Stafford, *Theology for Disciples* (Anderson, Ind.: Warner Press, 1996), 180.

10. See, e.g., Ambrose, *On the Holy Spirit*, probably written in 381.

11. Gary D. Badcock, *Light of Truth and Fire of Love: A Theology of the Holy Spirit* (Grand Rapids: Eerdmans, 1997), 61.

12. See the glossary, chapter 10, and figure 4 for more detail.

13. Wolfhart Pannenberg, *Systematic Theology*, trans. Geoffrey W. Bromiley (Grand Rapids: Eerdmans, 1991), 2:317–19.

14. H. P. Owen, *Concepts of Deity* (New York: Herder & Herder, 1971), 1. These two origins may be seen as complementary or, as in the Clark Pinnock quote leading this chapter, in some ways standing in destructive tension.

15. Donald G. Bloesch, *God the Almighty* (Downers Grove, Ill.: InterVarsity Press, 1995), 205.

as a formal Christian response to early challenges to the faith's integrity and remains foundational for today's theology as well as the object of controversy in the Christian theological community.

In Response to Early Challenges

The key challenge for early Christian thinkers had to do with maintaining their Hebrew heritage of belief in Yahweh, the only God, and simultaneously relating this heritage to their experience of God in the person of Jesus and in the ongoing ministry of the Spirit of Jesus. It should be understood that what eventually evolved, the doctrine of the Trinity, is about the *unity* of the *one* God, not the multiplicity of gods. The first Christians were Jewish in heritage and thus inflexibly monotheistic. All that followers of the Christ believed, including the deity of the Son and Spirit, was being affirmed in relation to the one God. It is understandable, then, that the theological controversies of the first four centuries of church life wrestled with the relation of the "Three" to the "One."

The earliest impetus among Christians for clarifying the Hebrew-Christian understanding of God came from two challenges posed by anti-Jewish versions of early Christian teaching. The first challenge came from Marcion (ca. 100–160), who argued that the Creator God of the "Old" Testament and the Redeemer who is the God of Jesus Christ are so different that they are two different gods, with the earlier Jewish version of the divine clearly the inferior of the two. The other challenge was gnostic. This line of thought argued that the God who "seemed" (*dokeo*) to take on a literal body in Jesus was actually the One who came to save humans from the creator god of the Jews who had "trapped" humans in material bodies. Christ, in other words, came to destroy the god of the Jews. Both of these anti-Jewish challenges soon came to be judged heresies by mainstream Christianity. Even so, analysts such as John Howard Yoder speak sadly of the "fall of the church" and the "betrayal of the Jewishness of the early church" as Christian theologians of the second and third centuries after Jesus moved "creatively" into the Hellenistic and Roman cultures.[16]

There is only one God, and traditional Christian belief came to affirm that this only God is the One who became known progressively in the salvation story told in the histories of both Israel and the church, and who is known most fully in the life, teachings, death, and resurrection of the man Jesus. The God

16. Carter, *Politics of the Cross,* 167.

whom Christians worship is none other than the God of Israel. See figure 2 and note this:

> The God who created the world, liberated Israel from captivity in Egypt, was with Israel in the wilderness, in the entrance to the land of Canaan, who "dwelt" with Israel in the ark of the covenant, in the temple, who went with Israel into exile, the God whose "dwelling" . . . is with us even in the valley of the shadow of death, the God who became flesh in Jesus Christ and "dwelt among us, full of grace and truth," this "Emmanuel" (God with us), and this God who eschatologically will ultimately redeem God's good creation—this is the One of whom we speak when we name/identify God as "Trinity."[17]

Here surely is one of the key decisions ever made in the whole history of Christian doctrine. Marcion was excommunicated from the church. The truth established as "orthodox" is that the God and Father of our Lord Jesus Christ is none other than the God of Israel. There is a fundamental and continuing connection between creation and redemption, Israel and the church, the "old" and the "new" covenants.[18] Human perceptions of God may have progressed in their fullness and adequacy, but God has been constant in being, character, and intent (see figure 2).

Once the early anti-Jewish challenges had been met, however, another one arose. This new challenge involved a long conflict with paganisms of various kinds. The central question consistently was "Who really is God?" The final result of this reflective process for the Christian mainstream was the doctrine of the Trinity, which tries to make explicit the various strands of biblical teaching about God in the face of a range of imbalances and distortions. In frequent dialogue with the network of theistic implications arising from the general mindset of Greek (Hellenistic) philosophy, Christian theologians resisted some things and adopted others, all the while refining and freshly articulating their own thoughts about God (and sometimes subtly moving away from the moorings of Hebrew thought).

Plato was the dominant philosopher of the period of early Christian theologizing. For him, the universal is found in the "other world," with this immediate world a shadow of the true and ideal world beyond. He criticized ancient pagan mythologies, disdained anthropomorphisms (see glossary),

---

17. Clark M. Williamson, *Way of Blessing, Way of Life: A Christian Theology* (St. Louis: Chalice Press, 1999), 119–120.

18. See Timothy George, "Is the God of Muhammad the Father of Jesus?" *Christianity Today*, February 4, 2002, 34.

Figure 2
Yahweh as Trinity

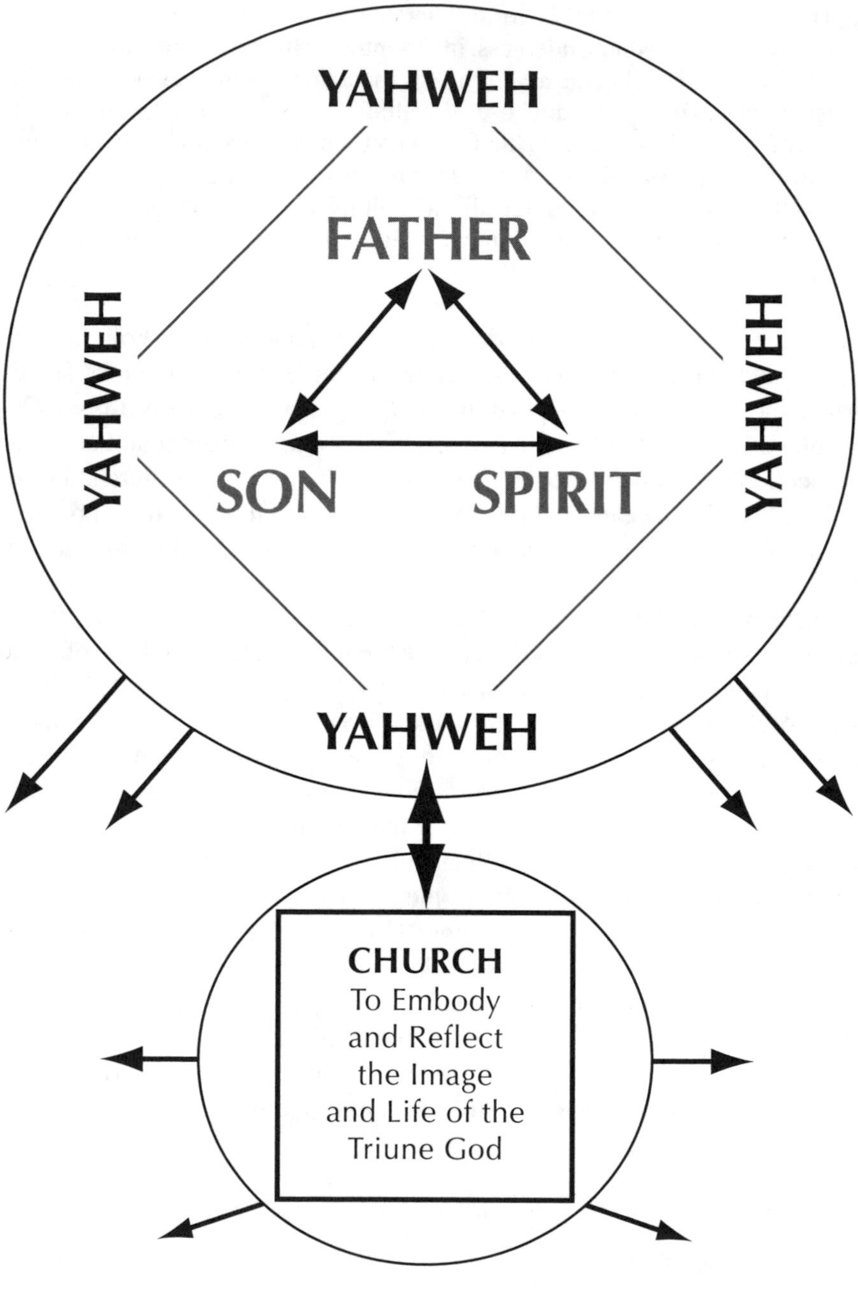

YAHWEH

FATHER

YAHWEH

YAHWEH

SON   SPIRIT

YAHWEH

CHURCH
To Embody
and Reflect
the Image
and Life of the
Triune God

and projected "perfections" onto whatever deserved to be called "God." An adequate God, according to this line of thought, must be conceived as having escaped the ravages of time. Plato argues in the *Republic* that the perfect being must be wholly self-sufficient and unchanging—after all, would not any change from perfection necessarily be for the worse? Christians, coming to reflect this vision in their first centuries, began to stress the mystery and sovereign transcendence of God. God is the *mysterium tremendum* whom we see only through a glass darkly. God is the "wholly other" who dwells in light inaccessible. Approaching God is a quest to know the unknowable—apart from a sheer gift of divine self-revelation. God is the perfection of perfections, quite other than the changeableness of the human scene.

The early church fathers, therefore, proclaimed that the "Father" of Jesus was in fact the universal God, not merely an ethnic "god" of the Jews. They did this under the influence of key Greek philosophical assumptions. The result was a biblical-classical synthesis about God.[19] This synthesis tended toward a conceiving of God as in every respect absolute, unchanging, the God whose relations to this world are necessarily external and nominal. It set Christian theologians over the centuries to the difficult work of mediating essentially contrasting understandings of the divine reality—the immutable and impassible God of the Greek philosophers and the dynamic and compassionate God of the biblical narrative and church experience. Certainly it is not wrong to emphasize God's *otherness,* certainly a key biblical motif, unless it is done at the expense of the wonder of the revelation about the amazing divine *relatedness.*

It was natural for early Christian theologians to develop expressions of Christian belief that were understandable and persuasive for thinkers in the largely non-Jewish world where disciples of Jesus increasingly lived and witnessed. The constant challenge then and now is to evolve fresh articulations of the faith that remain consistent with the biblical revelation and communicate effectively the good news about God in Christ to people who often do not share the Hebrew-Christian heritage. The danger always involved, however, is both subtle and substantial. Failure to communicate the good news effectively is intolerable; communicating the wrong message is also intolerable. Whether or not the early biblical-classical synthesis is fully biblical or is seriously compromised by certain alien Greek perspectives is a matter of keen debate to this day.

19. See the chapter "Historical Considerations" by John Sanders in Clark H. Pinnock et al., *The Openness of God* (Downers Grove, Ill.: InterVarsity Press, 1994), 59–100. The key early bridge from Greek philosophy to Christian faith was Philo of Alexandria, a Jew who sought to reconcile biblical teaching about God with Greek thought.

An early Christian communication of belief was the Apostles' Creed, which begins with the words "I believe in God the Father Almighty, maker of heaven and earth." The Nicene-Constantinopolitan Creed (A.D. 381) is the renowned Christian affirmation of the triune God that seeks to express the biblically revealed God who is unity in plurality. In part, it reads:

> We believe in one God,
> the Father, the Almighty,
> Maker of heaven and earth,
> of all that is, seen and unseen.

> We believe in one Lord, Jesus Christ,
> The only Son of God,
> eternally begotten of the Father,
> Light from Light, true God from true God,
> begotten, not made, of one Being with the Father.
> . . . .

> We believe in the Holy Spirit,
> The Lord, the giver of life,
> who proceeds from the Father.
> Who, with the Father and the Son,
> is worshipped and glorified.[20]

Behind this classic Nicene creedal statement lay a formidable challenge to the early Christian teaching about God. Arius (256–336) of Alexandria, Egypt, had envisioned Christ as above creation while not fully God. The creed of Nicaea, by intentional contrast to Arius, confessed the Son as "begotten, not made, of one Being with the Father." Thus, God is one; the Son is God, even as is the Father; the distinction between them is more than a mode of divine manifestation (modalism) but is real and personal—so that God's unity is one of distinguishable "persons" (but not separable parts). By the end of the fourth century after Christ, then, the doctrine of the Trinity as we now know it had emerged formally. Put most simply, this doctrine affirms that the *ousia* of God exists in three *hypostases,* making Jesus Christ and the Holy Spirit inherent in God's very being and in the process of our salvation.

Millard Erickson interprets as follows the meaning of the Nicene and similar creeds, the so-called orthodox or classical Christian conception of God:

---

20. This text is as found in *Confessing the One Faith,* Faith and Order Paper No. 153 (Geneva: World Council of Churches, 1991), 11–12. Note that the *filioque* phrase ("and the Son") had not yet been added, a later addition often seen as subordinating the Spirit to the Father and Son.

He [God] is a perfect, complete, and infinite being. He is perfect in all of his characteristics. . . . He is all-powerful, able to do all things. He is all-knowing, aware of and understanding all truth. He is eternal, without beginning or end. He is omnipresent, active everywhere within the creation. He is independent of the creation, not needing it. . . . He is free, not compelled by anything other than his own nature. He is completely good morally and spiritually. There is no lack of any kind in him. . . . The concept of *impassibility* was developed. . . . [It] basically meant the independence of God. He is not affected by anything. The tranquility of his emotions is not disturbed by anything humans do.[21]

Norman Geisler considers this the "traditional" Christian view of God. It is said to be "the God of Augustine, Anselm, Aquinas, the Reformers, the Puritans . . . [and] both classical Arminians and Calvinists." He elaborates:

Classical theism is characterized by its belief in a personal, infinite, eternal, and immutable God who created the world out of nothing (*ex nihilo*) and who has supernaturally intervened in the world from time to time. God has absolute unity (oneness), simplicity (indivisibility), aseity (self-existence), pure actuality, and necessity (rather than contingency). God is both eternal (non-temporal) and infinite (without limits). God is also omnipotent (all-powerful) and omnipresent (everywhere present). God is also fully omniscient, knowing the future perfectly and infallibly, including what free creatures will do in the future.[22]

This general pattern of theistic emphases was formalized later at the Synod of Dort (1618–1619). It is the so-called TULIP theological model that soon became the widely influential teaching typically associated with John Calvin. The TULIP consists of the five affirmed articles of Dort issued in response to the Arminian Remonstrance of 1610. The articles are: (1) *T*otal depravity; (2) *U*nconditional election; (3) *L*imited atonement; (4) *I*rresistible grace; and (5) *P*erseverance of the saints. These five theological petals form the tightly interconnected logical chain that would become standard theological thinking for much of evangelicalism in the twentieth and early twenty-first centuries. They appear clearly in the famous Westminster Confession of 1646.[23]

21. Millard J. Erickson, *The Evangelical Left: Encountering Postconservative Evangelical Theology* (Grand Rapids: Baker Books, 1997), 87–88. See the glossary for more on *impassibility*. Augustine (A.D. 354–430) profoundly affected the thought about God among later Roman Catholics and Protestants. He maintained a list of divine attributes, including God as self-sufficient, impassible, immutable, omniscient, omnipotent, timeless, ineffable, and simple.

22. Norman L. Geisler, *Creating God in the Image of Man?* (Minneapolis: Bethany House Publishers, 1997), 25–26. See the glossary for terms such as *aseity*.

23. The section "Of God and of the Holy Trinity" of the Westminster Confession begins, "There is but

Such was the culmination of a long theological process. Early in Christian church history, the core biblical message about God—in Jesus Christ, through the Spirit—had interacted with prevailing non-Jewish assumptions about the Divine, some of which appear resident in the above description of what became the orthodox Christian view. It is one thing to affirm the biblical witness to the God who is unchanging in existence and essence—God always was and will be and God always functions in a manner consistent with the unchanging divine nature. It is quite another thing to also affirm with Greek philosophy that God *in all respects* is immutable and impassible (incapable of any change and unaffected by the life of the creation). Is there nothing contingent or relational in God's ongoing experience with the now fallen creation? If not, is God thereby exempt from any meaningful involvement in time and history? It often is argued persuasively that many of the major Christian theologians of the earliest centuries of church life demonstrated the strong influence Greek philosophy had on them in their acceptance of complete divine immutability and impassibility, assertions not warranted by biblical teaching. Whether the biblical-classical synthesis did or did not accommodate unacceptably to a nonbiblical worldview is an important matter of ongoing debate among Christian theologians.

Current Readings of the "Classic" Christian Tradition

The Christian doctrines about God formulated in the earliest centuries after the earthly life of Jesus—the "common era" before the big divisions of Christians into Eastern Orthodoxy, Roman Catholicism, and Protestantism—have become known as "classic." Under pressure from inside and outside the church community, vigorous and often hotly contested attempts were made to clarify pressing questions about how best to understand God and communicate this understanding in non-Hebrew settings. A keynote of the classic stance is Augustine's view of human salvation as the wholly free and even surprising gift of God. All human turning to God is said to originate solely in God's good pleasure (thus, predestination). Martin Luther, John Calvin, and Ulrich Zwingli later stood with Augustine in exalting God's free grace against

one only, living, and true God, who is infinite in being and perfection, a most pure spirit, invisible, without body, parts, or passions; immutable, immense, eternal, incomprehensible, almighty, most wise, most holy, most free, most absolute; working all things according to the counsel of His own immutable and most righteous will, for His own glory; most loving, gracious, merciful, longsuffering, abundant in goodness and truth, forgiving iniquity, transgression, and sin; the rewarder of them that diligently seek Him; and withal, most just, and terrible in His judgments, hating all sin, and who will by no means clear the guilty."

any exaltation of human free will. "Let God be God!" was the cry of Luther.[24] The results of such a focused Christian theism now are read in two basic ways, one positive and one negative.

A Sympathetic Reading

Sharply criticizing what has been called "neotheism," classic theologians today deny vigorously the charge that their traditional Christian theology is permeated with a significant and essentially alien strain of nonbiblical assumptions about God, supposedly drawn largely from the Greek philosophical world. One classicist insists that "the roots of biblical theism are not found anywhere in Greek thought. No pagan Greek looked to an infinite, personal God, to say nothing of a Triunity of Father, Son, and Holy Spirit—united in one essence."[25] To the contrary, an early high point of Christian thought is said to be Augustine, with such thought being soundly based on biblical revelation and not Greek philosophy. The Christian tradition has sought to relate wisely to various philosophies over the centuries, but without violating the biblical base of authentic Christian theism. Anselm and Aquinas are good examples.

Anselm (ca. 1033–1109), archbishop of Canterbury, developed the "ontological proof" for God's existence while insisting that faith is a necessary foundation and support for philosophical speculation. Thomas Aquinas (1224–1274), whose work was the apex of medieval Christian theology, sought to harmonize the biblical-classical synthesis with the freshly discovered work of Aristotle. He inherited the traditional list of "perfect" divine attributes and "epitomizes the tensions of the biblical-classical synthesis in attempting to reconcile the God of historical action depicted in the Bible with the understanding of God as metaphysical principle, which was needed to explain the cosmos."[26] Rather than telling us what God is, he focused on what God is not, seeking to undermine all idolatrous attempts to turn God into something understandable or controllable. He wanted us to stop trying to reduce God to our human level and rather allow ourselves to be drawn ecstatically into God's mystery. In summary:

> Thus, the *simple* God is the God who cannot be understood and controlled; the *good* God is the one who captivates us and draws us out of ourselves; the God *who is present to the world* is the divine power that will not leave

---

24. Typical emphases of the Protestant Reformation of the sixteenth century were authority in Scripture alone and salvation only through Christ because of grace and by faith alone.

25. Norman L. Geisler and H. Wayne House, *The Battle for God: Responding to the Challenge of Neotheism* (Grand Rapids: Kregel Publications, 2001), 189.

26. Sanders, "Historical Considerations," 87.

us alone, that insinuates itself into our blood and bones; the *eternal* God is the one who invites us into the ecstasy of being beyond time; the *immutable* God is the rock upon which we can build our lives; the God of *knowledge and love* is the spirit who searches us and knows us, who seeks us and who will never abandon us.[27]

Later, John Calvin (1509–1564) sought to escape scholastic speculation and rigidity by returning to a more biblically oriented theology. Although preferring biblical language, Calvin continued to reflect the influence of Neoplatonic philosophy when speaking of the attributes of God. Augustine was

---

Faith and Reason in Search of God

O Lord my God, teach my heart where and how to seek you,
Where and how to find you.
Lord, if you are not here but absent,
Where shall I seek you?
But you are everywhere, so you must be here.
Why then do I not seek you?
Surely you dwell in light inaccessible—
Where is it? And how can I
Have access to light which is inaccessible? . . .

Let me seek you by desiring you,
And desire you by seeking you;
Let me find you by loving you,
And love you in finding you. . . .

I do not seek to understand so that I may believe,
But I believe so that I may understand;
And what is more,
I believe that unless I do believe I shall not understand.

—Anselm of Canterbury, *Proslogion*, select lines from chapter 1

---

27. Robert Barron, *Thomas Aquinas: Spiritual Master* (New York: Crossroad, 1996), 108.

his mentor. Calvin said that God is self-existent, simple, impassible, and immutable.[28] Martin Luther (1483–1546) focused Christian theology on the cross of Jesus, where we see the God who is dramatically and sacrificially *for us*. God is the One redemptively with us, not a theoretical and distant being. Luther contrasted the God of the Bible and the "god" of Greek metaphysics. Even so, Augustine was also Luther's mentor.

Luther and Calvin clearly qualified the Christian theistic tradition with more dynamic, active, and consciously biblical analogies for God. However, while introducing a limited challenge to the biblical-classical synthesis, they essentially retained it. This persistent and sympathetic reading of the classic Christian theistic tradition has been sustained by works such as Stephen Charnock's classic *Discourses on the Existence and Attributes of God*. Since God is presumed to be perfect, immutable, pure spirit, and so on, it apparently is not possible for God to repent or have emotions, to not know something or to change his mind in response to human decisions. Since many biblical texts in fact speak of God's changes and emotions, they are relegated to the category of anthropomorphism (see glossary). The biblical witness is divided into two levels, the upper defining God as God really is within the independent divine being (transcendent, immutable, etc.) and the lower as God sometimes appears to us humans (immanent, suffering, changeable, etc.). Leading evangelical theologians such as Carl F. H. Henry insist that God foreknows because God foreordains. Prayer cannot change God's mind. Divine "repentance" is impossible.

Thomas Oden and Robert Webber have recently popularized a new appreciation for the foundational nature of the common Christian era (prior to the Roman/Orthodox/Protestant divisions), without necessarily affirming unconditionally all aspects of the biblical-classical synthesis. The early fathers of the church are said to have hammered out their theologies in the contexts of polytheism, Gnosticism, cults, political pressures, and prominent philosophies of the day. They did so, however, in close proximity to the New Testament era and its Hebrew tradition. The result formed a classic theological foundation still judged pivotal for Christians. Webber observes that "the early church has defined the theological issues and established the framework or the 'rules' in which the church does its theological reflection. . . . To give special attention to the period of classical Christian thought is to be orthodox, evangelical, and ecumenical. Novel ideas of the faith will come and go, but the classical Christian tradition will endure."[29]

28. See John Calvin, *Institutes of the Christian Religion*, ed. John McNeill, 2 vols. (Philadelphia: Westminster Press, 1960).
29. Robert E. Webber, *Ancient-Future Faith: Rethinking Evangelicalism for a Postmodern World* (Grand Rapids: Baker Books, 1999), 28–29.

An Unsympathetic Reading

Today there is much criticism of the classic theism of Christian theological history. Clark Williamson represents an influential body of thinkers who see as much harm as good in the theistic teaching of the common era of church history. Christian thinking of that early time is thought to have departed from biblical foundations by formulating views of God that tell us "more about pre-Christian, Greek understandings of God than about the living, covenantal God of the Bible." The God of the Bible, Williamson argues, was transformed into the "impassible absolute" of Greek thinking, the "unmoved mover" of Aristotle, the God who affects all but is affected by none.[30] Accordingly, Clark Pinnock has countered Aristotle with his book *Most Moved Mover,* in which he says, "From early times, under the influence of alien ideals of perfection, theology has lost somewhat the biblical focus. A package of divine attributes has been constructed which leans in the direction of immobility and hyper-transcendence, particularly because of the influence of the Hellenistic category of unchangeableness."[31]

Is it not the case that an impassible-absolute understanding of the Divine is too philosophically oriented and focused on the intradivine relationships of God to God, God being thought of (speculated about) unbiblically and apart from the relationship of God to us humans through Jesus Christ and in the Holy Spirit? Catherine LaCugna certainly thinks so and argues that excessive metaphysical focus is a central problem of much of Christian theism. She calls for a new beginning based on the original basis of Christian faith, "the experience of being saved by God through Christ in the power of the Holy Spirit." This should be the necessary beginning premise "because the mystery of God is revealed in the mystery of salvation, [implying that] statements about the nature of God must be rooted in the reality of salvation history."[32]

Classical theism has made it difficult to speak meaningfully of a God who covenants with humanity, makes humans significant partners in introducing the reign of God in human affairs, and actively loves all creation. If God is changeless and invulnerable to human evil, one is made to wonder about what was really going on as Jesus hung on that old rugged cross. Was not God in the midst of a world-shaking act of self-giving love? Western thought has tended to define divine freedom as something unaffected by time and humans. But is it not more biblical to use the metaphor of persons in loving, respon-

30. Clark M. Williamson, *A Guest in the House of Israel: Post-Holocaust Church Theology* (Louisville, Ky.: Westminster/John Knox Press, 1993), 202–3.

31. Pinnock, *Most Moved Mover,* 65–66. His general perspective is that "the available philosophical resources for the early church were not altogether suitable for rendering Christian ideas" (150).

32. Catherine Mowry LaCugna, *God for Us: The Trinity and Christian Life* (San Francisco: Harper-SanFrancisco, 1991), 3–4.

sive, and faithful relationship? Evangelical theologian Donald Bloesch, for instance, affirms that through human prayer "God makes himself dependent on the requests of his children," since love does not force its will.[33]

Many Christian theologians have come to make room for the significance of human responsiveness as God's chosen way of working and relating with the fallen creation. Thomas Oden, drawing on the early church fathers of the common era, insists that God has a name, enters into history, has emotions, responds to humans, and takes new initiatives in light of human decisions.[34] John Sanders calls for a reevaluation of classical Christian theism "in light of a more relational metaphysic . . . so that the living, personal, responsive and loving God of the Bible may be spoken of more consistently in our theological reflection and not merely in our devotional practice."[35]

Delwin Brown is one of the voices critiquing the classical Christian view of God. For him, "a loving God is necessarily a related God. . . . Far from the remote, all-powerful deity of classical thought, a God accessible to modern Christian piety would be always incarnate in the world, accepting the risk of that involvement, bearing the world's sorrows and sharing its joys."[36] Juan Luis Segundo has even insisted that the idea of God as absolutely independent of the world—the ultimate abstraction bearing no resemblance to the biblical story of God deeply engaged with history—is an idol holding Latin Americans in bondage. He says that this abstract idol is a projection on God of what is wrong with modern human society—otherworldliness, passivity, and individualism.[37] Clark Pinnock stands in the center of this criticism of classical theism but is less open to formulating an alternative view in the politically oriented categories of liberation theology (Segundo) or the process philosophy categories of Alfred North Whitehead (Brown). Rather, Pinnock seeks to stay close to the Judeo-Christian categories of the biblical narrative that are clearly relational, worrying that a prominent alternative such as process theology also results in an inadequate view of God because of its excessive and reductive relationalism.[38]

---

33. Donald Bloesch, *Essentials of Evangelical Theology* (New York: Harper & Row, 1982), 1:31. See also 1:27–31; 2:57–58.

34. Oden, *Living God,* 53–130. Oden presents a paradox in that he reads the church fathers in a consistently favorable light, recognizes the various dynamics of divine responsiveness, and yet is not clear about how such a recognition can fit with his general acceptance of the biblical-classical synthesis. For example, he affirms divine simplicity, timelessness, and exhaustive foreknowledge.

35. Sanders, "Historical Considerations," 100.

36. Delwin Brown, in Clark H. Pinnock and Delwin Brown, *Theological Crossfire: An Evangelical/ Liberal Dialogue* (Grand Rapids: Zondervan, 1990), 86.

37. Juan Luis Segundo, *Our Idea of God* (Maryknoll, N.Y.: Orbis Books, 1974), 178–79. See chapter 8 of this volume for more on this concern.

38. See John B. Cobb Jr. and Clark H. Pinnock, eds., *Searching for an Adequate God: A Dialogue between Process and Free Will Theists* (Grand Rapids: Eerdmans, 2000), especially chapter 4.

From the perspective of traditional Christian orthodoxy, the process God is much too passive, failing (even being unable) to take defining initiatives in the world on behalf of the divine will and reign.[39] Even so, Clark Williamson's statement is telling:

> [I]f God is utterly immutable and impassible, then you and I and what we do make literally no difference to God. If, however, God is the One to whom all things happen, if everything that happens to each of God's creatures happens also to God (because those creatures are perfectly included in God's life), then what happens matters.[40]

In fact, the biblical narrative clearly affirms that what happens does matter to God. Jesus said it quite directly: "And the king will answer them, 'Truly I tell you, just as you did it to one of the least of these who are members of my family, you did it to me' " (Matt. 25:40). The Bible reveals God as a dynamic personal agent who by sovereign choice is deeply and vulnerably involved in human joys and sorrows, sins and salvation. While classic theology tends to speak more of God's power than of God's "weakness," more of eternal majesty than temporal engagement, the key fact of Christian faith is that the Word became *flesh,* a dramatic statement of God's relational engagement and changing unchangeability![41] In the paradox of this changing and unchanging lies the pulsating heart of biblical revelation, which includes both the sovereign God who stands above creation and the compassionate God who stoops to significant involvement with the creation. Concludes Walter Brueggemann, in God *"self-giving graciousness* and *undoubted sovereignty* are identical."[42]

Theological Types in Church History

Historian and theologian Justo González has identified three theological types that have appeared in the history of the Christian faith. While not mutually exclusive, they provide good perspective. Christian theology has proceeded

39. Pinnock and Brown, *Theological Crossfire,* 96. See also Barry L. Callen, *Clark H. Pinnock: Journey toward Renewal* (Nappanee, Ind.: Evangel Publishing House, 2000), 145–49.

40. Williamson, *Way of Blessing, Way of Life,* 130.

41. While sympathetic with the openness emphases of free-will theists like Clark Pinnock, Gabriel Fackre identifies several points of necessary caution so that corrections of the classic tradition do not themselves deteriorate into the opposite problems ("An Evangelical Megashift? The Promise and Peril of an 'Open' View of God," *Christian Century,* May 3, 1995, 485–87).

42. Walter Brueggemann, *The Bible Makes Sense,* rev. ed. (Louisville, Ky.: Westminster John Knox Press, 2001), 94.

Figure 3
Theological Types in Christian Church History

Type A
Tertullian: Concern with "law,"
seeking to show that Christianity
was compatible with Roman law
and order.

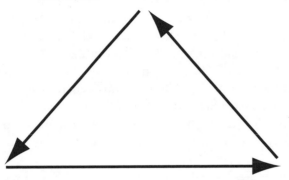

Type B
Origen: Intellectual concern
about "truth," seeking to show
that Christianity was compatible
with Greek philosophy.

Type C
Irenaeus: Pastoral concern with
"history," not seeking compatibilities
outside the church, but oriented to
participating with God's emerging
victory in the present and future.

These types are identified and tracked in detail by Justo L. González, *Christian Thought Revisited* (Nashville: Abingdon Press, 1989; Maryknoll, N.Y.: Orbis Books, 1999). The types are not mutually exclusive. Type C is said to be the oldest. Type A became dominant for much of church history. González sees A and B as most acceptable to the established political-social orders of the Roman Empire that came to adopt the Christian faith—once it was seen as compatible. He prefers type C now that the "Constantinian" era has ended for the church and "modernity" is in decline.

over the centuries with various concerns being dominant in changing political-social contexts, a variety that often has been influential on the development of Christian doctrine. Using the categories in figure 3, the formative patristic centuries in the early history of the church (the "common era") saw types A and B prominent. The most recent centuries and certainly the present reflect all three types, with varieties of type C gaining increased prominence in recent generations. Critics of the biblical-classical synthesis see it as too reflective of types A and B, while a more relational theology reflects type C.

One might picture the classical view of God in architectural terms. On a transcendence-immanence scale, God is perceived heavily on the transcendence side. Based on the very influential theology of Augustine (354–430), God is believed to stand at the apex of reality and authority as the God who creates, predestines, and becomes involved in the world primarily through Jesus Christ and the grace imparted through the divinely established life of the church. Throughout the Middle Ages this general view was symbolized by towering Gothic cathedrals. Revelation and the church's teaching authority dominated. God was high above the turmoil of this world. But times changed and so did theological approaches to conceiving and knowing God.

The Importance of Theological History

The next chapters of this book trace these changing times and approaches. They assume that wisdom is found in knowing the history of Christian theism. Doing theology well requires understanding how theology has been done before. Surely God has been with the church as it has sought to understand divine revelation and then carefully conserve and appropriately adapt its expressions to the changing settings of its life and mission. Focusing on this history is in some contrast to the stance of Thomas Oden, who says, "My aim has not been to survey the bewildering varieties of *dis*sent, but to identify and plausibly set forth the cohesive central tradition of general lay *con*sent to apostolic teaching, not through its centrifugal variations but in its centripetal centering."[43] I agree that the early centuries of Christian theology are valuable milestones of consensual orthodoxy and always must be kept clearly in view. I also contend that the centuries since, complex and troubling as they sometimes have been, offer guidance, warning, and language that informs

43. Thomas C. Oden, *Life in the Spirit*, vol. 3 of *Systematic Theology* (San Francisco: HarperSanFrancisco, 1992), vii.

today's Christian exploration of the nature and work of God. Without this history it is difficult if not impossible to address today the subject of God with perspective, wholeness, and public understanding.

So we proceed. We will keep the biblical base always in view as authoritative and honor appropriately the theological formulations of the earliest Christian centuries. We will not abandon the affirmation that proper Christian belief is that which is faithful to divine revelation and the "Great Tradition" (see note 2), which confesses that God is both perfectly good (truly immanent) and unsurpassably great (truly transcendent). Even so, we recognize the need to consider seriously more than the ancient past and only one stream of orthodox thought about God. Influential Christian thinkers have emphasized God's transcendence or immanence in special ways, usually seeking to address a perceived imbalance and/or to restate Christian thought for the sake of more effective Christian mission in new times. These special ways of considering God, so prominent in the ongoing theological enterprise of Christians, must be understood for both their values and dangers. Therefore, we recall the theological life of the Christian community over the centuries—particularly the last two—as the quest has gone forward to know who God is, how God works, and what faithfulness to God entails in each new time. This review of theological searching will aid in our being able to proceed with maximum wisdom into the demands of the immediate future.

Chapter 5

Disappearance and Reappearance

God is neither an object of scientific investigation nor something that we can insert in the treasure of our knowledge, as one mounts a rare stamp in a special place in an album. . . . God is not within your knowledge, your knowledge is in God. . . . It is only because of God that anything is to be known at all. . . . Our conscience tells us that God is, but does not know who He is. . . . The world with a million fingers points toward God, but it cannot reveal Him to us.
—*Emil Brummer,* Our Faith[1]

Know then thyself. Seek not God to scan. The proper study of mankind is man.
—*Alexander Pope*

God is not dead, but some of the ways we have presented God are dead. By distancing God so far from the world and from human affairs, theology has prepared the way for secularism and atheism.
—*Clark H . Pinnock,* Most Moved Mover

*T*he so-called classical theological tradition of Christians reviewed in the last chapter settled a range of key questions about God—at least for the majority of Christian believers for the centuries that followed the early patristic period. This tradition highlights a truly transcendent God who has come near through the divine incarnation in Jesus and has remained near through the continuing ministry of the Spirit—three divine "persons," but only one God. However, this Trinitarian tradition would not remain unchallenged. Time has a way

---

1. Brunner also says, "The first and most important fact that we can know about God is ever this: we know nothing of Him, except what He Himself has revealed to us.... God desires one thing absolutely; that we should know the greatness and seriousness of his will-to-love, and permit ourselves to be led by it" (*Our Faith,* trans. John W. Rilling [New York: Charles Scribner's Sons, n.d.], 11, 16).

of raising old questions again and spawning new answers in new settings. The need for theological renewal seems unending. Also unending are the theological dangers that lie close to the innovations suggested by many renewal efforts.

One renewal trend particularly prominent in the theologies of the eighteenth and nineteenth centuries altered significantly the Christian approach in the West to discerning the divine. It was hailed by some as a great advance and ridiculed by others as the path of dangerous compromise. Its impact is very evident yet today. Often it is called "liberalism." The cultural landscape had changed. As the featured quotations above highlight, questions had arisen about God and the new science, and about God and the new focus on the study of humankind. If the biblical-classical synthesis of earlier centuries had not prepared the way for secularism and atheism, it at least now was being challenged vigorously by new "materialistic" emphases that were disruptive of the theological status quo.

Disappearance: Domesticating Deity

Something major happened in the intellectual world of the West and in the world of Christian theism between the Protestant Reformation of the sixteenth century and the opening of the twentieth century. It often is called the "Enlightenment," a new human mindset reflecting considerable contrast to the revelation oriented and creed controlled older theologies. Functioning in the world of Christian theology, some of this new mindset came to be known as *liberalism,* an approach highlighting a freedom to affirm as worthy of careful consideration anything drawn from human experience. Fresh scientific perspectives such as evolution and a creed-eroding historical relativism grabbed public attention and were certainly controversial. Some Christian theologians saw such perspectives as providing important contributions to the thinking of "modern" Christians. They championed views stemming from Friedrich Schleiermacher (1768–1834) and Albrecht Ritschl (1822–1889) in theology, Immanuel Kant (1724–1804) and Georg Hegel (1770–1831) in philosophy, and David Strauss (1808–1874) and Julius Wellhausen (1844–1918) in biblical studies. Their more inclusive and exploratory spirit typically reflected the following logic:

> To say in advance that Christian theology must consider only Biblical evidence or that it must take into account only the Bible, the creeds, and the church fathers—perhaps adding the Reformers—is too much like demand-

ing that God must speak to me in the way I prescribe and in no other. To be sure, I must "test the spirits to see whether they are of God" (1 John 4:1), but I must pay sufficient attention to any kind of voice or evidence that offers some prima-facie relevance to test it. Sometimes the intellectually as well as the humanely hospitable are surprised to find that they "have entertained angels unawares" (Heb. 13:2).[2]

Put otherwise, the new science could help in the truth quest of intelligent Christian believers; God's revelation is not limited to the Bible, which is historically conditioned itself and should be studied with this very much in mind.

The term *Enlightenment* embraces a cluster of ideas and attitudes that involve the elevation of the constructive use of human reason in the attempt to demolish old "myths" judged to be binding individuals and societies inappropriately to the oppression of the past. Reason was now considered able to penetrate the world's mysteries and to guide Christians to a better human future and a wiser faith community. This new emphasis opened a period of considerable innovation and unsettledness for Christian theology. A spirit of critical inquiry about classic Christian dogmas was encouraged, and there began a "quest for the historical Jesus" on the assumption that the real man Jesus likely differed somewhat from the overly theologized Christ of faith who is enshrined in the historic creeds. Such a quest led to a "humanizing" of Christian theology. The God of biblical revelation was coming to be seen as more rationally approachable, definable, silent, disconnected, even nonexistent—or at least beyond human determination and possibly even an unnecessary faith hypothesis.

The Enlightenment, illustrated by deism (see glossary), became a strong intellectual movement in the Western world by the eighteenth century. Major catalysts were René Descartes (1596–1650) in philosophy and Isaac Newton (1642–1717) in science. Their general goal was to develop knowledge of the spiritual world with more certainty attached than comes from mere church tradition. New knowledge was available, and an "objective" science and universal morality and law presumably would lead to a more rational and humane organization of everyday social life. Immanence increasingly replaced transcendence as the perceived primary characteristic of God—or at least the primary way that humans can come to know God. The insights of human experience were beginning to prevail over the claims of divine revelation. Featured was an increased confidence in human ability to know truth and then use it wisely. No longer were many Christian thinkers willing to accept classic

---

2. L. Harold DeWolf, *The Case for Theology in Liberal Perspective* (Philadelphia: Westminster Press, 1959), 14.

Christian dogmas merely on the basis of their status as supposed divine revelation or revered church doctrine. Instead, the light of reason was understood
to be possessed by each person. It was time to dethrone church hierarchy and
tradition as the controlling agents of Christian authority. Denied or at least
neglected in this dethroning process was the element of the supernatural, thus
the common charge by "conservatives" that "liberals" were domesticating the
Divine by restricting their consideration of God to the human categories and
methods of the modernist agenda.[3] Alexander Pope offered this advice to
Enlightenment people: "Know then thyself. Seek not God to scan. The proper
study of mankind is man."[4]

Much of the philosophical background of the Enlightenment's reconsider-
ation of God lay in Immanuel Kant's *Critique of Pure Reason,* where he contended that we humans cannot have knowledge of anything that lies outside
our sense experience. "Theoretical" reason cannot come to know any reality
transcending the phenomenal world. God's existence cannot be proved. Does
this eliminate all awareness of God? Not necessarily, concluded Kant. There
is a "practical" reason that involves a human sense of ought or obligation
through which we can experience that which is unconditioned by time and
space. This sensed moral imperative presupposes a highest good or "God" as
its ground. Such a spiritual sensing is necessary for the moral direction and
governance of our world.

This liberal theological focus on divine immanence (the knowledge of
God realized primarily within the realm of human experience) was soon redi-
rected somewhat by Friedrich Schleiermacher. Taking seriously Kant's
rejection of speculative metaphysics, he chose to affirm *feeling* as the proper
domain of religion.[5] Schleiermacher lived at the height of the Romantic

---

3. The modernist agenda has been summarized this way: "Enlightenment-modern thought tended to
focus on the omnicompetence of reason and its authority over tradition or faith, the uniformity of nature
rather than supernatural control and interventions, and inevitable progress of humanity through education,
reason and science. . . . Religion's main role in modernity would be moral education of humanity rather
than metaphysical speculation or indoctrination in dogmas about things beyond rational investigation"
(Roger E. Olson, *The Story of Christian Theology* [Downers Grove, Ill.: InterVarsity Press, 1999], 540).

4. Georg Hegel (1770–1831) sought to rethink God as fully immanent in the world, the "World Spirit"
(*Geist*) underlying and evolving with nature and history. God is humanity and human culture coming to
their self-conscious maturity. God and the world are to be thought of together. God, rather than being the
transcendent Creator, is better conceived as a Spirit permeating all, so that God is realizing the fuller potential of divine being in concert with the upward evolution of history. The whole world process is the activity of the Spirit, a product of the Spirit-mind, and thus intelligible to mind. Truth, rather than fixed and
revealed church doctrine, is more the reasoning process itself.

5. "Feeling" may wrongly convey a shallow emotionalism as the essence of religion for Schleiermacher. A better translation of the original German here probably is "deep inner awareness." He was no mere
sentimentalist, but a stout believer that "Christian doctrines are accounts of the Christian religious affections set forth in speech."

movement, when many people were awakening to dimensions of human existence that are ignored by a narrow rationalism. He would become known as the "father" of liberalism, breathing new life and interest into the Christian theology of his time by taking actual human experience as theology's primary datum. Feelings, he insisted, constitute the ground of reality, and Jesus was the man in whom the feelings of God-consciousness had attained their highest perfection.

The Christian life was said by Schleiermacher to be less rationally grasped and conceptualized and more intuited. It is not essential for true religion that God be thought of as a separate being behind and outside the world.[6] The essence of true religion is "the immediate consciousness of the Deity as we find him in ourselves as well as in the world."[7] The foundation of religion is the feeling of absolute dependence, and God is the "whence" of this feeling. Divine revelation is thus removed from the center of the Christian faith, being replaced with the universal human experience of being aware of something infinite that is beyond the human self and on which the self is fully dependent. For Christians, theology is said to be less the reflecting on a supposed supernatural revelation and more giving attention to Christian "religious affections," the central affection being the feeling of total dependence on the redemptive work of Jesus Christ for one's relationship with God.[8] The feelings of humans constitute the ground of religious reality, with Jesus the one man in whom these feelings of "God-consciousness" existed in their highest perfection. Such subjectivistic liberalism desired a much more dynamic and undogmatic form of the faith than had been traditional among "orthodox" Christians for centuries.

The new, revolutionary, and rationalistic environment of "modernism" helped lead to the Pietistic and Romantic movements. These perspectives came to see excessive rationalism as itself enslaving. The mysteries of reality surely cannot be reduced to neatly intellectualized formulae. The Infinite is to be found in the finite, often through religious "affections," feelings, and imagination. The realm of spiritual experience was said to be crucial to knowledge of the divine. The doctrine of divine immanence (see glossary) was not prominent in much of early Christian thought. This changed,

6. It is unclear whether Schleiermacher's understanding of God involves a being distinct from us humans or is essentially a projection of human self-consciousness. At a minimum, God is perceived as very immanent.

7. Friedrich Schleiermacher, *On Religion: Speeches to Its Cultured Despisers* (New York: Harper & Brothers, 1958), 101.

8. Friedrich Schleiermacher, *The Christian Faith,* ed. H. R. Mackintosh and J. S. Stewart, 2d ed. (Philadelphia: Fortress Press, 1928), 76.

especially in the nineteenth century and in line with the new theories of bio-logical, psychological, and social evolution (Darwin, Freud, and Marx). Christian liberalism arose with fresh focus on God as present and active in the processes of nature and human consciousness. If Christian faith were to remain credible to modern people, some philosophers and theologians with Christian orientations had come to think that it was necessary to ground the faith in human reason and/or experience and culture.

Christian "liberalisms" had seen Kant bring a *moral* focus, Hegel an *intellectual* focus, and Schleiermacher an *intuitive* focus. They were seeking to reconstruct Christian faith and its view of God on fresh and more human-oriented bases, bases thought more credible to their times. Throughout, the supernatural agency of God was largely replaced "by an immanence that is continuous with nature and history, dispensing with awkward claims for mir-acles or divine interventions which run counter to the predictable laws of sci-ence."[9] Talk about God became primarily talk about the human experience of God, not what God is inherently and apart from creation. Most liberal the-ologians emphasized the continuity between God and nature, an emphasis that suggested to conservative critics a subtle form of pantheism, or at least panen-theism (see glossary). The idea of God's "wholly otherness," God as a sover-eign person existing eternally and separately from creation, was questioned and sometimes rejected.

For many prominent Christian intellectuals of the nineteenth century, the agenda became a reducing of the concept of God to a spiritual force creatively immanent in all things. The utopian dream of the Enlightenment rested on rea-son and aimed at human happiness, liberty, and social progress. The human-istic ideals of the earlier Renaissance had come to flood tide, even inside the arena of Christian theology. Humans and their societies were now thought perfectible, and in a context of domesticated deity. The deism common among influential Enlightenment leaders saw the Creator God now largely discon-nected from direct involvement in the life of the world. If God still was, at least there was general silence from the divine voice. Initiative lay with the world itself and on its own behalf. For classical Christians, this reduction was read as dangerous, perverting, and unacceptable, a denial of the true and tran-scendent being of God.[10] For the liberal theologians, it was a necessary read-justment of the faith to the wisdom of the times, a readjustment thought to

---

9. Henry H. Knight III, *A Future for Truth: Evangelical Theology in a Postmodern World* (Nashville: Abingdon Press, 1997), 139.

10. See Francis A. Schaeffer, *How Should We Then Live? The Rise and Decline of Western Thought and Culture* (Old Tappan, N.J.: Fleming Revell, 1976). He calls for a renewal of commitment to God's transcendent reality and revelation, and to the personal and social ethics that are biblically defined.

regain for God the credibility required to allow belief to continue. Once God was "saved," however, the result was a view of God greatly reduced from that of the biblical-classical synthesis.

With all its optimism and good intentions, the triumphalist vision of the liberal Protestant theologians proved premature. World War I erupted and soon was socially and theologically devastating. Finally, Karl Barth stepped forward in the early twentieth century to proclaim that the God of the Bible must not be confused with human ideas about God, ideas that usually are self-reflective and self-serving. On the Christian theological scene, there had been a disappearing and now, he insisted, there must be a reappearing of the true God who is known dependably only through the definitive divine revelation in Jesus of Nazareth. This "neo-orthodoxy" of the twentieth century (particularly in the 1920s–1960s), with Karl Barth as its fountainhead, argued vigorously against the immanence orientation of the nineteenth-century liberals.[11] Liberals were said to have lost sight of the distance between God and humans. God had virtually disappeared by being reduced to working within the human self. Humans had become seen as continuous with God— and maybe they were the only god there is if the traditional view of God was only an idealized projection by humans of the best of humans. The reign of God had become viewed as God working through humans so that there could be built on earth the functioning kingdom of God. God was judged so immanent that the laws of nature were seen as revealing the Divine at work.

The struggle was to determine the true identity of God and how this identity can best be determined. For many liberals, God became less of a "person" and more the rational order of the universe, often identified with the Absolute of idealist philosophy. The primary exponent of this rationalistic idealism was Georg Hegel, who understood reality as mental, one great thinking mind, the Absolute. All that happens are thoughts in the mind of God, who thinks and acts through us humans and our historical process. The biblical-classical synthesis was broken in a new philosophical environment.

William Placher recently has looked at classical Christian theology (particularly Thomas Aquinas, John Calvin, and Martin Luther) and contrasted it with the modern teaching about God. He argues that useful lessons can be drawn from premodern thinking about God (see chapter 4), since "some of the features contemporary critics find most objectionable in so-called 'traditional' Christian theology came to prominence only in the seventeenth century." Therefore, some current concerns should not be directed against the

11. See Karl Barth's substantial systematic theology titled *Church Dogmatics,* which appeared in sections from 1936 to 1969.

ancient Christian tradition, "but against what modernity did to it."[12] And what did modernity do? Roger E. Olson describes the specific response of deism:

> Deism was an effort to demonstrate Christianity to be the highest and best expression of a purely natural religion of reason. In order to carry out this project, the Deists had to lop off much of traditional Christian theology or radically reinterpret it. . . . The deity of Jesus Christ and the Trinity were two closely related dogmas of classical Christianity that many if not most Deists gladly neglected.[13]

Intentionally or not, these modern thinkers dimmed an earlier awe in the face of divine mystery, devalued the wonder of the sheer grace of God, and came increasingly to think that they could talk clearly, confidently, and categorically about a reconceived and science-compatible God.

In fact, however, we sinful humans cannot simply fit God into our intellectual systems as one key component. The divine "disappearance" created a substantial vacuum in Christian theism. Part of the way back to theistic adequacy today involves shaking off the urge to theological precision and human confidence about knowing God and God's ways. We must again learn "to rest more content with how little we can understand about God and to be more willing to live with ambiguities and puzzles than much of modern thinking about God has been."[14] For instance, lying outside rigid modernist categories (including Christian fundamentalism) is the possibility of the following biblical paradox: God is engaged in all the realities of the world around us; this engagement is compatible with saying *both* that we humans act freely and that our actions are nonetheless part of God's providential plan. Human reason struggles with such a paradox and is not ready to accept the fact that we humans can know the transcendent God, not as an *object* available to our intellectual grasp, but only as a *subject* who is apprehended through the essential aid of divine self-revelation.

Divine revelation comes as a free gift, an absolutely necessary gift. In the biblical narrative we encounter the God who makes available to human knowing the essential nature of the Divine. The center of this availability is the person Jesus, who is best understood through the biblical account as it is illumined by the Holy Spirit. But Enlightenment thinking elevated the

---

12. William C. Placher, *The Domestication of Transcendence* (Louisville, Ky.: Westminster John Knox Press, 1996), 2.

13. Roger E. Olson, *The Story of Christian Theology* (Downers Grove, Ill.: InterVarsity Press, 1999), 520.

14. Ibid., 3.

autonomous human self, reduced truth and value to what the individual can discern through reason or feeling, and sacrificed relationships on the altar of immediate utility. With individual "rights" reigning, social relationships deteriorated into optional choices of free people (including believers choosing or not choosing an active church association for themselves). This brought drastic consequences for relationships with God. More important than personal relationship became a rational affirmation of God's existence. Largely absent was the sense that God desires real relatedness with us humans. Autonomous and isolated selves also projected a similar disconnected circumstance onto God's very nature:

> God's nature, like ours, is reducible to His rational functions, rather than being defined by the limitless, expansive possibilities of love. Many moderns see God as a self-contained, autonomous and lonely rational agent removed from all those things that we experience but cannot account for rationally. . . . He was often visualized as a set of rational principles, devoid of personal characteristics. In these accountings God is not the Covenant-Maker of Scripture but an entity to be rationally probed and admired for his strength and independence.[15]

Assuming that philosophy and Christian theology are impacted significantly by cultural change, why was there a significant and sustained tendency toward the immanence of God as a central focus in the nineteenth century? Greater contact with different religious traditions had heightened the thought that maybe God is not as far removed as once thought from the masses of humanity who were not immediately informed by the good news in Jesus Christ (see chapter 9). The perceived distance between humans and God had been reduced, as the meaning of *sin* was softened and the presumed innate worth and goodness of all people was elevated. Thinking about God as "up there" and "out there" was questioned by modern astronomy and physics. As societies in the West moved toward a more classless status, respect for the legitimacy of hierarchy was lessening. Thus, there was less of a tendency to think of God as the idealized king of the universe. In addition, the increased presence of Eastern religions within countries traditionally Christian elevated a fresh consideration of pantheistic views of God (see glossary).[16] The spirit and guiding ideas of that time had come to be

---

15. C. Leonard Allen and Danny Gray Swick, *Participating in God's Life* (Orange, Calif.: New Leaf Books, 2001), 146.

16. In the United States, such views, often mixed with Christian vocabulary, are often now referred to as "New Age."

scientific, immanentist, optimistic, and progressivist. Prevalent was the idea that reality is an immanent and evolutionary process of development moving things over time from relative chaos to higher forms of life and culture. For many thinkers, God came to be considered as intimately *in* or even inherently *as* this process.

Reappearance: Let God Be God!

Trends tend to generate countertrends. The way of protest against the liberal changes on the larger scene was led by the Danish philosopher-theologian Søren Kierkegaard (1813–1855). He reacted to the immanent view of God inherent in Hegel's philosophical system and the shallow religiosity of the members of the Danish state church of his day. He countered with an insistence on the "infinite qualitative distinction" between God and humans that has only widened because of sin.[17] Knowing God, he insisted, necessarily involves the risk (leap) of faith. One must leave the objective position of religious observer and dare by faith to participate in an actual relationship with God. Kierkegaard explains in his *Fragments* that truth is not latent in us humans, just waiting to be recalled, but rather resides in God alone. God must bring the truth to the individual. It is fruitless to posit arguments for God's existence—no one will be brought to faith by cleverly cogent arguments.

In 2001 Donald Bloesch expressed great concern about why there was an "increasing vacuity of much Protestant preaching and worship." His analysis was that worship had become "performance rather than praise," something "far more egocentric than theocentric," "a spectacle that appeals to the senses rather than an act of obeisance to the mighty God who is both holiness and love." Many churches, he sadly observed, create an atmosphere that is "clubby and convivial rather than adoring and expectant."[18] The Divine has been submerged in a mass of human rational and moral activity, but must be allowed to reappear as truly God in our midst. Bloesch joins a long list of critics of Christian liberalism who see it as having adopted "naturalistic and anthropocentric viewpoints" that feature "an immanentist, sub-Trinitarian idea of God as working chiefly in cultural developments, philosophical, sociological, moral and aesthetic," and hold an excessively

17. Søren Kierkegaard, *The Sickness unto Death* (Princeton, N.J.: Princeton University Press, 1941), 192, 199, 207. The word "infinite" in Kierkegaard's famous phrase should not be read to mean that, given the divine initiative, God is wholly unknowable by humans.

18. Donald G. Bloesch, "Whatever Happened to God?" *Christianity Today,* February 5, 2001, 54.

optimistic view of "cultural humanity's power to perceive God by reflecting on its experience."[19]

Bloesch's critique of the current scene is similar to the earlier fundamentalist and neo-orthodox criticism of Christian liberalism, which exploded in the early decades of the twentieth century. H. Richard Niebuhr's famous characterization was that the liberal tradition featured "a God without wrath [who] brought men without sin into a kingdom without judgment through the ministrations of a Christ without a cross."[20] The liberal stance concerning authentic Christian faith has been characterized this way. It centers in right relation to God and neighbor, with little necessary relationship to specific theological affirmations or metaphysical speculations. The fatherhood of God, the common community of all people, and the infinite value of the human soul are to be the foci of the faith, leading to a "social gospel" that tends to think of truth as essentially subjectivity. That was the nineteenth century before the world suffered the depressing horror of World War I that was hard on all shallow optimisms about the innate goodness of humans and their supposed ever improving societies.

Some Christian theologians now reacted sharply to what they saw as skeptical rationalisms and earth-bound reductions of God. They returned to a renewed focus on the transcendence of God. Let God again be truly God! Fundamentalism was one resulting movement, with leading theologian J. Gresham Machen (1881–1937) seeking to expose liberalism as a false gospel.[21] Christian theology should not deny that God works immanently in the world, of course, but it certainly should emphasize that God is not the world or merely the best of human idealism. The divine essence is quite other than the world. God is hidden, known only through divine revelation, and transcends all that we know about him. Neo-orthodoxy was another reacting movement, but with key differences from fundamentalism. The great Swiss theologian Karl Barth (1886–1968) was a leading neo-orthodox spokesperson for the Protestant reaction against nineteenth-century liberalism. His highly influential thought was the flowering of seeds seen in the earlier work of Kierkegaard.

It has been said that in 1919, with the publication of his *Epistle to the Romans,* Barth dropped a bombshell on the playground of the liberals. He called for an acknowledgment of the genuine divinity of the Divine. Speaking of the "strange new world of the Bible," Barth explained his view that the

19. J. I. Packer, in Packer et al., eds., *New Dictionary of Theology* (Downers Grove, Ill.: InterVarsity Press, 1988), 385.
20. H. Richard Niebuhr, *The Kingdom of God in America* (Chicago: Willet, Clark & Co., 1937), 193.
21. See especially Machen's book *Christianity and Liberalism* (New York: Macmillan, 1923).

Bible is "not the history of man but the history of God! Not the virtues of men but the virtues of him who hath called us out of darkness into his marvelous light! Not human standpoints but the standpoint of God!"[22] The Scriptures bring us face to face with the God who is "wholly other." Here is no domesticated, cozy, manageable deity, but the God who is holy, beyond, sovereign. Humans are idolatrous when they fail to take seriously the radical abyss between Creator and creature. Thus, revelation is a critical category in any adequate Christian theology because "God is known *by God* and by God *alone*." If God is God, then unaided and finite human thought cannot arrive at any coherent synthesis of truth about God. "Natural" theology—humans managing to draw wisdom about God from observations of the natural order of things—is not an option.[23]

Such a dramatic call to theological renewal, a call for the "reappearance" of God among Christian theologians, assumed that there had been a serious diminishing of the Christian doctrine of God, a virtual disappearance of the Divine as biblically conceived. This theistic diminishing was the work of the Enlightenment and the rise, at least within Western Christianity, of liberalism, pietism, romanticism, deism, and so forth. These "isms" tended to alter the classic biblical-theological synthesis that had stood for centuries. They encouraged varieties of divine "disappearances" rooted in a revised human mentality that soon gripped much of Europe and that was evident in the eighteenth-century Enlightenment, the French Revolution, and philosophical idealism.

Barth's 1919 commentary on the book of Romans was intended to shock the theological world out of its liberal complacency. It announced the failure of the liberal experiment and launched a new and influential school of thought. The orthodoxy of the sixteenth-century Protestant reformers was now revived, although admittedly informed by select Enlightenment perspectives (thus, *neo*-orthodoxy). It was freed from what was judged the naive subjectivity and doomed social idealism of the liberal experiment. What was needed for Christian preaching, teaching, and pastoral care, according to Barth, was a "wholly other" theological foundation—namely, the biblical God. God should be understood as existing in a way that is independent of human subjectivity. The wholly otherness of God requires divine self-revelation if we sinful humans are to know anything dependable about God. We can know God, but not on our own, not apart from God's revelation in Jesus Christ. The human subject is not to be the beginning point or focus of theological reflec-

---

22. Karl Barth, *The Word of God and the Word of Man* (New York: Harper & Row, 1957), 45.
23. Emil Brunner countered Karl Barth at this point, affirming that there is some room for a natural theology in support of divine revelation.

tion. The proper beginning point is God, God as known in Jesus Christ. In short, neo-orthodoxy was concerned "to attack the tendency to make man's life, religion, moral experience, etc., the center of theology."[24] In place of this, it asserted the absolute centrality of God for Christian faith. Neo-orthodoxy was more willing than fundamentalism to adjust Christian belief to some aspects of modernity, but it nonetheless was clear that liberalism had gone much too far in the direction of an earthbound faith. Barth sought a renewed theological objectivity based on divine revelation in Jesus Christ, a transcendent Word known in and through the Bible.[25]

We humans are dependent on God alone for salvation—and God is not to be equated in any way with humanity at its best. In fact, "there is no road that leads from man to God. . . . God in his freedom chooses when and where he will be made known. . . . Our relationship to God is first and above all the result of God's activity, not of ours. . . . As a result, man never possesses God in his church, his creed, or his theology."[26] Knowing God is necessarily a participation in God's revelation, the essence of which is Jesus Christ. In fact, as Craig Keen notes:

> [T]he three letter word "God" is not for Barth a generic term for any object of exceptionally intense reverence. Rather, "God" . . . is that which happens as one is drawn in a very particular way into the very particular history of Jesus. It is in this sense that, because all that *is known* of God and, therefore, all that *can be known* of God is what is known of God in the history of Jesus, that what is known there is what one must say God *is*.[27]

Barth insisted that the holy, transcendent, and true God should be allowed to reappear on the center stage of Christian theology. God is sovereign, transcendent, and knowable only through his own Word. This Word is God's speech to humanity in the history of Jesus Christ. To know Jesus is to know God since Jesus is God's Word. The Bible may *become* God's Word, but it is not identical with it. God's Word is never merely a verbalized object available to human control, as God himself never is. God reveals *himself,* not propositions about himself, and the revelation is specific (Jesus), as opposed to some

24. William Hordern, *The Case for a New Reformation Theology* (Philadelphia: Westminster Press, 1959), 111.

25. By contrast, Henry Nelson Wieman (1884–1975) began with human experience, but tried to transcend its subjectivity and relativism by using an empirical method similar to the sciences. He wanted to establish the objectivity of God in such a way that God's reality could not be denied. God is the source of the highest of human meaning and values, he taught; God is the creative process that brings meaning and value into being.

26. Hordern, *Case for a New Reformation Theology,* 19, 165.

27. Craig Keen, "The Transgression of the Integrity of God," *Wesleyan Theological Journal* 36, no. 1 (Spring 2001), 92.

vague and universal human experience of the Divine (Schleiermacher). Such is the logic of neo-orthodoxy. Jesus has come; it is in him and only in him that God is self-revealed and thus knowable.

Coming, Going, Coming Again

If the radical-immanence focus of nineteenth-century liberalism was an extreme, it soon was judged by many that so was the radical-transcendence focus announced by Karl Barth early in the twentieth century. In fact, Stanley Grenz and Roger Olson have argued convincingly that the complex paths of Christian theology in recent generations can be analyzed with reference to the various ways that divine transcendence and immanence have been conceived and interrelated.[28] If God had virtually disappeared among the subjectivities of classic liberals and then had dramatically reappeared among the fundamentalists and neo-orthodox, the pendulum would keep swinging back and forth. Divine transcendence would again be challenged, this time in the twentieth century by existential and process philosophies. It is difficult to maintain a balanced perspective on how best to approach knowing God.

Before the next chapter explores additional challenges to divine transcendence that soon emerged, let us hear Orthodox Bishop Kallistos Ware's warm and wise affirmation of thoughtful balance between the distance and nearness of God, the God who is well known and yet never fully known:

> God is both further from us, and nearer to us, than anything else. And we find, paradoxically, that these two "poles" do not cancel one another out: on the contrary, the more we are attracted to the one "pole," the more vividly we become aware of the other. . . . Advancing on the Way, each finds that God grows ever more intimate and ever more distant, well known and yet unknown—well known to the smallest child, incomprehensible to the most brilliant theologian. God dwells in "light unapproachable," yet man stands in his presence with loving confidence and addresses him as friend. God is both end-point and starting-point. He is the host who welcomes us at the conclusion of the journey, yet he is also the companion who walks by our side at every step upon the Way.[29]

28. Stanley J. Grenz and Roger E. Olson, *20th Century Theology* (Downers Grove, Ill.: InterVarsity Press, 1992).

29. Kallistos Ware, *The Orthodox Way,* rev. ed. (Crestwood, N.Y.: St. Vladimir's Seminary Press, 1995), 12.

Such theological balance has been more difficult to maintain than to state. The next two chapters recount how in the middle decades of the twentieth century, despite the vigorous call of Barth and others, the Christian theological world was freshly bathed in radical subjectivity. The doctrine of God was even subjected to the bold declaration that God had actually died!

Chapter 6

In Experience, Myth, and Symbol

At best, Thomas Aquinas suggested, we can speak of God only ana-
logically, in which there is a partial resemblance between our
words and the transcendent reality to which they point. . . . While
analogy yields real knowledge, it is not complete knowledge. Anal-
ogy, moreover, does not overcome the infinite distance between
God and man for, Thomas insisted, God is always more unlike than
like the creaturely world that reflects his glory. Although we begin
from below in our analogizing, the norm for the truth of our anal-
ogy lies in the object, i.e., in God's self-revelation, rather than in
the subject.
    —*Donald G. Bloesch,* The Battle for the Trinity

Some want to restrict revelation to the past or at least make all reli-
gious claims answerable to their ability to show coherence with the
self-communication of God given in Jesus Christ. Others believe that,
without denying the central importance of Jesus, there is need to take
with deep seriousness the reality of the Holy Spirit. The Spirit is not
restricted to the past but is alive and active today.
    —*Donald G. Luck,* Why Study Theology?[1]

*T*he previous chapter recalls the theological move inward that brought to
Christian theism first a liberal "disappearance" of God and then a vigorous
neo-orthodox "reappearance" as some theologians reacted to liberalism's
extensive erosion of several core affirmations of traditional Christianity, especially transcendent theism. The quest for intellectual relevance in the present
time and a fresh focus on the historical relativity of Christian creeds, and of

---

1. Conservatives caution that John 16:13–14 says that the Spirit teaches the things of God *as revealed*
in Jesus Christ, not anything genuinely new and different from him.

the Bible itself, had brought into serious question for many Christian thinkers the continuing adequacy of "classic" Christianity.

The two quotes heading this chapter help to set the ongoing theological scene. There is a limitation to the full adequacy of religious language. There must be serious attention given to the dynamics of inward Christian life (the ministry of the Spirit), hopefully without devaluing the historical foundation of the faith itself (the sovereign God and the saving ministry of the Son). The revealed Word and the experienced Spirit are coordinate and both are key to the fullness of Christian faith. So say the classic Christian creeds. So said the Wesley brothers in the eighteenth century:

> [John] Wesley's own occasional unguarded comments . . . left him open to accusations that he taught a religious "enthusiasm," encouraging people to make their individual inward impulses the guides of their actions and beliefs. Wesley's consistent response to such accusations was that all present inward revelations must be tested by Scripture. As Charles [Wesley] once put it, "Whate'er his Spirit speaks in me, must with the written Word agree."[2]

Despite this traditional tie between inward spiritual experience and outward biblical authority, the middle decades of the twentieth century spawned several new Christian thinkers who pushed the limits of theological innovation in the direction of a substantial, even exclusive focus on experience, myth, and symbol. This brought into question the "objective" role of the Bible as the authority that traditionally has been assumed will check the subjective vagaries of believers anxious to be open to present experiencing of the Spirit. This focus on experience, myth, and symbol rests in part on the work of philosopher Immanuel Kant (1724–1804), who denied that humans can ever have conceptual or theoretical knowledge of the world behind the phenomenal world of appearance. He only saw a place for symbolic knowledge of God that centers in intuitive awareness.

Emphasis on the Holy Spirit has increased greatly in the field of Christian theology in recent generations. There were several reasons why this had not been the case earlier. The theology of Augustine seemed to depersonalize the Spirit into merely the bond of love between Father and Son by divesting the Spirit of full "personality." The church fathers and others often introduced the Spirit as the "unknown third," emphasizing that the Spirit steps to the background to avoid showing himself, but rather chooses to highlight the face

2. Randy L. Maddox, *Responsible Grace: John Wesley's Practical Theology* (Nashville: Kingswood Books, 1994), 31.

of the Father in the face of the Son. Over the centuries, like in the early struggle with Montanism and again in the eighteenth-century "enthusiasm" charge against John Wesley, the church often has been ambiguous or even antagonistic toward the contemporary work of the Spirit. The fear has been the outbreak of chaos, subjectivity, and lack of order in theology and church life. The Spirit is trustworthy, of course, but our human subjectivity is notorious for misreading the Spirit to the benefit of our own needs and goals.

It was not until the 1980s that the Christian ecumenical movement became especially aware of the need to enter seriously into dialogue about pneumatology (the doctrine of the Spirit). This long lack of awareness changed with the entrance into the World Council of Churches of the Eastern Orthodox churches and their rich pneumatological tradition, the dramatic spread of the pentecostal movement throughout the world in the latter decades of the twentieth century, and actions such as that of Pope John Paul II, who assigned the year 1998 as one of special devotion to the Holy Spirit for the world's largest Christian family, the Roman Catholic Church. The tide had turned in the Spirit's favor. It is now widely affirmed that Christian faith is more than mental affirmations and traditional sacred practices. "Experiencing" God in the immediacy of actual living surely is both possible and essential to being fully Christian. God's self-disclosure is not restricted to some ancient past and locked mechanically in creedal formulations created in distant cultural circumstances. Surely God remains present, active, self-revealing, and personally significant for believers. The important issues involve how best to relate past and present, historic foundation and current experience, order and spontaneity.

A Response-Able God

The inwardness of faith may represent a theological danger when it is made the norm for controlling Christian truth claims; nonetheless, the revealing and transforming ministry of God's Spirit lies at the heart of vital and truly relevant Christianity. John and Charles Wesley knew this in the eighteenth century. Randy L. Maddox has provided clarity on the Wesleyan model of God that is founded on biblical revelation, controlled by the person of Jesus Christ, and yet dynamically alive with the present ministry of the Spirit.[3]

---

3. See Randy L. Maddox, "Seeking a Response-Able God," in *Thy Nature and Thy Name Is Love: Wesleyan and Process Theologies in Dialogue*, ed. Bryan Stone and Thomas Oord (Nashville: Kingswood Books, 2001).

In the debate over predestination in the eighteenth century, John Wesley became convinced that the disagreement was less over how to interpret select Bible verses and how much freedom humans possess, and more over a disagreement about the nature of God. He saw in his predestinarian opponents a prior commitment to a sovereign-monarch model of God, even at times an omnipresent almighty tyrant. Guided by their understanding of biblical revelation, the contrasting model of Wesley was God as a loving parent. Says Maddox, "The God whose prevenient gracious empowerment makes us *response-able* is like a truly loving parent in also finally respecting the integrity of our *responsible* appropriation of that grace."[4] John Wesley laid greater stress on the genuinely *response-able* nature of God. God is able to respond to human responses because of his loving nature. The Christian life is characterized by the process of such responses, both human and divine.

In the larger Christian tradition, it had become widely assumed for centuries that there could be no type of change in God. Would not any change imply or lead to divine imperfection? Wesley countered that a God who did not take into account the changing response of humanity would surely cease to be unchangeably just and gracious! In fact, central to the very concept of the God of Christians is love, the "reigning attribute" of God that sheds its amiable glory on all of God's other perfections. Accordingly, Wesley construed God's sovereignty or power in terms of *empowerment* rather than control or *overpowerment*. This was thought not to weaken God's power but to determine its character. God's power should not be defined in any way that would undercut the integrity of responsible grace—God's grace that enables the human ability to respond and thus to be truly responsible. Wesley insisted that "affirming a place for God awaiting our uncoerced response to the divine initiative did not detract from God's glory, provided that it was God's grace that enabled us to respond."[5]

This open conception of God has cultivated receptivity of many Wesleyans to various themes and concerns of today's process theology. There are, however, points of remaining tension between these two traditions. Primary among them is the tendency of process theologians to place significant restrictions on the ability of God to act. Can God do any more than "lure" humans toward the good? Is God, if so "limited," truly *response-able* and thus truly the sovereign God of biblical revelation? Are there not places and ways for God to engage fallen humanity and the flawed historical process more actively than mere persuasion, without resorting to a coercion that disables

4. Ibid., 113.
5. Ibid., 116.

human responsibility? For Wesley, "the decision would be made in favor of the approach that best captures the balance of the biblical God—a God that works 'strongly and sweetly.'"[6]

John Wesley, then, was vulnerable to his approach being criticized as "enthusiasm" since he affirmed the great significance of the work of the Spirit in the contemporary life of the church and in the process of the salvation of each individual. He became the leading edge of the current struggle to affirm both Word and Spirit. Donald G. Bloesch has continued this struggle in the current evangelical environment, insisting that we "must affirm both the sovereign unpredictability of the Spirit and the faithfulness of the Spirit to honor Jesus Christ by kindling the gift of faith in those who hear the church's proclamation of Christ."[7] Other prominent theologians in the twentieth century also entered this arena, but with models of the Spirit and human spiritual experience that championed the inward dynamic of faith while altering significantly the traditional understanding of the historic foundations of the biblical revelation about God. To some of these we now turn.

Contemporary Priority of the Existential

The issues of subjectivity and existentialism have been major players in Christian theism in recent generations. They have drunk deeply of certain contemporary philosophical trends and have been quite influential in the fields of theology and biblical studies. They also have been very controversial and have troubled particularly evangelical Christians who desire to protect "sound doctrine" from what is viewed as the slippery slopes of human subjectivity. We now give attention to four related schools of Christian theism that have impacted heavily the contemporary theological scene. They are represented by two towering figures, Rudolf Bultmann and Paul Tillich. Their theologies dramatize in different ways the key issues of human experience and Christian truth. Who is God? Where is God? How is God to be known? What has God to do with what happens on the historical scene of humans? Is God to be found primarily in the Christ-shaped experiences of human existence, in the philosophical and symbolic concept of "being" itself, and/or in the concrete and even objective historical existence that is claimed by faith and open to public examination?

6. Ibid., 142.
7. Donald G. Bloesch, *The Holy Spirit: Works and Gifts* (Downers Grove, Ill.: InterVarsity Press, 2000), 13.

The liberalism of the nineteenth century may have been challenged and sobered by the neo-orthodoxy of Karl Barth and others early in the twentieth century, but it certainly did not go away. It continued unabated in what we will consider in this chapter—the "demythologization" and "resymbolizing" programs of Rudolf Bultmann, Paul Tillich, and others. Elements of the liberal mindset still persist. They emphasize the conviction that God ought to be defined and defended in light of the broader wisdom drawn from the increasing body of modern knowledge generally. Delwin Brown, for example, insists that today we should "no more absolutize the first-century worldview on the topic of God than on women's roles, monarchy, and slavery." Instead, the Christian concept of God "must cohere with the rest of modern knowledge" as liberal theology "examines the past in light of present insights and the present in light of the past, seeking always from this encounter a revised perspective that is more adequate."[8]

Following such reasoning and embracing an existentialist philosophy, some Christian theologians now have proceeded to recast Christian theism by removing what are seen as past husks and focusing only on the remaining kernels of *experienced* truth. They set past and present in a tense dialogue and typically grant priority to the present. They tend to remove Christian faith from the outer world of history and "demythologize" many of its creedal statements and apparent historical claims (such as the literal resurrection of Jesus). As a result, there have emerged emphases about the nature of God, revelation, and salvation that are quite different at points from classic or orthodox Christian thought.

The most recent wisdom of humans may or may not turn out actually to be wisdom, but surely some level of significance should be granted to the present reality and work of the Holy Spirit. The Spirit is God's active presentness. Spiritual things can be known only in the context of right relationship with God through the Spirit. To be "in Christ" through the present life and guidance of the Spirit of Christ is the way to be set free and put on the path of Christian being and knowing. The Hebrew verb *yada* ("to know") means to encounter, experience, share relationship in an intimate way. Paul's theology champions the concept of "in Christ," which has intimate, immediate, and relational implications. Even so, how is such divine reality and relating to be separated from the vagaries of mere human subjectivism?

Where does divine revelation end and human "enthusiasm" begin? See the chapter-leading quote about John Wesley. Is revelation intensely inward in

---

8. Delwin Brown, in Clark H. Pinnock and Delwin Brown, *Theological Crossfire: An Evangelical/Liberal Dialogue* (Grand Rapids: Zondervan, 1990), 82–83.

nature, or is it also, even primarily, historical and somehow "objective" apart from an individual's experience of it? Traditional Christian theology is pleased to affirm that God's Spirit is very much alive and active and that this dynamism is not to be disconnected from the baseline theistic understandings derived from the historical incarnation of God in Jesus. Wrote Charles Wesley, "Whate'er his Spirit speaks in me, must with the written Word agree." Even so, many theologians of recent generations have struggled to address what they have seen as a "currency crisis," the perceived breakdown of traditional means of Christian communication in relation to modern and now postmodern people.

Henri Nouwen makes an initial point that is widely affirmed. He highlights the central importance of a deep personal relationship between the believer and God, concluding that fruitful Christian leadership relies on "a movement from the moral to the mystical."[9] This is intended as anything but a retreat from the suffering of the world; in fact, Donald Bloesch insists that "meaningful identification with the oppressed rests upon a prior identification with the Savior of the oppressed."[10] Of course, Christian life and ministry require knowing about the faith and being able to function, to do various tasks of ministry. The issue, however, is not only what one *knows* and can *do*. It also and significantly is about *who one is* and *to whom one is significantly related*. To be effective representatives for Christ requires being genuinely Christian, rightly related to Christ. The call is first to be "in Christ" by relationship through the Spirit, then to develop the related knowledge and skills that can verbalize and implement the central reality of true life with God and mission for God. This being said, there nonetheless are many questions that arise when Christian experience is a key focus of faith.

Often we humans tend to dress God in the clothes of our personal choice, consciously or otherwise. We easily manage to see what we look for and adapt that which we see to suit our own presuppositions, needs, and even feelings. Feelings are both deeply human and notoriously undependable as a source of religious truth. Theologians seek for disciplined ways to compensate for this tendency to self-deception and self-serving, to making God in our own image. The search for a balanced and self-critical approach is helped by reference to a quadrilateral of interacting authority sources—the Bible, church tradition, reason, and experience. Often identified as the Wesleyan Quadrilateral (see figure 1), it is important to note that—at least as John Wesley would have it—

    9. Henri Nouwen, *In the Name of Jesus* (New York: Crossroad, 1989), 28–32.
    10. Donald G. Bloesch, *The Struggle of Prayer* (Colorado Springs, Colo.: Helmers & Howard, 1988), 166.

the Bible is to be highlighted as the basic authority source, with the other three forming a trilateral pattern of responsible biblical interpretation. Conservatives typically have emphasized the authority of biblical revelation, while being especially fearful of the misleading potential that lies in the subjectivities of religious experience (with church traditions seen as long-standing collective experiences). Now, however, there are "post-conservative" Christians who exhibit a lessening of the "obsessive fear of liberal theology" and are open to a "fusion of the practical-spiritual with the theoretical-intellectual in evangelical theological methodology."[11]

There certainly is an important connection between lived experience and theological reflection. Numerous contemporary theologians place great emphasis on the experience dimension of the life of Christian faith, sometimes bringing into question the foundational nature of the Bible. They strongly disagree with positivists who claim that the empirical sciences are our primary or even our only means of acquiring dependable knowledge. In fact, the sciences are not able to grasp the reality at the depths of human existence. Subjectivity needs to be stressed, since it is a key route to significant religious knowledge. Such knowledge comes through the human's own participation in actual being. In recent generations, for example, there has been a worldwide surge of interest in the Holy Spirit. The rapid growth of pentecostal and charismatic movements (inside and outside of mainline Christian bodies) highlights a considerable sense of past neglect that has contributed to a feeling of God's remoteness that is no longer tolerable.[12] Calling this fresh Spirit focus the "nearer side of God," John Macquarrie observes:

> It is a strange irony that God has so often been understood in terms of the "farther side"—his transcendence, majesty, rationality, immutability, masculinity, and so on. A renewal of the doctrine of the Holy Spirit would go far toward bringing a richer and more balanced understanding of God in his immanence, humility, accessibility, openness, and love.[13]

Most of Christian pentecostalism is orthodox in its general theological stance, but emphasizes, in addition to theological orthodoxy, the intensity and crucial nature of Christian religious experience, gifting, and community. On

---

11. Roger E. Olson, in John G. Stackhouse Jr., ed., *Evangelical Futures* (Grand Rapids: Baker Books, 2000), 202, 206.

12. The nonpentecostal theologian Donald G. Bloesch, for example, works nonetheless from the premise that "formalism" is one of the "deadliest enemies of true faith" (*Holy Spirit,* 13).

13. John Macquarrie, *Thinking about God* (New York: Harper & Row, 1975), 131.

the other hand, the subjective slant of much of contemporary theology openly questions aspects of the God of supernaturalistic theism. Such questioning of "up there" and "out there" language for God, claiming that it should be abandoned as no longer meaningful in the space age, means that increasingly it is difficult to distinguish between theism and atheism. Macquarrie thinks of belief in God as "faith in *being*," confidence that "reality is trustworthy at the deepest level." For him, special place belongs to the language of "being" because "it strives to open up for our time and culture new glimpses into that mystery, at once awesome and fascinating, which we designate by the word 'God.' "[14] Thus, there have arisen schools of Christian thought that reconceive God in terms of "being," with Christian meanings lying in the relatively undefinable spiritual depths of experienced existence.

Seeking the Essence of Being

Prominent at the scholarly level in relation to this recent emphasis on subjectivity are the highly influential works of Rudolf Bultmann (1884–1976) and Paul Tillich (1886–1965). In various ways they were major shapers of twentieth-century existential Christian theology.

Rudolf Bultmann

Rudolf Bultmann began with the assumption that theology speaks out of faith, so that "speaking of God . . . is only possible as talk of ourselves."[15] He claimed that the original oral content of the New Testament Gospels had been wrapped in layers of mythological tradition. He concluded, therefore, that the distinctive existential content of the good news in Jesus comes to us now in symbol-language packages made up of diverse cultural-religious patterns extending far beyond the ancient Jewish. Thus, he insisted on a distinction between the *Jesus of history* (the man who actually lived and taught) and the *Christ of faith* (the God present in Jesus who transcends any particular history or culture). The kerygma, the essential proclamation of the New Testament, must be "demythologized"—freed from the shell of its mythical settings and expressions. Speaking in part from a pastoral concern, Bultmann assumed that the theological statements of the New Testament are to be interpreted in a way that clarifies their understanding of human existence. Only in this way

14. Ibid., 109.
15. Rudolf Bultmann, *Faith and Understanding* (London: SCM Press, 1969), 61.

can they offer to new hearers the possibility of understanding themselves in the same way that the original writers understood themselves.

The philosophy of Martin Heidegger became the interpretive lens through which Bultmann determined he could perceive the dimensions of the New Testament kerygma that are relevant for all times. The focus shifted for him to the immediate, inner self-consciousness of the individual. Providing an antimetaphysical account of Christian faith, Bultmann held to the experienced realm of religion separate from the natural, social, and historical worlds. Through the biblical record God is said to confront humans with a divine graciousness that makes possible the recovery of the authentic existence that was supremely actualized in Jesus. The promise to us is transformed existence.

When once asked whether he believed that Jesus had actually risen from the dead, Bultmann responded, "I am a theologian, not an archaeologist." This makes clear that "instead of defining the Christian proclamation in terms of what God has announced and accomplished 'out there' in biblical history . . . Bultmann defined it in terms of what individuals experience in their own personal confrontation with existence."[16] He was convinced that if the modern person were going to take seriously the question of God, the "mythological" element of Christianity must be removed. The key question is whether or not the gospel of God's graciousness in Jesus can be salvaged from its early cultural and linguistic expressions and separated from its traditional historical moorings. The quest to discover the enduring meanings beneath what is presumed to be the dated mythological packages of the text is a legitimate one, according to Bultmann, because the "myths" of Scripture were intended to portray, not historical and cultural incidentals, but the ways in which the narrators understood their own existence in relation to "ultimate concerns" that persist for humans.

A common criticism of Bultmann's agenda is his failure to affirm that the biblical witness and traditional Christian doctrine are intentionally concerned *both* with God in his relationships with humans (the existential aspect of God's nature and work) and with God as he actually is in himself (quite apart from all human existence and experience). A key question is *where* knowledge of God is to be found. Bultmann locates saving truth in the faith community that is responding with heart and mind to the foundational revelation of God, the Jesus-event, *whose power is to be experienced in the present.* While such transformation clearly is a New Testament teaching, the danger of Bultmann's approach, as many of his conservative critics have pointed out,

---

16. Ed. L. Miller and Stanley J. Grenz, *Introduction to Contemporary Theologies* (Minneapolis: Fortress Press, 1998), 51–52.

is an individualistic subjectivism that reduces history only to a process of self-understanding and silences along the way much of the historical dimension of the biblical witness that is more than incidental to the text's long-term intentions. There surely is more to theology than anthropology, more in the Christian proclamation about God than what is experienced immediately by believers.

Bultmann believed that personal experience made God-talk intelligible in the modern world quite apart from any metaphysical overlays found in the New Testament and subsequently added in Christian history. For example, Bultmann said that talk of "Trinity" was beside the point for the most part since this dogma emerged from accommodation to the ancient Hellenistic ethos and thus distracts the believer from the prime existential question. In fact, Bultmann said that God cannot be thought of theoretically at all, but only existentially as the power of new life within us. We can assume *that* God is, but not *what* God is.[17] The best approach, therefore, is to adopt a new existential language that resonates with the ethos of modernity. Bloesch understandably concludes that Bultmann "in effect gives up his claim to be a biblical theologian and becomes instead an existentialist philosopher."[18]

Admittedly, human language is fragile at best when speaking of God and inevitably is conditioned culturally. Does this mean, however, that all theological language is secondary to the experience to which it refers? Does this mean that there is little firm and necessary historical grounding to the Christian proclamation, only existential insight and power? Such are key theological questions.

Paul Tillich

Another German theologian, Paul Tillich, fled to the United States in the 1930s when the Nazis began persecuting nonconforming theologians. Unlike Karl Barth, who was resisting the incursions of philosophy and culture as serious distractions to true Christian identity, Tillich joined Bultmann in affirming the necessity of translating the Christian message in relation to the existential questions being posed by contemporary cultural situations. The 1936 publication of *On the Boundary*, Tillich's autobiographical reflections,

---

17. For reflections on Bultmann's belief about God, see Macquarrie, *Thinking about God*, 179–90. Bultmann resisted as illegitimate any attempt at objectification of God. God cannot be talked about in abstractions or reached through a purely intellectual speculation. While his "actual thought of God is very elusive" (179), Bultmann nonetheless said that Christianity is not merely another religious existentialism, but that it knows of an act of God that enables access to authentic life.

18. Bloesch, *Holy Spirit*, 236.

positioned his own vocation at the intersection of the Christian tradition and major movements in secular culture. He sought to reinterpret Christian symbols so that secular people could understand and be moved by them. His famous "method of correlation" sought to take "religious" questions as they were commonly posed and link them to answers that are implied in the best of the Christian tradition.

Tillich wanted to make Christianity understandable and persuasive to religiously skeptical and secularly inclined people who nonetheless wrestle with issues of "ultimate concern." He assumed that divine revelation gives us a true awareness of the spiritual, but not objective knowledge about it. We can speak only symbolically about God. Although the key Christian symbols are not fixed religious propositions of truth, they do participate in the truth toward which they point. Knowledge of God is more quest than possession.

What about God? Part 2 of Tillich's *Systematic Theology* correlates the "symbol" of "God the Creator" with modern culture's expressions of finitude.[19] How can we withstand the destructive forces that threaten to disintegrate our lives? People often are nearly overwhelmed by meaninglessness, guilt, and death. Their "being" is threatened by "non-being." Tillich said that God is the welcome presence of the "power of being," the very ground of our human being. He did not speak of the *existence* of God, but of "Being itself," utterly unconditioned and present to everything ("God is Lord"). He has been called a "Christian atheist" because of his denial of sure knowledge about the existence of a traditionally understood God "out there." For him, thinking of God as personal is to speak transformingly to modern humans in their anxiety and loneliness. There is a difference between a "person up there" and a personal ground of all existence. God is not to be thought of as a "person," but as the name for what concerns us humans ultimately.[20] Tillich insisted that faith must transcend the "God of theism" in order to apprehend the "God above God."[21]

To avoid idolatry, insisted Tillich, we must deny both the supernaturalist idea of God as another being-entity beyond our world experience and the naturalist idea of God not being distinguished from the universe and thus not adequate for our experience of the holy. Note Alvin C. Porteous's clarification:

19. Tillich's *Systematic Theology* was released in three volumes (Chicago: University of Chicago Press, 1951, 1957, 1963).
20. Tillich does not mean that our ultimate concerns are secondary seductions such as gaining wealth or staying young. Even so, his concept is easily cheapened, misunderstood, and usually does not equal what the classic Christian tradition has meant by "God."
21. Tillich, *Systematic Theology*, 1:205.

What he [Tillich] means to convey . . . is not that God is not real and distinguishable from ourselves and our world; but that he [God] is precisely that reality with which we are most intimately, profoundly, and, indeed, disturbingly confronted. He is not a being who resides somewhere "up in the blue." . . . He is the creative ground of everything that has being, without whose sustaining power nothing could exist. We meet him not in some extramundane spiritual retreat, but in the depths of our intramundane existence as life confronts us with the unconditional demands of truth and righteousness and love in our daily relationships and forces upon us questions of ultimate meaning and purpose.[22]

Shaking the Foundations

Why were the [Hebrew] prophets able to face what they knew, and then to pronounce it with such overwhelming power? Their power sprang from the fact that they did not really speak of the foundations of the earth as such, but of Him Who laid the foundations and would shake them; and that they did not speak of the doom of the nations as such, but of Him Who brings doom for the sake of His eternal justice and salvation. As the 102nd Psalm says: "Thy years are throughout all generations. Of old thou has laid the foundations of the earth, and the heavens are the work of thy hands. *They vanish,* but *thou shalt endure;* they wear out like a robe, thou changest them like garments. But thou art the same and thy years shall have no end. . . ." When the earth grows old and wears out, when nations and cultures die, the Eternal changes the garments of His infinite being. He is the foundation on which all foundations are laid; and this foundation cannot be shaken. There is something immovable, unchangeable, unshakeable, eternal, which becomes manifest in our passing and in the crumbling of our world. On the boundaries of the finite the infinite becomes visible; in the light of the Eternal the transitoriness of the temporal appears.

—From the sermon "The Shaking of the Foundations" by Paul Tillich, based on Jeremiah 4:23–30, Isaiah 54:10, and Isaiah 24:18–20, in *The Shaking of the Foundations*

22. Alvin C. Porteous, *Prophetic Voices in Contemporary Theology* (Nashville: Abingdon Press, 1966), 109.

Leaving behind all special images (God *in* or *above* the world), Tillich thought that the best image is God as "Being itself," the depth, ground, condition, and power of all that is.

Seeking to rise above traditional Christian theism without reverting to pantheism (see glossary), Tillich taught that God is not a "person" in the sense in which we humans are persons, but the ground of all that is personal—and thus God is suprapersonal (as opposed to impersonal). God transcends that of which he is the ground, but has subjected himself to the conditions of human estrangement (the Christ incarnation). God also has transformed the estrangement through Jesus who, as the Christ, "united with the ground of his being and meaning without separation and disruption."[23] The cross symbolizes the shared estrangement and the resurrection its conquest, with Christ now bearing and mediating the "new being" for those who receive him in faith. The important thing about the story of the resurrection of Jesus, according to Tillich, is not whether it happened historically in a particular place and way, but (like Bultmann) that it is a powerful *symbol* of the potential of new being available to all people by the grace of Being itself.

God in Revelation and Real History

Christian theologians Rudolf Bultmann and Paul Tillich look inward for wisdom and locate authority in the dynamics of Being itself. Human experience, mythical expression, and Being itself are featured as crucial for the credibility of Christian faith on the contemporary scene. Such related approaches raise significant questions about faith's relation to actual (outward) human history.

The structure of Tillich's argument, for instance, makes the historical facticity of Jesus secondary to theological claims about his significance existentially. The existentialism of Bultmann makes the literal resurrection of Jesus from the grave relatively unimportant in favor of what really counts, namely, the message that new life within one's being is an ongoing possibility because of God's renewing grace. This approach leaves hard questions to be answered. Is there any meaningful content in Tillich's "Ground of Being" idea? Was God really incarnate in Jesus? Is it adequate to think of the cross and resurrection of Jesus as only primary Christian symbols that are devoid of necessary historical content? What is the relation between the Jesus who once lived and the Christ who now lives in and for our existential situations? The sharp contrast

---

23. Tillich, *Systematic Theology,* 1:133.

is this: Tillich judged that the contemporary significance of the Christian faith is relatively independent of whether or not Jesus even lived, died, or rose again; by contrast, the apostle Paul saw Christian faith as inseparable from its historical moorings (1 Cor. 15:14). Was Paul's view incidental to his time or inherent in the faith itself? Are the more recent existentialist views serious compromises of the faith with a contemporary philosophy or crucial and fully appropriate adaptations of the faith for our time?

God gets clothed in the inner dynamics of existence by Bultmann and Tillich, and God also tends to get removed from historically rooted reality. Christian faith certainly must have existential significance; such significance, however, surely depends on some substantive historical foundation—God *is* and has really *done something,* at least so says the more traditional view of Christian theism. Clark Pinnock speaks to this point:

> This trend toward the interiorization of faith, where Christianity becomes an ideal of life rather than a truth claim about an objective God beyond the natural world, is something we deplore. Evangelicals stand with all those who contend that God exists truly and objectively as the rewarder of those that diligently seek him. Belief in God is not just a projection or function of the human psyche, but exists in a realist sense as the source and power of the world.[24]

Thomas Oden broadens the meaning of religious "experience" so that much more than subjective personal consciousness is in view. He insists that it is misleading to pit "experience" against church "tradition," since tradition is the memory of the "vast arena of social and historical experiencing." Of course, past experience that is corporately remembered must intersect with one's own immediate experiencing if it is to be personally meaningful and effectively appropriated. Even so, "Scripture and tradition are received, understood, and validated through personal experience, but not judged or arbitrated or censored by it."[25] The Spirit works to make experiencing possible, but the Spirit's working does not lead in a direction contrary to the written Word of God as faithfully interpreted and conveyed in the believing tradition of the church. This tradition holds vigorously to a firm historical basis for the faith, one transcending the presumption that ancient "myths" are now to be removed from the essential witness. Substance and conveyance are not that separable in spite of changing culture and language.

---

24. Pinnock, in Pinnock and Brown, *Theological Crossfire,* 67.
25. Thomas Oden, *The Living God,* vol. 1 of *Systematic Theology* (Peabody, Mass.: Prince Press, 1998), 338–39.

Christian spirituality, then, should begin by recognizing reality and revelation rooted *outside* of us humans, as opposed to primary attention being focused *inside* our realms of immediate human experience. God's Spirit does come to dwell within us, but there are other spirits mingled with our finite inner worlds. To distinguish between God's Spirit, our own spirits, and foreign and even demonic spirits, we are called to look to Scripture to learn who God's Spirit is and what God's Spirit intends, has done, and still does.[26] To experience God's true presence and to become what God graciously enables require awareness of and openness to the true identity of God as God has been made known historically in Jesus Christ. Therefore, says Shirley C. Guthrie:

> If I want to know what God is doing and promises to do in my life, I cannot just analyze and tell *my* little story (or listen to the little stories of others); I must interpret my story (and theirs) in light of *God's* story with ancient Israel and the first Christian community. If I want to know what it would mean for me to be a truly spiritual person, I must first of all look at the life of Jesus Christ and the kind of person he was, not at my own life and the kind of person I would like to be.[27]

Clark Pinnock has come to value the "pietistic" in approaching Christian believing, encouraged in part by his understanding that postmodern developments in the last quarter of the twentieth century—emphasizing the particular and experiential—favor a biblical and "evangelical pietism."[28] He has found himself being "filled with the Spirit" and increasingly seeking to revitalize evangelical doctrine by the fresh illumination of God's Spirit.[29] For him, however, it is not that spiritual experience is the *norm* of truth, but that to really know God requires prayerful receptivity to the present revealing and re-creating work of the Spirit. Such divine work is never to be separated from the historically rooted and definitive revelation of God, which necessarily includes the key narration of divine actions and self-revelation available in the Bible. Experience *confirms* the gospel that history validates, but experience does not *create* the truth or finally *define* it. In his exploration of his own complex identity as an evangelical, Stanley Grenz agrees, noting that he is a

26. For an identification of the key functions of God's Holy Spirit and extensive commentary on how they should shape Christian spiritual life, see Barry L. Callen, *Authentic Spirituality: Moving beyond Mere Religion* (Grand Rapids: Baker Academic, 2002).

27. Shirley C. Guthrie, *Christian Doctrine,* rev. ed. (Louisville, Ky.: Westminster John Knox Press, 1994), 298–99.

28. Clark H. Pinnock, "Evangelical Theologians Facing the Future: Ancient and Future Paradigms," *Wesleyan Theological Journal* 33, no. 2 (Fall 1998), 11.

29. See Clark H. Pinnock, foreword to *Authentic Spirituality: Moving beyond Mere Religion,* by Barry L. Callen (Grand Rapids: Baker Books, 2002).

"Pietist with a Ph.D."[30] Experience is crucial, but must remain rooted in divine revelation and disciplined reflection.

To "know" in the realm of faith is intimately and necessarily related to knowing the knower (God). Spiritual knowledge, of course, is much more than a mere collection of religious information. Beyond information is spiritual discernment and formation. Beyond ideas is the God in whose vast mystery lies real understanding. To know God necessarily is to be changed by God in the direction of God-likeness. To know the truth involves the sheer grace of first being known by the truth—God. For Christian theology, truth finally is awareness of and right relationship with God. Theology "has no obvious subject matter since God is not an object of human knowledge and is not scientifically accessible as most physical objects are. . . . Seeking for truths about God is not to precede or overshadow actually knowing God."[31]

Recognizing that authentic life in Christ should be rooted in the Christ of historical revelation, Christian faith is certainly to have a profound inward impact. In fact, a strong Christian tradition speaks of the goal of *deification* (see glossary). As opposed to much of the Western church, early Greek and later Eastern Orthodox theologians saw the essential human need as therapeutic—the need to be healed by recovering the likeness of God in actual experience. God "has given us his very great and precious promises, so that through them *you may participate in the divine nature*" (2 Pet. 1:4, emphasis added). As Athanasius put it, "God became like us so that we might become like God."[32] God is source, model, resource, and goal. Rather than the legal focus of the West (being "justified" before God, for example), the East has stressed the mystical focus of being healed by and actually united with God— not to become part of God, of course, as in pantheism (see glossary), but to share by divine grace in the "energies" of God (see glossary).[33] The goal of life, triumphing over death, will only be complete in the age to come; even so, the process is now very real. Believers ascend from the image of God possessed by all people to sharing in God's very likeness, a sharing enabled for those who cooperate with the divine love and grace that has come historically in the Christ and truly transforms the present through the Spirit's ministry.

The paradox now being confronted might be put like this. There is fixed

30. See Stanley J. Grenz, "Concerns of a Pietist with a Ph.D.," *Wesleyan Theological Journal* 37, no. 2 (Fall 2002), 58–76.

31. Callen, *Authentic Spirituality,* 137.

32. Athanasius, *On the Incarnation of the Lord,* article 54.

33. Daniel Clendenin says wisely, "The East emphasizes the crucial idea of mystical union and divine transformation, while the West tends to stress the believer's juridical standing before a holy God. Both conceptions . . . find biblical support and deserve full theological expression" (*Eastern Orthodox Christianity* [Grand Rapids: Baker Books, 1994], 159).

truth for Christians, a definite understanding of God and God's ways. This truth is available through divine revelation, but it is centered in the personal presence of God in Christ through the Spirit. It can be known only in the context of believers (the church) who are being transformed by the truth of God that is in Jesus Christ and now is active in the ministry of the Spirit. Experience is essential to authentic faith, but uniquely Christian experience is not to be left without some definition and historical roots.

Charles Colson recently reacted to a popular theologian who had exhorted a crowd of Christian educators not to fight postmodernity, but to take advantage of it. If postmodernity represents the current mood of questioning the arrogance of human reason, instead championing a broad range of ways of knowing—including the experiences of intuition, feelings, and so on—it also represents a sharp narrowing of the presumed possibility of knowing any "truth" that is true for all people in all places. Knowing is thought to be locked in the confines of the knower's own communities of gender, race, social location, and so forth. Any claim to objectivity is to be forfeited in favor of a pervasive subjectivity, since this is just the way things apparently are. A recent poll revealed that the most common basis for moral decision making among Christians is "doing whatever feels right" in given circumstances. Colson responded by insisting that the Christian gospel is "not a matter of soothing feelings or rewarding experiences (although it may produce both). It is *the Truth.*"[34]

Seekers after God seek the truth within, and usually assume or at least hope that the truth found within corresponds to reality without. We seek transformation free of self-delusion. Continuing questions of Christian theology center in the roles of experience, myth, and symbol and their relationship to human understandings of God and God's truth.

---

34. Charles Colson, "More Doctrine, Not Less," *Christianity Today,* April 22, 2002, 96. Emphasis added.

Chapter 7

A Near-Death Experience

We shall understand the death of God as an historical event: God has died in our *time, in* our *history, in* our *existence. The man who chooses to live in our destiny can neither know the reality of God's presence nor understand the world as His creation.*
　　　　　　　　　　　　—*Thomas J. J. Altizer and William Hamilton,*
　　　　　　　　　　　　　　Radical theology and the Death of God

The rationalism that inspires the entire Death of God theology should be unmasked for what it is. The disease is not in the atheism nor in the shocking expression, "God is dead." These are but symptoms of a deeper disease and that disease is a theological rationalism that refuses obedience to the solemn authority of Scriptures.
　　　　　　　　　　　　　　—*Bernard Ramm, in* Is God Dead?

*M*artyrdom is a well-known concept. On occasion a deeply committed believer will accept death as a consequence of persistent faith in the face of violent opposition. Less common is the concept of *God dying,* abandoning the believer to the travail of nothing other than oneself and this troubled and now forsaken world. At the hands of various professing Christian thinkers in recent times, the God of the Bible—or at least the transcendent deity of the classic tradition's interpretation of the Bible—has faced a series of near-death or actual-death experiences. The history of Christian theology has witnessed God appearing, disappearing, and reappearing. But *dying*? Yes, the living God of biblical revelation has been pronounced dead by various Christian teachers.

In a local grocery store, I once saw a headline on the cover of one of those sensational tabloids that read, "Ventriloquist in Coma, But the Dummy Is Still Talking!" Such outrageous "reporting" has its counterpart in relation to none other than God who, according to some serious thinkers, supposedly has fallen silent, is gravely ill, or even has died, while many people are said to be going right on talking about or even for him! This has raised the most serious of questions in recent generations. Has God survived the intellectual challenges of modern times, or has the Divine quietly expired?

God as Irrelevant, Then Abhorrent

By the beginning of the nineteenth century, atheism (see glossary) was definitely leading the agenda in several intellectual circles of Europe and North America. A spirit of human autonomy and independence was growing, in part encouraged by the advances in science and technology. This spirit led some prominent people to declare their independence from old ideas about a transcendent and all-controlling God. New philosophies arose that left little or no place for even the idea of such a God. The resulting judgment was that the God traditionally affirmed by Christians was now largely irrelevant to quality human life and often obstructive to the fresh potential of social progress, maybe even antithetical to them and thus actually abhorrent to the well-being of humanity. "God" had become an optional religious theory that tended to retard personal development and social progress. Some liberal Christian thinkers, sensitive to progressive thought but not prepared to yield the cornerstone of Christian faith, reacted to this anti-God bias by trying to "save" God in a variety of innovative ways.

Friedrich Schleiermacher (1768–1834) and others drafted new theologies that largely disconnected God from threatening systems of empirical thought. But some Romantics, such as William Blake (1757–1827), rebelled against the God of Christianity because the divine idea supposedly had been used to alienate people from their natural dignity and humanity, repressing sexuality, liberty, and spontaneous joy. God himself, for the sake of humanity's well-being, needed to fall into the world and die. In fact, it was said that God actually had died in the person of Jesus so that the alienating "transcendent" God would be no more. In Jesus, God had gracefully eliminated himself for the sake of the creation. The cross of Jesus was the voluntary grave of God!

It is true that the early twentieth century witnessed a resurgence of emphasis by some theologians on the continuing reality and genuine transcendence of God (Karl Barth and others). It is also true that linguistic studies began calling into question the objective meaningfulness of all language about God. So, with God rising "out of this world" unless choosing to engage it (Barth), being depersonalized in the philosophical abstraction of "Being itself" (Tillich), and being "existentialized," moving outside the range of the certainty of human perception and articulation (Bultmann), it was only a matter of time before some theologians would conclude that, at least for all practical purposes, God was now "dead."

The words of theologian Thomas J. J. Altizer could hardly be more straightforward: "If there is one clear portal to the twentieth century, it is a passage to the death of God, the collapse of any meaning or reality by and beyond the newly discovered radical eminence of modern man, an eminence dissolving even the memory or shadow of transcendence."[1] The radical claim was that the era of "Christian" civilization had come to an end, along with many of the moral standards and restraints associated with the God tradition-ally proclaimed by Christians. This was not a mere publicity stunt. Altizer and others seriously contended that God *was no more*. The house of Christendom had collapsed, and with the collapse was a disintegration of its divine foun-dation. He insisted that God is dead both in the sense that transcendence is irrelevant to modern people and in the sense that God, having become incar-nate in Jesus, literally died in his primordial form.

The skeptical and revolutionary 1960s did not exempt God from its gallery of establishment targets, but such radicalism soon brought opposing and vig-orously resisting voices. Father Vincent Miceli echoed the forthright denun-ciation of atheistic communism written by Pope Pius XI in 1937 (*Divini Redemptoris*). He observed, however, that communism was hardly alone in its anti-God bias. There was a range of "Christian" thinkers attempting to do theology via human introspection and within a context of nontranscendent categories. They were building on but going farther than Bultmann or Tillich had gone, now actually announcing that God had died. Miceli insisted on the inevitable folly of opting for a view that denies the classic Christian category of absolute transcendence and seeks to avoid—even to kill and seek to bury—a God who is truly real quite apart from us arrogant humans and our troubled societies. He presented seventeen case studies of leading modern apostles of atheism, ranging from "Feuerbach: Humanity Becomes God" and "Marx: Cosmic Classless Society Becomes God" to "Van Buren: Annihilator of a Lin-guistic Deity." In every case, what he found was someone whom he judged had "equated their espousal of atheism with their adventure to achieve man's mental emancipation and personal liberation from the tyranny of a Deity who imposed upon mankind from above the shackles of crystalloid creeds and moral dictates."[2]

---

1. Thomas J. J. Altizer, *The Gospel of Christian Atheism* (Philadelphia: Westminster Press, 1966), 22.
2. Vincent P. Miceli, S.J., *The Gods of Atheism* (New Rochelle, N.Y.: Arlington House Publishers, 1971), as quoted in Barry L. Callen, *Christian Scholar's Review* 2, no. 1 (Fall 1971), 73.

Humans supposedly had come of age and thus needed less of the Divine as they pursued the achievement of their own legitimate independence, maturity, and self-realization. The secularized world was now largely empirical and pragmatic in approach to religious matters. Traditional belief in a transcendent God "up there" or "out there" had become essentially meaningless for many. John A. T. Robinson drew on a range of ideas from Rudolf Bultmann, Paul Tillich, and Dietrich Bohnhoeffer and proceeded to popularize such a dire conclusion in his popular 1963 book *Honest to God*. God was being reduced to the being of humans, and theology was becoming essentially a form of anthropology. Transcendence was now being understood as a this-worldly depth, not an otherworldly externality where God resides before and beyond the creation. Conservative Christians naturally judged such a conclusion idolatrous to the extent that it encourages humans to fall down before themselves in narcissistic love and adoration.

Given the traditional Christian teaching that humans by nature seek the Transcendent beyond themselves, is it not the case that atheism is less pure disbelief and more an inverted faith that finally names oneself as God?

Perspectives on Atheism

An atheist is a man who looks through a telescope and tries to explain what he can't see.

—O. A. Battista, *Power to Influence People*

My atheism . . . is true piety towards the universe and denies only gods fashioned by men in their own image to be servants of their human interests.

—George Santayana

To believe in God is impossible—not to believe in Him is absurd.

—Voltaire

The God I believe in is not so fragile that you hurt Him by being angry at Him, or so petty that He will hold it against you for being upset with Him.

—Rabbi Harold S. Kushner

Regardless of the answer, understanding the God who is biblically revealed has been challenged across the centuries by assertions of uncertain ways of knowing the ultimate and of claims to the independent adequacy of humans.

Obituary for the Divine

There is an ancient teaching in the world of Christian theology called *patripassianism* (see glossary). Finally judged heretical, it claimed that God the Father was so identical with the Christ of the incarnation that God "died" when Christ was crucified and died. Toward the end of the second century, Praxeas taught that the Godhead was emptied into the person of Christ *without remainder*. God came down into the Virgin's womb and was born as the Son. When the Son suffered, the Father suffered. When the Son died, the Father "died"—although the Father raised himself from the tomb to live on with us as the Spirit. Various forms of such thought have persisted for centuries around the outer edges of orthodox Christian teaching.

Today, whether one speaks of the perceived absence or presumed actual death of God, the reference is in the context of the atheistic tendency of modern secular culture. It is shaped by the science, technology, and consumerism that tend to explain the world and form definitions of human happiness without reliance on the "hypothesis" of God's existence. As early as 1802, Hegel spoke of the Good Friday experience of the death of God as the basic religious awareness of modern times. William Blake and Friedrich Nietzsche (1844–1900) interpreted human freedom as emancipation from all external authority, especially the religious authority of the Christian tradition. For Nietzsche, humans have finally managed to kill God and, to be worthy of their deicide, they must themselves become gods or supermen, taking charge of history and building a better world on the corpse of God. In *Thus Spake Zarathustra* (1883), Nietzsche proclaimed the birth of enlightened people who were heralding a powerful new humanity that would dispense with the feeble Christian virtues of love and pity. It should be noted, however, that Nietzsche's theories were used by a later generation of Germans to justify key Nazi policies, a warning to us that an atheistic ideology, supposedly liberating humanity, can easily lead to a cruel march toward humanity's destruction!

The new "gospel" of atheism holds that apparently there no longer is need or room for God in the world. Science can explain things without reference to the Divine, and the God traditionally taught by Christians is too otherworldly to be relevant to real life here and now. After all, argued Ludwig

Feuerbach in his influential *The Essence of Christianity* (1841), all along God had been nothing more than a human projection. Sigmund Freud (1856–1939) insisted that the idea of God was a device of the human unconscious, nothing more than an exalted father figure needing elimination. "Modern" people increasingly were inclined to think that new understandings of the universe (such as evolution) dealt a deathblow to the traditional idea of a sovereign creator God. This deathblow was greeted with a dismissing smile by some and with fearful dismay by others. The great Victorian poet Alfred, Lord Tennyson, wrote in 1850 about such loss of faith that reduces a person to "an infant crying in the night; an infant crying for the light, and with no language but a cry."[3]

In 1961 Gabriel Vahanian used the phrase "the death of God" in his analysis of contemporary culture. He became the father of the short-lived movement called the "theology of the death of God." His view was that contemporary culture, with its anthropocentric attitude, was expressing the presumed irrelevance of God to concrete existence.[4] People had lost all experience of God and awareness of transcendence. An even harsher judgment was that the anti-God revolt in progress was really against the Christian community, which Vahanian identified with an outmoded system of thought that was itself a social order now perceived to be impeding the needed progress of humankind. For the sake of real progress, the church and its God had to go. One conservative Christian leader recognized some truth in this dire judgment and issued this warning to the churches:

> No wonder some have felt that the church's God is dead when the church has been so dead to the cries for freedom and justice in our land and around the world. Ours is a day of almost idealistic concern for the rights of others, especially among our young people. A calloused church will gain no hearing on our university and college campuses. In fact, some students may go so far as to rejoice in the reports of the death of a God whose people have been so careless about the humane causes that preoccupy them.[5]

It is one thing to join Rudolf Bultmann, Paul Tillich, and others in trying to resymbolize God in order to address more effectively today's secularized people at the level of their experienced being. It is quite another thing to speak of getting rid of religion and even God altogether. Many of the radical the-

---

3. Alfred, Lord Tennyson, *In Memoriam*, 54.
4. Gabriel Vahanian, *The Death of God: The Culture of Our Post-Christian Era* (New York: George Braziller, 1961), 175–87.
5. David Hubbard, in *Is God Dead?* (a published multi-author symposium; Grand Rapids: Zondervan, 1966), 114–15.

ologians in the middle decades of the twentieth century were either Paul Tillich's students or were strongly influenced by him, but in revolutionary times they took themes in Tillich's work to a new level (or a new low), one more reflective of the earlier German existentialist Friedrich Nietzsche. In his 1882 *The Gay Science,* Nietzsche pictured a madman running wildly in the streets in a failed attempt to find God. God apparently was dead, meaning that we fragile humans would have to step into the void.

Where had God gone? "We have killed him, you and I!" What is left? "Do we not stray, as though through an infinite nothingness?" Nietzsche was saying that the classic Christian understanding of God was no longer believable. The decks must somehow be cleared for a fresh theological beginning in the vacuum of departed deity. While biblical believers would readily affirm that God is hardly disturbed about premature reports of his death (see Ps. 2), many modern people believe what they hear—and want to hear. God is gone; biblical obedience is no longer necessary; human rights and reason are supreme; the future is finally open for whatever people want it to be and on their own are able to make it be.

A key voice among the radicals of the twentieth century was Dietrich Bonhoeffer (1906–1945). He was a highly educated German pastor who was ousted by the Nazis from his theology professorate at the University of Berlin in 1936. Soon he was heading an underground seminary and writing influential books such as *The Cost of Discipleship* and *Life Together*. Bonhoeffer developed the dramatic thesis that the world had "come of age" and could do without "religion." As God was being pushed out of modern life, he saw and approved of the trend to a "completely religionless time."[6] It is important, however, to be fair to this courageous and deeply believing Christian martyr. What he presumably meant was essentially that the world now can do without *religiosity*—that is, faith based on "cheap grace," preoccupied with the traditional institutions and rituals, individualistic in character, much too isolated from the pain of public life, rationalized for privilege, a perpetuation of dependency.[7] Traditional religion, as Bonhoeffer saw it in the troubled 1930s and 1940s, featured the default position, a "God of the gaps." Theism had become little more than a temporary compensation for what we advanced

6. Dietrich Bonhoeffer, *Letters and Papers from Prison*, rev. ed., ed. Eberhard Bethge (New York: Macmillan, 1965), 139, 168.

7. Bonhoeffer's contrast, new life versus mere religion, echoes the earlier contrast made by John Wesley between new life in Christ and the mere formalities of establishment religion. Wesley was careful, however, to keep God first, followed by care for the neighbor (but never God without the neighbor). He argued that "real" Christians are those whose inward and outward lives have been transformed by the bountiful sanctifying grace of God. See the Wesley biography *A Real Christian* by Kenneth J. Collins (Nashville: Abingdon Press, 1999).

humans still could not understand or were yet unable to do for ourselves. The true God demands of his people disciplined righteousness and the practicing of social justice.

With the rise of such things as Darwinian evolution and Freudian psychology, the gaps seemed to be getting much smaller and were forcing people to learn to live almost as though the concept of God were not a given at all. As the world "comes of age," Bonhoeffer argued, the way was opening for the true God of the Bible to be seen again. This God was said to come to us in weakness. Rather than solving our problems and ignorance through an otherworldly and unlimited power and knowledge, God breaks down our pretensions and leads us to a "worldly holiness" in which we are called to live "for others." Being authentically "religious" and truly Christian, then, means the actual participation with God in the sufferings of secular life. We are being called to *new life,* not *new religion.* Bonhoeffer himself felt compelled to be involved in the horrific political and moral crisis of his time, including resisting the accommodating ("religious") German Christians of the Third Reich and helping with a plot to assassinate Hitler, which led to his own execution in April 1945. He had joined Bultmann and Tillich in a radical reimaging of Christianity for the sake of practical relevance in the modern world.

Some interpreters see continuity between Bonhoeffer and radicals such as Baptist theologian Harvey Cox. In 1965 Cox wrote *The Secular City,* which announced that traditional religion was collapsing in the face of rising urban civilization. The secularizing process was "the loosing of the world from religious and quasi-religious understandings of itself, the dispelling of all closed world-views, the breaking of all supernatural myths and sacred symbols."[8] Meaning and morality were no longer to be found in religious traditions and rituals. People were being released to their own maturity and freed of any "god" beyond in favor of the well-being of this world at hand. Cox dipped into the Bible to find themes that were seen as encouraging such "maturity" and freedom. He echoed the earlier work of Bishop John A. T. Robinson, who had leaned on some insights of Dietrich Bonhoeffer to prepare his own 1963 theological bestseller, *Honest to God.* To be really honest, announced Robinson, God was in big trouble!

More radical yet were two Americans, William Hamilton and Thomas J. J. Altizer who together in 1966 published *Radical Theology and the Death of God.* They announced boldly nothing less than the demise of the Divine—a "death" that made the cover of *Time* magazine (April 8, 1966). On a solid black background, the magazine cover contained only the red-

8. Harvey Cox, *The Secular City* (New York: Macmillan, 1965), 2.

lettered question, "Is God Dead?"[9] Richard Rubenstein added to the new graveyard theology his *After Auschwitz,* a pessimistic view of post-Holocaust Judaism that saw people living in a time of the death of God—not necessarily that something had happened to God, but an expression of the way people were experiencing the world in which assumptions about the presence and gracious purposes of God had been crushed and rendered virtually incredible. But Altizer and Hamilton went further. God had really died. Said Hamilton: "There really is a sense of non-having, of non-believing, of having lost, not just the idols or the gods of religion, but God himself."[10] Here is his bottom line:

> God has been transformed, the supernatural has become immersed in space and time, the spirit has become flesh, the transcendent God has become wholly immanent, and not only has our way of talking about God changed—*God* has changed.[11]

Reflecting Ernst Bloch, the Marxist philosopher who taught that in the incarnation the Son replaced the Father, Altizer speculated that the transcendent God had annihilated himself in the act of incarnation and thereby had achieved the liberation of his human creatures. The finality of God's death liberated humans to authentic selfhood. With God dead, humanity could finally live!

The social turbulence of the 1960s was the perfect setting for a secular theology that saw God being pushed out of the world altogether. God had become flesh (began dying in Jesus) and now was said to have achieved a complete union of the sacred and profane that finally was liberating people from an "alien transcendent" so that they could live freely and responsibly in the present. An abolished transcendence apparently allows an absolute immanence released from all bondages of the past.[12] Liberation from what was claimed to be an artificially induced guilt rooted in arbitrary rules ("sin") and attributed to life in another world was thought to yield a celebration of present life, a focus on the now, and a responsibility to love.

9. This 1966 cover story turned out to be one of the more provocative stories *Time* had ever run. Interestingly, the cover of the December 26, 1969, issue of *Time* splashed the words, "Is God Coming Back to Life?" According to the publisher, "Recently, the death-of-God theologians have fallen silent, while ministers of all denominations have embarked on new, dynamic ways of bringing the divine back into daily existence" (5). Maybe the obituary for the Divine had been published prematurely.

10. Thomas J. J. Altizer and William Hamilton, *Radical Theology and the Death of God* (Indianapolis: Bobbs-Merrill, 1966), 28, 46–47.

11. Ed. L. Miller and Stanley J. Grenz, *Fortress Introduction to Contemporary Theologies* (Minneapolis: Fortress Press, 1998), 83.

12. Altizer, *Gospel of Christian Atheism,* 154.

What can "God" still mean if God is "dead"? The work of Dorothee Soelle (1929–2003), a radical German theologian, attempted an answer. She began her career in the 1960s, deeply affected by her home country having produced the Holocaust and then the United States bombing peasants with napalm in Vietnam. She concluded that, because of a fundamental change of public consciousness, the idea of a God as omnipotent ruler of the world was now inconceivable. The old God "is out of work as soon as man begins to think in a scientific way and orders his world according to scientific laws."[13] Drawing on insights of Bultmann, Bonhoeffer, and Marx, she reinterpreted the meaning of Christian theism in ways she saw as immediately relevant to the transforming of social structures. Instead of omnipotent superiority, God is actually loving solidarity. She demythologized like Bultmann, but rejected his existential privatization of Christianity in favor of a political hermeneutic. How can Christ become Lord even for those without God? Turning to God, she said, is a turning to each other, engaging in a radical existence for others (a reflection of Bonhoeffer). We can still speak of "God" as the existence of trust in the world and the transcendental possibility of love. Soelle said that we can believe in God if we affirm that the totality of the world "is not meaningless, empty, capricious and indifferent to man, but instead for him."[14] In light of this view of God, Perry LeFevre says that prayer means the following:

> In a post-theistic age prayer is still a dialogue; it is the conversation which we ourselves are. It does not presuppose an external God whom we address, to whom we send messages, but it does presuppose having heard that word [of God], of coming to the awareness of the transcendental possibility of love, of acknowledging the distance between the way things are and the way things might be.[15]

One might conclude that such a radical theology was merely part of its times, a rush for the worldly relevance of religion, the end product of human arrogance, a romantic idealism. As a formal theology, "death of God" itself died a rather quick death. It now appears to have been more theological posturing than serious theology, having been "40 percent poetry, 40 percent social commentary, and only 20 percent theology."[16] Bernard Ramm sees it as having been a symptom of the deep disease of "theological rationalism that

---

13. Dorothee Soelle, *The Truth Is Concrete* (New York: Herder & Herder, 1969), 26.
14. Dorothee Soelle, *Suffering* (Philadelphia: Fortress Press, 1975), 157.
15. Perry LeFevre, *Modern Theologies of Prayer* (Chicago: Exploration Press, 1995), 216.
16. Miller and Grenz, *Fortress Introduction to Contemporary Theologies*, 86.

refuses obedience to the solemn authority of Scriptures."[17] Wolfhart Pannenberg's assessment is probably correct. The experience of the absence of God "should alert every serious observer to sound an alarm, not so much for God, or for the future of Christianity, but for Western secular culture with its proud science and technology."[18] The living God of biblical revelation is not dead, of course, but some of the ways that Christians have presented God to the public are on emergency life support at best.[19]

The "Finite" God of Process

More influential and lasting than the "death of God" theology was another man's personal experience of God's "death" and his own attempt to find some approach to a divine resurrection. John B. Cobb Jr. (b. 1925) was a sincere Christian believer who enrolled at the University of Chicago to expose his faith to "the worst the world could offer." He faced the modern objections to Christianity and soon found his own faith shattered. Not satisfied with the death of his God, he began to challenge the acids of modernity by developing a fresh way of conceiving God and the world. The results have been significant and influential, and they raise the following question for many people: How does one distinguish the fine line between God having *died* in human view and the traditionally understood biblical view of God having been *diminished* to the point that even using the word "God" is no longer really appropriate?

Charles Hartshorne guided Cobb's doctoral studies in Chicago and led him to the philosophy of Alfred North Whitehead (1861–1947). Here Cobb encountered the view that to live transformingly in the world, now being experienced as a place of constant becoming, one must have a process view of reality and deity. Reality is not a static essence. God is not the all-powerful, all-knowing, and unchanging deity of classic Christian theism. This God now is essentially dead. What was being judged alive instead is God as deeply interdependent with the world, a fellow sufferer in the ongoing world process, the one who remembers all of the becoming and seeks to persuade it in a divinely intended direction, luring all nature forward to ever new and ever better possibilities. Cobb pursued this course of thought and replaced the God

---

17. See the Ramm quotation at the head of this chapter.
18. Wolfhart Pannenberg, *Christian Spirituality* (Philadelphia: Westminster Press, 1983), 91.
19. See the introduction to Clark H. Pinnock, *Most Moved Mover* (Grand Rapids: Baker Academic, 2001).

he critiqued as cosmic moralist, unchanging absolute, and sanctioner of the status quo with the idea of God as "Creative-Responsive Love" enmeshed in the dilemmas of the historical journey of creation. This God risks deep involvement with the cosmic experiment; in fact, God cannot even be conceived by humans except as the one present in the midst of the ongoingness of the world process. Such divine involvement is often painful for the God who does not fully know the outcome of the adventure with a sinful creation that yet is very much in process.[20]

The God resurrected from death in John Cobb's thought clearly goes beyond pantheism, since Cobb does not simply equate God and the world or the world process. More accurate for Cobb's view is the word *panentheism* (see glossary), meaning that the world, especially humankind, cocreates with God and thus contributes to God's own life, so that God is other than but cannot be conceived apart from the world. Cobb, a Methodist, sees an important connection between the work of Whitehead and John Wesley. The connection is their common affirmation of the "primacy of God's activity in a way that gives a significant role to human responsibility."[21]

But even with the advance of panentheism over pantheism, there remains this significant caution: "Where does this leave the holy God of the biblical story, who rejects sin and evil to the point of defeating them within the program of salvation history?"[22] Given this question and its concern that God not be excessively "limited" by an undue stress on human freedom and responsibility, Donald Bloesch understandably judges that the process thought of Cobb and many others teaches an unacceptably "finite" God, a teaching that "veers dangerously close to pantheism."[23] Delwin Brown disagrees. A leading exponent of process theology, he speaks approvingly of liberalism as that school of Christian thought that seeks to dwell critically and creatively "at the intersection between the sensibilities of the historic faith and the best intellectual resources of its own time." For him, a philosophy of reality-in-process is a key contemporary resource that yields the following about God:

20. This picture of God involved in the world process should be distinguished from the more biblical and transcendent understanding of God as portrayed by John Sanders in *The God Who Risks* (Downers Grove, Ill.: InterVarsity Press, 1998).

21. John B. Cobb Jr., "Human Responsibility and the Primacy of Grace," in *Thy Nature and Thy Name Is Love,* ed. Bryan Stone and Thomas Oord (Nashville: Kingswood Books, 2001), 95. There are lyrics from Charles Wesley affirming that "the immortal God hath died for me" and "how greater still the Savior's grace, when God doth for His creature die!" These words, however, came in an orthodox and not a process set of assumptions.

22. Miller and Grenz, *Fortress Introduction to Contemporary Theologies,* 102.

23. Donald G. Bloesch, *God the Almighty* (Downers Grove, Ill.: InterVarsity Press, 1995), 19.

If God is genuinely related to, and thus affected by a contingent historic process, then there will be real contingency, even uncertainty in the divine life. In a world of freedom, chance, and unpredictability, a God who really is with us and for us can hardly be conceived apart from the contingency that characterizes our lives. This must mean that in some important way the realization of God's own goals in and for the world are themselves uncertain. There is genuine risk in the life of God.[24]

For traditional Christian believers, such a process concept of a "finite" God can be viewed positively and negatively. It can be beneficial in emphasizing that God really is related to the world, that this relating involves some changing on God's part as relationships evolve, that God is a compassionate comforter who can be loved rather than merely feared, and that theology is a fragile human enterprise that is both fixed and dynamic. The "finite" view, however, has been less than positive in that, although process thought says that God is distinct from the world, God nonetheless is viewed as so mutually interdependent with the world as to be virtually inconceivable apart from the world—thus the lurking danger of pantheism.

A key question remains. Cannot God be both absolutely sovereign over the world and also really attached and related to it in truly caring and saving ways? Need the God of classical Christian theism "die" in order for him to be the loving Father of our Lord Jesus?[25] Need God's role in the ongoing historical process be restricted to only that of "lure"?[26] A serious search for adequate answers has involved key Christian process thinkers such as John Cobb and evangelical thinkers such as Clark Pinnock.[27] This discussion continues and keeps taking new turns. Today, for instance, some Christian thinkers are seeking to rediscover the Spirit of God in an age of increased ecological concern. Mark Wallace tends to understand the Spirit not as a metaphysical entity but as a healing life-force, so that nature itself is construed as the primary mode of being for the Spirit's work in the world.[28] In fact, the Spirit, according to Wallace, may be so related to the universe that the specter of "ecocide" raises the risk of "deicide"—if the world should die, would the Spirit not die also?

24. Delwin Brown, in Clark H. Pinnock and Delwin Brown, *Theological Crossfire: An Evangelical/ Liberal Dialogue* (Grand Rapids: Zondervan, 1990), 85–86.

25. See John S. Feinberg, *No One Like Him: The Doctrine of God* (Wheaton, Ill.: Crossway Books, 2001), 149–79.

26. See Randy L. Maddox, "Seeking a Response-Able God," in Stone and Oord, eds., *Thy Nature and Thy Name Is Love* (Nashville: Kingswood Books, 2001), 142.

27. See especially John B. Cobb Jr. and Clark H. Pinnock, eds., *Searching for an Adequate God: A Dialogue between Process and Free Will Theists* (Grand Rapids: Eerdmans, 2000).

28. See Mark Wallace, *Fragments of the Spirit: Nature, Violence, and the Renewal of Creation* (New York: Continuum, 1996).

Evil and the Threat of a Divine Demise

Evil in its many forms often has assaulted persons and rendered their belief in God problematic at best. Note this description of the relation between the God brought to Africa by white people and "Ngai," the name for God among the Gikuyu, Masai, and Wakamba peoples of East Africa: "God who is Jesus, the God who was brought by the white Westerner, was *nothing other than the white Westerner*. What we thought was God was nothing but a shadow drawn very artistically in the form of Jesus, the white man. . . . It was not Ngai who is alone Ngai. When that shadow disappears, and it has happened to some of us, it leaves a terrifying darkness and void. It also brings theological anger."[29]

Elie Wiesel has shared a similar perspective from a white European setting. In his autobiographical novel *Night,* a young Jewish boy is hanged cruelly and senselessly for some minor infraction of a rule in the Nazi death camp of Auschwitz. His body dangles limply, deliberately displayed for all other prisoners to stare at as an object lesson. Someone asks prisoner Wiesel in response to this sickening scene, "Where is God now?" Wiesel reflects to himself in profound remorse: "Where is He? Here He is—He is hanging here on this gallows!"[30] Such unaddressed injustice, in other words, surely means that God is also dead. A God traditionally thought to be both good and almighty seems in as much difficulty as the dead boy. Can anyone still believe in God after an Auschwitz? Karen Armstrong puts the concern bluntly:

> The idea of a personal God, like one of us writ large, is fraught with difficulty. If this God is omnipotent, he could have prevented the Holocaust. If he was unable to stop it, he is impotent and useless; if he could have stopped it and chose not to, he is a monster. Jews are not the only people who believe that the Holocaust put an end to conventional theology.[31]

The troubling presence of such evil is clearly a challenge to traditional Christian theism. Doubt stalks most believers in God when crisis comes and evil appears to prevail. The ancient psalmist explored the frustration and even despair typical when prolonged trouble does not seem to attract God's atten-

---

29. Kamuyu-wa-Kang'ethe, "The Death of God: An African Viewpoint," *Caribbean Journal of Religious Studies* 6, no. 2 (September 1985), 18.

30. Elie Wiesel, *Night* (New York: Bantam Books, 1982), 62.

31. Karen Armstrong, *A History of God* (New York: Ballantine Books, 1993), 376. Christian process thought insists that evil comes from the free choices of people, a freedom that God will not limit. God persuades toward the good, but to a significant degree is himself finite and thus unable to actually stop evil from happening. A process paraphrase of 1 Peter 5:7 might thus be: "Cast all your cares upon God who, although he has limited ability to do anything about them, nonetheless really cares for you."

tion and result in corrective action: "I think of God and I moan" (Ps. 77:3). The prophet Jeremiah asked, "Why does the way of the guilty prosper? Why do all who are treacherous thrive?" (Jer. 12:1). Even Jesus said in his time of agony, "My God, my God, why have you forsaken me?" (Matt. 27:46). Is God only a fair-weather fairy tale that fades off the stage when the pressure of evil is on? The questions are persistent and painful.

How God is conceived is often related significantly to one's social circumstance. For instance, Benjamin Mays's 1938 study titled *The Negro's God* clearly demonstrated how the "Negro" idea of God was related to the social situation in which African Americans had found themselves. William Jones carried this analysis further in his 1973 *Is God a White Racist?* He insisted that African Americans must resolve this tension between black suffering and the will of God. If they do not, the tension leads to the conclusion that their suffering has been sanctioned by God—thus, God is evil and should die for them. Theology is a very human enterprise carried on in the midst of very real history.

David Hume (1711–1776) stated clearly the problem confronted by anyone who believes in the God revealed in the Bible and thoughtfully observes the sordid drama of ongoing historical existence. Is God willing to prevent evil but not able? Then God is impotent. Is God able but not willing? Then God is malevolent. Is God both able and willing? How then is continuing evil to be explained? The reality of evil appears to challenge all that Christians believe about God. Biblical faith affirms that God is at once aware, willing, and able—thus the problem. Why is there still evil? The effort to understand and vindicate the justice of a good and able God in the face of persistent evil is known as *theodicy* (see glossary). The Bible as a whole yields no simplistic answers. The wisdom it offers involves going to Calvary, gazing at the broken Son of God, and contemplating suffering in light of this amazing act of God on our behalf. God is one with us in our suffering and can use suffering to achieve the highest good (see chapter 8). God does not originate evil and ultimately will prevail over it. The issues lie in the meantime.

The Negro spirituals were surely songs in the night, songs of sorrow and protest. But in many of them, beyond the obvious social commentary, lies a persistent perspective regarding God. This music is "spiritual" because it comes from searchers who found something eternal and someone immortal. Speaking as an African American about his rich heritage of faith in the face of great injustice, James Earl Massey says of the Negro spirituals, "They give us our history. They honor our heritage of hope. They witness to our faith. They nurture our self-respect. These songs echo our theology, voice our theodicy, and mirror our souls."[32] Faith can exist and prevail in the face of evil. The presence of evil does not eliminate the possibility of God being all that the Bible claims.

Many who suffer, however, have handled their travail in a way that has ended in denying faith in God. Through their pain there emerges the assumption that either God does not care, cannot make a difference, or does not even exist. There is no tolerance for cheap or evasive answers—such as the one sometimes called the "omelet theory" (eggs have to be broken to make an omelet, so evil contributes to an eventual good and thus is not really evil). Even ancient Israel, God's chosen, faced defeat and suffering and experienced devastation rather than divine protection from evil. Writers of Hebrew Scripture were realistic about the apparent contradiction between how life actually was and how they thought it should be in light of their belief in God. The Psalms repeatedly express complaint about the distance, silence, absence, hiddenness, and maybe even demise of God. "Why" is the troubling question, leading to our finding in the Psalms

> not orthodox confession of the "omnipresence" of God, but the heretical confession of the omni-absence of God. Not triumphant confession of the "omnipotence" of God, but confession of the omnipotence of those who rape, oppress, and destroy the innocent, weak, and needy. Not confession of the saving love of God, but confession of a God who refuses help just when it is needed most. Not comforting assurance that God answers prayers, but bitter complaint that God refuses to answer prayers. Not "resting on the promises of God," but the hostile charge that God has not kept God's promises. In short, "My God, my God, why have you forsaken me?" (Ps. 22:1)—a shockingly honest acknowledgment of the experience of godlessness and godforsakenness in a suffering world.[33]

Such apparent evil can bring to the despairing sufferer the threat of a divine demise—if God *has* not, maybe God *is* not!

God May Yet Be Alive!

How else might the being and activity (or apparent inactivity) of God be conceived in the face of persistent evil? Is there a way to face the fact of evil with-

---

32. James Earl Massey, *Sundays in the Tuskegee Chapel: Selected Sermons* (Nashville: Abingdon Press, 2000), 17.
33. Shirley C. Guthrie, *Christian Doctrine,* rev. ed. (Louisville, Ky.: Westminster John Knox Press, 1994), 184.

out relinquishing belief in God? Can we avoid the conclusion that faith in God is no more than wishful thinking, or that, at least, God is trapped with us in our human plight? The radical death-of-God theologians of the twentieth century tried in their own ways to resurrect God from total oblivion. God is really "incarnate," they said, not in the classical sense of being eternal in the heavens and also with us miraculously in Jesus of Nazareth, but in the more radical sense of being fully and *only* with us. The divine presence affirms the value of the mundane, but at the expense of affirming the God who also is transcendent, other than the mundane. God is so with us in our suffering that God also suffers (see *patripassianism* in the glossary). Missing was the power of divine transcendence that rises above the coordinate truth of God being present with us.

Might the truly transcendent God of classic Christian tradition yet be alive despite appearances to the contrary? The psalmist helps. After venting frustration, anger, and sometimes despair because of the apparent absence of God, memory returns concerning what God has done in the past for his people: "I consider the days of old, and remember the years of long ago. . . . I will call to mind the deeds of the LORD; I will remember your wonders of old" (Ps. 77:5, 11). God often has been present and has answered the cries of his people. Such memory yields hope, so that faith affirms, even in a seemingly godforsaken present, that God nevertheless somehow is near and still is on the side of the brokenhearted, crushed, and needy (Pss. 34 and 72). The One who has acted to liberate surely will do so again, somehow, sometime.

One helpful answer to the troubling question Why is there evil if God is good and all-powerful? is called the "logic of love" theodicy. This logic presumes that God originally created for the sake of enabling loving relationships, a purpose requiring the granting of real freedom to the created. God wills love, but in the process opens the door to the potentially wrong use of freedom, which is evil ("live" spelled backward). Thus, "though God does not protect us from ourselves, God is there redeeming every situation, though exactly how, we may not yet always know."[34] Only because God is present and lovingly at work in all things can Romans 8:28 affirm, "We know that all things work together for good for those who love God, who are called according to his purpose." Walter Wink speaks helpfully of "the powers" that were created good, are now fallen, and can be redeemed. What has become institutionalized evil presents the Christian with this difficult but unavoidable dilemma and mission:

---

34. Pinnock, *Most Moved Mover,* 132.

God at one and the same time *upholds* a given political or economic system, since some such system is required to support human life; *condemns* that system insofar as it is destructive of fully human life; and *presses for its transformation* into a more humane order. Conservatives stress the first, revolutionaries the second, reformers the third. The Christian is expected to hold together all three.[35]

The first Christians remembered Jesus, the tragic and innocent victim of evil who cried, "My God, my God, why have you forsaken me?" only to remember also that Jesus later had been raised by God's power, victorious over the worst that evil could do. Christ is risen! From the beginning there were signs among believers that the Spirit of Jesus was inaugurating the kingdom of life in the face of the still present kingdom of death. The reality of resurrection provided a new way of viewing the cross of Jesus. More than a sign of God's powerlessness in the face of evil, the cross became a sign of God's amazing love that transforms the worst of evil into the fullness of life (see Gen. 50:20). Faith in a just and loving God is not based on good or bad experience in the immediate present. The longer view is required. What God *has done* in the history of his people, and particularly in his Son, God surely *will do* for the faithful at the time and in the way of God's own choosing.

Stubborn faith persists. Despite all, God is! God still lives in the face of all reports to the contrary. But where is God to be found? The following two chapters review prominent ways in which some leading Christian theologians in recent generations have located God. It just may be that God, being a fellow sufferer with us humans, is the comforter, the liberator, and the source of hope that the tomorrow of God's fuller reign should and can be realized even today. Where is God? Maybe God is found most readily among the poor and oppressed, or maybe in the future that already is coming into our troubled present.

35. Walter Wink, *The Powers That Be: Theology for New Millennium* (New York: Galilee, Doubleday, 1998), 32.

Chapter 8

Seen in Suffering and Marginalization

The Israelites groaned under their slavery, and cried out. Out of the slavery their cry for help rose up to God. God heard their groaning, and God remembered his covenant with Abraham, Isaac, and Jacob. God looked upon the Israelites, and God took notice of them.
—Exodus 2:23

When we look for the conquering hero to make his move, to enter into the royal city on his white charger to signal to the people that the time has come to establish his kingdom, we find instead a Jesus who enters into Jerusalem astride a humble donkey. . . . When we look for a deliverer who will crush the opposition by superior force, we find instead a servant-messiah who allows himself to be crushed and bruised for us. What kind of God is this?
—Philip D. Kenneson, Life on the Vine

*H*ow easily human self-perception leads to selfish and distorted God-perception. Dominant groups often create God in their own image and then make a convenient idol of that image at the expense of others. The elite and powerful tend toward self-serving actions that are costly for the powerless under their control. According to Rosemary Ruether, most images of God in the world's religions are modeled after the ruling class of their associated societies.[1] The proclaimed identity of God gets mangled in the process. There surely is some truth in what Theodore Dreiser reportedly once said: "Religion is a bandage that man has invented to protect the soul made bloody by circumstance." Self-protection easily becomes self-service. Much of what has passed for "orthodox" theology has been colored by alliances between the

---

1. Rosemary Radford Ruether, *Sexism and God-Talk: Toward a Feminist Theology* (Boston: Beacon Press, 1983).

church and the power structures of the societies where the church has resided. This is not to discount the inspiration of God's Spirit; it is to admit that theology always proceeds in influential cultural contexts.

Sometimes it is necessary for prophetic voices to emerge and pay the high price of telling the truth. Let the church be the church and let God be God! Rather than serving those comfortably in power, the Almighty God is robed in compassion for the powerless. As the Hebrew Scriptures report extensively, God is engaged in rescuing and redeeming the enslaved and exiled. Indeed, God may be understood best when viewed through the eyes of the poor and in the face of pain. Powerful church establishments often have difficulty reflecting adequately the God seen in Jesus astride a humble donkey.

While it is true that much of the heritage of Christianity has been identified with Europe, too often even captured narrowly by a Western and often colonial mentality, one should recall the great African tradition of Christian theology. Thomas Oden confesses his great debt to this non-European tradition and often quotes Athanasius, Augustine, Origen, Clement of Alexandria, Tertullian, and Cyprian. He says, "I am especially troubled when Christianity is portrayed as an essentially European religion, since it has its roots in cultures that are far distant from Europe and preceded the development of modern European identity, and some of its greatest minds have been African."[2] Many people today are troubled when Christians think and act as though Christian faith is finally defined by only one culture, tradition, or gender—although sometimes they seek to correct the problem by redefining it with excessive reference to their own social locations and personal experiences and preferences.

If there were to be a preferential location for the focus of the current concerns of the biblical God, it would not be geographical in nature. God as biblically revealed is associated closely with suffering and is related particularly to those marginalized by others. Such divine associating and relating surely says much about who God really is and what God actually intends. To know the God revealed in Israel and Jesus leads to a serious consideration of the issues of evil and justice. The righteous and merciful God is in the seeking and saving business, and thus is most immediately encountered where such activity is needed. The sorry business of domination and exploitation easily conjures up for the powerful of a society images of God they choose to create, which are usually quite reflective of themselves. Karl Marx insisted that the ruling ideas of each age have ever been the ideas of its ruling class. Walter Brueggemann has argued in similar fashion that "church interpretation [of the Bible] . . . has tended to trim and domesticate the text not only to accom-

---

2. Thomas Oden, *The Living God,* vol. 1 of *Systematic Theology* (Peabody, Mass.: Prince Press, 1998), 9.

On God and Human Suffering

God will provide—ah, if only He would till He does!

—A Yiddish proverb

The believer in God must explain one thing, the existence of suffering; the nonbeliever, however, must explain the existence of everything else.

—Dennis Prager and Joseph Telushkin,
The Nine Questions People Ask about Judaism

God is weak and powerless in the world, and that is precisely the way, the only way, in which he is with us and helps us. Only the suffering God can help.

—Dietrich Bonhoeffer

And the king will answer them, "Truly I tell you, just as you did it to one of the least of these who are members of my family, you did it to me."

—Jesus (Matt. 25:40)

modate regnant modes of knowledge, but also to enhance regnant modes of power."[3]

Our Suffering and God's

While the pervasive and persistent presence of evil in this world may be a threat to the credibility of God's existence in human eyes, it also can be a fresh seedbed for faith. Suffering is sometimes the very matrix in which God's presence is most readily realized. Philosopher Alfred North Whitehead (1861–1947) saw God as deeply involved in the struggling world process, not self-contained and invulnerable to the ongoing pain and progress of this flawed creation. He keynoted a prominent theme in much of contemporary Christian theism:

3. Walter Brueggemann, *Texts under Negotiation* (Minneapolis: Fortress Press, 1993), vii.

I affirm that God does suffer as he participates in the ongoing life of the society of being. His sharing in the world's suffering is the supreme instance of knowing, accepting, and transforming in love the suffering which arises in the world. I am affirming the divine sensitivity. Without it, I can make no sense of the being of God.[4]

Christian teaching has struggled to determine how best to relate the reality of human suffering to the reality of God. How does one coordinate divine sovereignty and divine sensitivity? The classical tradition often has insisted that, despite the troubling paradox of a good God and persistent evil, the very presence of evil is not inconsistent with divine power and goodness. Oden distinguishes four aspects or levels of God's "parenting" of the creation: permission, restraint, overruling, and limiting the threat to the good.[5] In the face of any and all negative circumstances, faith stubbornly affirms that God somehow is working out the divine purpose in the conflicted historical setting (see Isa. 40:1–11).

Often it has been claimed in the history of Christian teaching that God the Father cannot be acted upon since God is pure actuality. To suffer is to be acted upon, and surely God cannot be at the mercy of the creation. Therefore, the suffering in the human experience of Jesus should be understood as somehow separated from the direct experience of God. Or should it be? This ancient debate continues. One view, *patripassianism* (see glossary), reasons as follows. If Christ is God, he must be identical with the Father and, if identical and since Christ suffered, the Father also must have suffered—maybe even died! But classic theologian Christopher Hall cautions that God suffers only in the sense that God was joined to human nature in Jesus and in that conjoined nature experienced suffering and death. The divine suffering is possible only because of the human dimension of the hypostatic union in Jesus. As for the very nature of God, however, "God remains wondrously and ineffably impassible and immutable."[6]

Who is God in relation to the troubling reality of suffering? Much of the classic Christian tradition has joined Hall in insisting on divine impassibility (see glossary), God's perfection which presumably renders the divine invulnerable to suffering. But much theological thought in the twentieth century— such as that of Karl Barth—has come to insist otherwise. As Roger Olson summarizes:

---

4. Alfred N. Whitehead, as quoted in Karen Armstrong, *A History of God* (New York: Ballantine Books, 1993), 384.

5. Oden, *Living God,* 300–2.

6. Christopher Hall, in Hall and John Sanders, *Does God Have a Future?* (Grand Rapids: Baker Academic, 2003), 63.

God's being is being-in-act, not a static essence aloof from God's dynamic relationship with the world. God's love for the world means that he is truly involved and that the world affects God. Barth broke radically from classical Christian theism insofar as he saw it infected by static Greek categories of being. And yet, on the basis of divine revelation, Barth insisted that even in his loving, suffering, thoroughly involved relationship with the world, God remains ever the Lord of that relationship.[7]

Nicholas Wolterstorff adds this penetrating judgment:

> God is love. That is why he suffers. To love our suffering, sinful world is to suffer. God so suffered for the world that he gave up his only Son to suffer. The one who does not see God's suffering does not see his love. God is suffering love. Suffering is down at the center of things, deep down where the meaning is. Suffering is the meaning of our world. The tears of God are the meaning of history.[8]

The biblical witness pictures God as the Sovereign who *stands above* and also as God the Savior who *stoops below*. This stooping, far from being unrelated to and unaffected by the world, reveals a God who, in Jesus Christ, so utterly related to the world as to become incarnate in humanity and so utterly affected by the world as to die on a cross. The particular place where the God of the Bible intersected the life process of creation was at the point of pain, the pain of sin and injustice. Here emerged a distinctive view of God, a dynamic theism that sees God as simultaneously sovereign over creation and suffering with creation because of its sin. Israel experienced great pain because of its own waywardness and that of others, and through this pain gained a distinctive discernment of the God who identified with and even shared the pain. God became known as responsive, vulnerable, suffering because of human sin, and long-suffering on behalf of human redemption.

The Lord said, "I have observed the misery of my people who are in Egypt; I have heard their cry on account of their taskmasters. Indeed, I know their sufferings, and I have come down to deliver them from the Egyptians" (Exod. 3:7–8). According to the gospel of Christ, God hears, loves, comes, takes risks, suffers over sin, and reveals the divine self most fully in a man of sorrows who was acquainted with grief (Isa. 53). God both rules over and is moved by the creation. Biblically speaking, God suffers *because of* his

---

7. Roger E. Olson, *The Story of Christian Theology* (Downers Grove, Ill.: InterVarsity Press, 1999), 584.

8. Nicholas Wolterstorff, *Lament for a Son* (Grand Rapids: Eerdmans, 1987), 90.

people, *with* his people, and *for* his people.[9] God is willing "to relate responsively to the intrinsically unpredictable development of human freedom." Even so, continues Oden, with God's goal being the regeneration of the disordered world (Rom. 8:19ff.), "nothing can finally thwart this divine purpose (Isa. 11:1ff; Dan. 7:13ff)."[10] In the meantime, God's purpose is sufficiently clear in the ministry of Jesus, and its ultimate accomplishment is assured by reference to Jesus' resurrection (Acts 17:18ff.; Rom. 6:1–5; Phil. 3:10–11). The cross and resurrection of Jesus were for the early Christian community the lens through which the meaning and the end of human history and the nature and way of God are to be understood.

In one key sense, God never changes—at least not in existence, character, or intent. In another sense, the unchanging and grace-full God, by an uncoerced divine choice of love, is in the historical process with those of us who sin, suffer, and hope for an undeserved salvation. God's way with the world, as experienced by Israel and seen in Jesus, features a divine love that chooses a cross. Love engages, suffers, bears, and is patient (1 Cor. 13). We come to know God best as the One who willingly and healingly engages and embraces our human pain. It truly is amazing grace![11] Note these very direct words from Clark Pinnock: "Augustine was wrong to have said that God does not grieve over the suffering of the world; Anselm was wrong to have said that God does not experience compassion; Calvin was wrong to have said that biblical figures that convey such things are mere accommodations to finite understanding."[12]

In sharp contrast to popular health-and-wealth teaching and the churches that are burdened awkwardly with their own substantial possession of the world's goods and friendship with its political powers, Isaiah 53 presents the Suffering Servant—God's unusual and special way of being. Disciples of Jesus are called to follow him and share in his sufferings (Mark 8:31–38). This is in dramatic contrast to any "what's in it for me" theology. There surely is no mystery so great as this: a suffering God, an almighty Savior nailed to a cross! The cross was at the center of Martin Luther's theology and much of the Protestant theology that has followed him. According to Alister McGrath, Luther declared that "the Cross alone is our theology," meaning that "the haunting image of the crucified Christ is the crucible in which all our thinking about God is forged. . . . Here is God at work . . . making mockery of the wisdom of the wise and showing up the futility of human ideas of strength."[13]

---

9. See Clark H. Pinnock, *Most Moved Mover* (Grand Rapids: Baker Academic, 2001), 56–57.
10. Oden, *Living God,* 306–7.
11. See Barry L. Callen, *God as Loving Grace* (Nappanee, Ind.: Evangel Publishing House, 1996).
12. Pinnock, *Most Moved Mover,* 27.
13. Alister E. McGrath, *Spirituality in an Age of Change* (Grand Rapids: Zondervan, 1994), 75–77.

Christ reigns from a cross! Christ is the faithful image of who God really is. The great irony is that the implacable tread of the persistent "Hound of Heaven" is the sound of suffering.

Jürgen Moltmann reflects theologically out of his own personal experience of human horror during World War II. He served as a German soldier, was captured and imprisoned in Scotland, watched his nation be crushed, and later reflected on the immense cruelty of the Holocaust. He came to believe that the presence of God is found primarily in the power of suffering, especially in the cross and resurrection of Jesus.[14] The cross is intrinsic to God's own being.[15] Breaking with classical Christian theism at this point, Moltmann argues that the cross of Jesus means that God is not immutable and impassible. God both affects the world and is significantly affected by it. God really suffered in the very real sufferings of Jesus. Paul proclaimed that "God was in Christ" (2 Cor. 5:19). Noting the common theological distinction between the *immanent* and the *economic* Trinity (see glossary), Moltmann elevates the economic by pointing to the cross of Jesus as the central event in the life of God. When the eschatological goal of salvation reaches completion and all is "in God" and God is "all in all," then "the economic Trinity is raised into and transcended in the immanent Trinity."[16]

Joining these reflections are the themes of divine suffering prominent among process theologians done in the wake of God's supposed "death"—at least the demise of aspects of the classical concept of God. It appears that a truly different understanding of God and the world has increasingly permeated Western thought beginning with the last decades of the twentieth century. Alfred North Whitehead and many subsequent process thinkers have been teaching the "fellow sufferer" God. Donald Bloesch is a concerned evangelical who calls this trend a "new immanentalism" that focuses inordinately on God's vulnerability at the expense of God's almightiness and that highlights "God's empathy with the world rather than his majesty, his pathos rather than his infinite beatitude."[17] Despite this understandable and appropriate caution, the newer thinking is significant and worthy of close examination.

14. See, e.g., Jürgen Moltmann, *The Way of Jesus Christ* (Minneapolis: Fortress Press, 1993), chapter 4, "The Apocalyptic Sufferings of Christ."

15. See Jürgen Moltmann, *The Crucified God* (New York: Harper & Row, 1974). Japanese Christian theologian Kazoh Kitamora essentially agrees with Moltmann. He sees God's very nature mediating an intense love for sinners and an equally intense wrath for the sin itself. The tension is said to generate pain within the life of God (*Theology of the Pain of God* [Richmond, Va.: John Knox Press, 1965]).

16. Jürgen Moltmann, *The Trinity and the Kingdom: The Doctrine of God* (San Francisco: Harper & Row, 1981), 160–61, 183.

17. Donald G. Bloesch, *God the Almighty* (Downers Grove, Ill.: InterVarsity Press, 1995), 17.

In the 1930s and 1940s the German theologian Dietrich Bonhoeffer represented this more immanent emphasis by encouraging a rethinking of the classic Christian view of God, with fresh stress on the One who *by weakness and suffering* is really with us in this troubled world.[18] Joining Bonhoeffer in reconceiving Judeo-Christian thought in light of the Nazi terror, Irving Greenberg was even more radical by offering the sobering judgment that no theological statement should now be made "that would not be credible in the presence of the burning of children." He resisted the conclusion of some Jews that after the Holocaust in the 1940s there is no longer even the possibility of belief in an all-powerful and truly good God. Rather than abandoning what was sacred to the Nazi victims and thus smearing their memory by judging their faith a mere illusion, Greenberg thinks that we should "err on the side of the moral necessity of a God who called this people to a sacred, albeit dangerous, mission of testimony." One also should resist the logic of unbelief in order to avoid absolutizing secular civilization—which would be a very misguided idolatry. The Holocaust has taught that we should maintain at least "a fundamental skepticism about all human movements, left and right, political and religious—even as we participate in them." God may be strangely silent in the face of gruesome injustice, but we must not merely validate the contemporary denial of God since "in pure secularity, humans appoint themselves God and thereby become the devil."[19]

Suffering has been so much a part of contemporary life. Teachers such as Jürgen Moltmann have helped make the idea of a suffering God a virtual orthodoxy in many Christian quarters today. The death of the Son of God on a cross outside Jerusalem is said to have been an event that reached deep into the very nature of God, in fact also took place in the innermost nature of God. Contemplating this leads one to the manifested mystery of the triune God. If among the persons of the Trinity "one suffers, the others suffer too. Christ's death on the cross is an inner-Trinitarian event before it assumes significance for the redemption of the world."[20]

18. This immanence emphasis is highlighted by John B. Cobb Jr. and David Griffin in *Process Theology: An Introductory Exposition* (Philadelphia: Westminster Press, 1976). They vigorously oppose traditional and popular views of God as "Cosmic Moralist," "Unchanging and Passionless Absolute," "Controlling Power," "Sanctioner of the Status Quo," and "Male" (8–10). In chapter 3 they develop their alternative view, "God as Creative-Responsive Love."

19. Irving Greenberg, "The Shoah and the Legacy of Anti-Semitism," in *Christianity in Jewish Terms,* ed. Tikva Frymer-Kensky, et al. (Boulder, Colo.: Westview Press, 2000), 27–28, 30. See also Clark M. Williamson, *A Guest in the House of Israel: Post-Holocaust Church Theology* (Louisville, Ky.: Westminster/John Knox Press, 1993).

20. Jürgen Moltmann, *Experiences in Theology: Ways and Forms of Christian Theology* (Minneapolis: Fortress Press, 2000), 305.

The prevailing view of God in a society usually issues in political applications of a similar nature. Moltmann warns that Christians must rediscover the biblical concept of God's triunity as three equal persons in rich community and fellowship rather than the monarchy of one dominant person in relation to the others (see *subordinationism* in the glossary). The dynamics of mutuality, he insists, have positive political ramifications, while the dominance of singular lordship within God's self has dangerously negative implications on the human scene. The forging of an intimate link between God's being and tragic historical events has been accomplished by highlighting the cross of Jesus as something in God's own heart as well as something that happened on a Palestinian hill two millennia ago. Concerns are sometimes expressed that this linking of God's being and the tortured path of the creation's history has come at too high a price. Some say that God's deity has been made ontologically dependent on world history to the extent that God truly comes to his fullest self only through the eschatological completion of world history. Edgar S. Brightman imagines a form of a presumed divine dependence on creation in which there is a limiting, even an evil, "given" element within the divine self, so that God is in some sense "finite."

God as finite? There is no way of avoiding the presence of evil in this world, and such presence surely does raise questions about the power and goodness and the infinite availability and adequacy of God. Historical experience regularly brings to human attention the pain of human sin, injustice, and death. Who and where is God in all of this? One simple line of thought appears justified. Recognizing a relational dynamism in the exercise of God's sovereignty is both biblical and called for by the reality of evil in this world. If God were an all-controlling power, it appears to follow that God would have to be seen as the author if not the sanctioner of evil—surely an unacceptable thought. But the mystery of evil is penetrated (although never removed) by the realization that there is a creaturely freedom granted room by God to function throughout the life of the creation. Evil originates in the misuse of this freedom, a misuse allowed by God in the divine pursuit of truly loving relationships with creatures who, as God's gift, have meaningful freedom to choose for or against God's will. Evil is completely ungodly, but nonetheless, for the sake of love, its possibility is allowed by God—at least temporarily. Divine determination of all things makes for robots, not willing, loving, rejoicing covenant partners.

I recently listened to a close friend of mine illustrate this dilemma with great personal emotion. He had been a Dutch slave laborer in Nazi Germany and one night watched helplessly as a young girl was raped repeatedly by four soldiers. My friend later became a biblical scholar and committed Christian believer, but he could never get free of a haunting question. How could a truly all-powerful and all-good God, the sovereign Father of all, just stand quietly in the heavens and let happen what a human father would have done almost anything to stop if it had been his daughter?[21] If God is truly God, then surely there is active divine governance of the creation. *Providence* is the Christian doctrine that seeks to explain the mode of such divine activity. The key question comes when the persistence of suffering suggests the apparent inactivity of God in the face of active evil. If God does not appear to act, is God inattentive to evil, helpless against it, waiting for another time to counter it, or what?

John Calvin thought it proper and comforting to affirm that the "Heavenly Father so holds all things in his power, so rules by his authority and will, so governs by his wisdom, that nothing can befall except he determine it."[22] But Philip Meadows counters that Calvin's view aggravates instead of alleviates the problem of evil. It seems to make God "*directly* responsible for human suffering" and reduces prayer to "a means of simple submission to the dominating and controlling providence of God."[23] John Wesley struggled to identify a better balance between the freedom of fallen human creation and the sovereignty of divine power and grace. For him, divine providence is not focused in control and power but in the active and loving guidance of humans who are set at liberty. God rules without overruling, thus creating the potential of true virtue—and also, necessarily, the potential of evil and suffering. Wesley's main point about divine sovereignty (directed at Calvin) was that it always should be related to the other divine attributes (especially love), thus avoiding abstract and mechanistic views of sovereignty that undermine God's love and justice, and essentially eliminate human responsibility.

This "open" circumstance of human freedom and responsibility, established by divine choice, is a divine act of love for the purpose of love. It may be thought of as a self-chosen "limitation" of God, at least penultimately, but it should never be understood as a diminishment of divine sovereignty.[24] Although ancient Greek philosophers tended to think of the divine majesty as

21. Gustav Jeeninga, *Doors to Life: The Stories of Gustav Jeeninga* (Anderson, Ind.: Anderson University Press, 2002).

22. John Calvin, *Institutes of the Christian Religion,* ed. John T. McNeill, trans. Ford Lewis Battles (Philadelphia: Westminster Press, 1960), 1.17.11.

23. Philip R. Meadows, "Providence, Chance, and the Problem of Suffering," *Wesleyan Theological Journal* 34, no. 2 (Fall 1999): 58.

24. Ibid. He elaborates: "Insofar as creation as a whole has been set free to flourish and fail, we cannot avoid the conclusion that God is indirectly responsible for the possibility and even the probability of evil and suffering. But this is the necessary condition for the nurture of genuinely free spiritual beings capable of loving and serving God" (75).

impassible, the good news of God in Christ is the dramatic countervision of divine responsiveness, vulnerability, and readiness for long-suffering, all without any abdication of true divine sovereignty. What will be in the penultimate tends to be at least in part dependent on human choice, action, and prayer. What will be ultimately is fully in God's control, will be shaped significantly for individuals by their present decisions, and always will be in accord with God's standards and judgments.

Through the Eyes of Justice

Evil leads to injustice and the dehumanization of the marginalized in human society. But God anointed Jesus with the Holy Ghost and with power (Acts 10:38), enabling him to liberate the captives and restore sight to the blind (Luke 4:18–19). John Wesley taught wisely that there is no faith in God that is not also love for those whom God loves. Indeed, "if we say that we have fellowship with him [God] while we are walking in darkness, we lie and do not do what is true" (1 John 1:6). There is no holiness that is not social holiness.[25] Gustavo Gutiérrez more recently has added that "the modes of God's presence determine the forms of our encounter with God. If humanity, each person, is the living temple of God, we meet God in our encounter with others; we encounter God in the commitment to the historical process of humankind."[26] According to James Cone, "the immanence of God means that God always encounters us in a situation of historical liberation."[27] God comes to where we are and has freedom and justice on his mind.

In the tradition of the ancient Hebrews, this means that to know God is to do justice. God takes sides in human conflict, as can be seen clearly in the Exodus story of the ancient Israelites enslaved in Egypt and in the later prophets of Israel who insisted that God renders judgment on those who oppress others, even if the oppressors are members of God's chosen people (Amos 8:1–14). Therefore, Canaan Banana affirms:

> I believe in a color-blind God,
> Maker of technicolor people,
> Who created the universe
> and provided abundant resources

25. Kenneth J. Collins has provided good perspective on John Wesley's general theological perspective and within it his particular emphasis on ministry to the poor. See Collins, "The Soteriological Orientation of John Wesley's Ministry to the Poor," *Wesleyan Theological Journal* 36, no. 2 (Fall 2001): 7–36.
26. Gustavo Gutiérrez, *A Theology of Liberation* (Maryknoll, N.Y.: Orbis Books, 1988), 110.
27. James H. Cone, *A Black Theology of Liberation*, 2d ed. (Maryknoll, N.Y.: Orbis Books, 1986), 76.

for equitable distribution
among all God's people.[28]

God notices, is pained by injustice, and brings hope by engaging the wrong. According to a Yiddish proverb, "If God lived on earth, people would break his windows." Dietrich Bonhoeffer wrote from his Nazi prison cell, "The Bible directs man to God's powerlessness and suffering—only a suffering God can help."[29]

In this spirit, the early history of the Free Methodist Church, particularly as expressed in the life and thought of its founder, Benjamin Titus Roberts (1823–1893), provides a vivid example of an evangelical expression of a "preferential option for the poor." Although differing in key ways from the more recent "liberation" theologians, the early Free Methodists were like them by being intentionally involved with the lives of the socially dispossessed. The denomination's very name reflected an antislavery stance (a major issue in 1860) and a determination to be a church body without aristocratic class distinctions—"free," for instance, from the detested practice of renting church pews to privileged families that was a reflection of the burgeoning capitalism of antebellum American society. Roberts charged that "money commands the pews, and the pews too often control the pulpit."[30] The story of God's Bible School, located on the "Mount of Blessing" in Cincinnati, Ohio, has reflected well this early Free Methodist resistance to monetary power and social pride in church life.[31] We have these two enduring questions: Who is the "God" who is too easily proclaimed in privileged church circumstances? To whom is God especially committed, and what does this commitment say about God's nature and will and divine expectations of proper church life?

It apparently is the case that truly knowing God requires sensing and sharing God's compassionate heart. Mother Teresa was quoted in 1982 as saying, "I am a little pencil in the hand of a writing God who is sending a love letter to the world." Her work among the dying in India surely composed an eloquent script. The life and work of Georgia Harkness (1891–1974) is one of the great stories of twentieth-century Christian theology. Coming from a con-

28. Canaan Banana, *The Gospel according to the Ghetto* (Geneva: World Council of Churches, 1974), 8. The theological implications of this "People's Creed" are explored by C. S. Song in *Jesus and the Reign of God* (Minneapolis: Fortress Press, 1993), 49ff.

29. Dietrich Bonhoeffer, *Letters and Papers from Prison* (New York: Macmillan, 1967), 188.

30. Benjamin T. Roberts, *Earnest Christian* (February 1865): 60. See also William C. Kostlevy's chapter in *Poverty and Ecclesiology: Nineteenth-Century Evangelicals in the Light of Liberation Theology*, ed. Anthony Dunnavant (Collegeville, Minn.: Liturgical Press, 1992), 51–67.

31. See Kevin Moser and Larry Smith, compilers, *God's Clock Keeps Perfect Time: God's Bible School's First 100 Years* (Cincinnati: God's Bible School, 2000).

servative rural background, she completed a masters thesis at Boston University School of Theology that was published in 1921 under the title *The Church and the Immigrant*. Her mentor, George Tupper, wrote the introduction, explaining that young people inspired by the "Social Gospel" to help their foreign-born neighbors in industrial centers "realized their helplessness as they invaded this great unknown realm where Old World backgrounds, race psychology, and myriad languages loomed large."[32] Harkness wrote to explain the condition of the new immigrants coming to America and the failure of society to welcome them humanely as brothers and sisters. The churches, she insisted, must address both the spiritual and social needs of this mass of dislocated people since "there is no necessary conflict between the spiritual message and the social gospel of Christianity."[33] The two, in fact, are to be inextricably bound together. To separate them is to violate the teachings of Jesus (Matt. 25:40) and to misunderstand the nature and will of God.

This concern for the social relevance of the Christian gospel typically is rooted in the assumption that key to God's very being is compassion for oppressed as well as sinful people. Therefore, many conclude, Christian theology should stop theorizing only abstractly about God and start participating with God, stop analyzing the world and start transforming it. Cheryl Bridges Johns observes that Pentecostalism "was birthed out of the hungering cries of simple people who desired to see the glory of God. Dead orthodoxy and creedal rigidity had hid the face of God from the humble, the contrite and the broken. God heard the cries of these people and filled their empty hearts with His fire."[34] How do God's nature and redemptive activity proceed? For C. Leonard Allen and Danny Gray Swick, they proceed "from His heart, through the cross and into our lives by the power of the indwelling Spirit."[35] The divine heart is one of compassionate love, and the Spirit's power is exercised justly and redeemingly on behalf of all whom God loves.

This line of thought was promoted in Latin America by a group of Roman Catholic bishops who met in Medellín, Colombia, in 1968 and condemned what they judged to be the church's traditional alliance with the ruling powers of that region. Soon after this meeting, a powerful theological movement was born, highlighted by the book *A Theology of Liberation* by Gustavo Gutiérrez.

32. George Tupper, introduction to *The Church and the Immigrant,* by George Harkness (New York: George H. Doran Co., 1921), vii–viii.

33. Harkness, *Church and the Immigrant,* ix.

34. Cheryl Bridges Johns, "The Adolescence of Pentecostalism: In Search of a Legitimate Sectarian Identity," *Pneuma,* Journal of the Society for Pentecostal Studies 17, no. 1 (1995): 13–14.

35. C. Leonard Allen and Danny Gray Swick, *Participating in God's Life* (Orange, Calif.: New Leaf Books, 2001), 164.

This priest from Peru endorsed God's "preferential option for the poor," criticized the destructive military dictatorships in Latin America, and praised the many new grassroots groups of Christians known as "base communities." Taking as their beginning the experience of the poor in their struggle for liberation and social justice, these "liberation" theologians began actively to link salvation and justice. They radically contextualized and practicalized their theologies. North American and European theologians may have been preoccupied with the question of how to speak credibly about God in a secularized world, but Gutiérrez insisted that the pressing Latin American question was "how to tell the nonperson, the nonhuman, that God is love, and that his love makes us all brothers and sisters."[36] The Latin American context was reported to be one of mass and deliberately imposed poverty. It therefore had to be said clearly by responsible Christians in that setting that the God who loves all people identifies especially with the poor and sides with them against every oppressor who exploits and dehumanizes. To know God necessarily involves working for justice, for that is who God is and what God is lovingly doing.

God surely revealed the true divine heart when Jesus touched the man lowered through the roof on a bed (Luke 5:17–26). God certainly was with us in a dramatic and self-revealing way when the body of Jesus was broken and his blood shed on the cross. Because of who God is, death and sin were allowed to touch God. Christ died "for" (Greek: *huper*) us (Rom. 5:8). This "for" can be understood as "in solidarity with" rather than only "instead of." As opposed to God requiring from Jesus the high price for human sin that we sinners must but could not pay, there is merit in thinking that God in Jesus came vulnerably to the side of sinful and marginalized people, affirming and loving them in the most costly way possible—a horrible and humiliating death on a cross. The ministry of Jesus was his journey of mixing sacrificially and healingly with the lost and the least, consciously being on the side of the people who were economically exploited, politically oppressed, and religiously alienated. To be sure, there is the danger of prematurely identifying God with current political agendas, so that the Christian gospel is reduced to being merely a religious veneer for socially driven concerns.[37] Even so, there also is the real danger of failing to recognize and join God in the midst of his redeeming mission.

36. Gustavo Gutiérrez, *The Power of the Poor in History* (Maryknoll, N.Y.: Orbis Books, 1983), 193. He observes: "Concern for preserving the gratuitous quality of the supernatural order led to the formulation of the doctrine of *pure nature*. This completely separated human nature from divine grace; it attributed to human nature not a strong orientation toward grace, but rather a bare 'lack of repugnance' for it. There was no interior desire for communion with God, but rather simple passivity. The supernatural was fundamentally alien to human beings, a perfection superimposed upon them" (43).

37. Says Donald Bloesch, "It is customary in both Neo-Protestantism and Neo-Catholicism today to

Theologians who are highly sensitized to God's caring for marginalized people go where they think Jesus would have gone and where God now is likely to be found most readily as the active Spirit of Jesus. Gustavo Gutiérrez went to the dispossessed masses of Latin America. In North America, James Cone went to his oppressed African American brothers and sisters.[38] He insisted that God "is Black" and that black power is Christ's timely message to racially divided America. Theodore Jennings now has reinterpreted the classic Apostles' Creed by removing supposed "mythological" elements and refocusing Christian faith on loyalty to "the way of God." God's task, and thus ours, he says, should center in relieving the oppressed of their exploitation and deprivation—just as the teachings and ministry of Jesus did.[39]

Such relief from injustice today is often related to the question of gender discrimination and the related impoverishment of the Christian faith. Who is God "the Father" in relation to women, especially ones who have had abusive earthly fathers? Are there second-class citizens in God's kingdom on the basis only of their gender? Are our gender-specific references to God, often exclusively male, unjust to females? Are the male references to God in the Bible incidental to the times, or are they part of the divine revelation itself?

Gender and God

Language is power. Reality—or at least the perception of it—is shaped significantly by how we think and then put our thoughts into words. Words both reflect and construct reality. There is no better example of the power of language than how we humans choose to speak about the Divine and relate to the much-debated issue of exclusive male language for God that generally is typical of the Bible and found in most churches. Is this practice of gender-privileged language part of God's self-disclosure, or merely a culture-bound ancient pattern that unfortunately has persisted and often has been used against justice for women in church and society?

Recent voices such as that of Sallie McFague judge that exclusive male language for God is inherently patriarchal, imperialistic, and oppressive for women. She insists that it is better in our day to replace the emphasis on God

---

deride the otherworldly piety of a past era and to emphasize the need for identification with the oppressed of the world in their struggle for liberation. It is possible to go so far in this direction that we lose sight of the fact that meaningful identification with the oppressed rests upon a prior identification with the Savior of the oppressed" (*The Struggle of Prayer* [Colorado Springs, Colo.: Helmers & Howard, 1988], 166.)

38. See especially Cone, *Black Theology of Liberation.*

39. Theodore Jennings, *Loyalty to God* (Nashville: Abingdon Press, 1992).

as lord, king, and patriarch with the divine models of God as mother, lover, and friend.[40] Ongoing debate centers on whether this is a fair reading of things and the best way to go. Does divine revelation include the precise language to be used in reference to God? Are there vital theological issues at stake, or only disadvantaged people scrambling to right the wrongs of their lives?

Divine revelation clearly points to God as personal, thus prompting numerous personal references to the Divine in the Bible, most of them male in nature. Like female and male human beings, God is a living, speaking, and very personal God who functions in active relationship with others. The Judeo-Christian tradition, however, affirms that God is neither "He" nor "She," and certainly uses neither of these in any way that would encourage injustice toward anyone. According to the second commandment, humans are forbidden to make God in the image of *any* earthly thing, women and men included. The actual reality of God is beyond everything we mere humans can conceive (Isa. 55:8–9; 1 Cor. 2:9–13).

There is in the religion of ancient Israel a clear and yet limited confession of the "fatherhood" of Yahweh, but this confession probably should be seen in the context of the polytheistic mythologies that surrounded Israel. In these mythologies, it was typical to ritually divinize sexual potency and fertility. The gods were portrayed as gender-specific sexual beings who lust, mate, and give birth. Further, the god called *'ab* (father) was nothing like the patriarchal figure sometimes depicted by contemporary feminist rhetoric. Most often, the father god in ancient Near Eastern mythologies was incompetent and inert, while the divine activity was conducted by his wife, consort, son, or daughter. In contrast, "Yahweh's fatherhood is wholly removed from the notion of physical procreation. In fact, it has been well said that the loudest silence of the Hebrew Bible is the absence of a consort for Yahweh. He is utterly and completely alone!"[41]

What is the best way to proceed with God-language in today's social setting? Rosemary Radford Ruether has focused her Christian theology on the discriminatory experiences of women. She sees salvation in large part in sociopolitical terms as God shows compassion for the oppressed and provides liberation from all kinds of bondage. She insists, for instance, that the

---

40. Sallie McFague, *Models of God: Theology for an Ecological, Nuclear Age* (Philadelphia: Fortress Press, 1987), xiii.

41. Peter Toon, *Our Triune God: A Biblical Portrayal of the Trinity* (Wheaton, Ill.: Victor Books, 1996), 133–34. John Wright cautions that, while the prophetic biblical voice is consistently in support of viewing Yahweh as without consort, cultic acceptance of Asherah in popular Jewish religion was more widespread than previously thought. See Wright, "Toward a Holiness Hermeneutic: The Old Testament against Israelite Religion," *Wesleyan Theological Journal* 30, no. 2 (Fall 1995): 68–90.

traditional image of God as male is inherently oppressive to women and must be replaced. Patriarchy is a basic evil to be abolished. It is male domination and the hierarchical structures of society that foster the control of father figures. Part of the structural problem is the traditional thought about God as the all-controlling being above all else. So Ruether turns to Paul Tillich's "Ground of Being" expression for the Divine, concluding that God should be called "God/dess." The Divine is the transcendent matrix of Being that underlies and supports both our own existence and our continual potential for new being.[42]

Ruether surely does well to highlight the historic and very real evils of androcentrism. The question remaining is whether, in the process, she and others like her translate Christian *theology* into a self-serving *ideology* by making their own experience the controlling norm of Christian thought. God is certainly far more than a timely social agenda, worthy as that agenda might be. What clearly was an agenda of Jesus was the elevation of a new family concept, the deep bond among those in solidarity with the work of God (Mark 3:35). The disciples of Jesus are to call none "father" except God (Matt. 23:9), effectively subverting all patriarchal structures, at least in church life.

Jürgen Moltmann also thinks that God should no longer be understood along unisexual and patriarchal lines, but rather "bisexually or transexually," embracing aspects of both sexes.[43] Donald Bloesch warns, however, that there is much theological danger in resymbolizing God in order to speak more forcefully to our times. To avoid the persistent dangers of deism and pantheism, he suggests that we "speak of masculine and feminine *imagery* concerning God rather than masculine and feminine *attributes* of God."[44] God, rather than being partly male and partly female, is better thought of as intensely personal, reflecting characteristics of both genders without being either. Bloesch readily affirms that the biblical God is the ground of both the masculine and the feminine, but also insists that God

> chooses to relate to us in the form of the masculine—as Lord, Father, Son, and so on. God is described [in the Bible] in feminine imagery as well, but the masculine is always dominant, and God is never addressed as "Mother."
> . . . Evangelical theology will declare its profound misgivings concerning nature mysticism and goddess religion, first because this kind of faith orientation subverts the discontinuity between God and nature, and second

---

42. Ruether, *Sexism and God-Talk,* 70–71.
43. Jürgen Moltmann, *Trinity and the Kingdom,* 164.
44. Bloesch, *God the Almighty,* 190. Emphasis added.

because it reduces God to an impersonal life force or creative process within nature.[45]

The continuing theological concern that Bloesch highlights is that the language Christians use for God not encourage a too-close identification of God with the creation, subtly encouraging human beings to worship the creation and not the Creator (Rom. 1:25). The Hebrew prophets generally avoided feminine language for God, at least in part because they knew well from the surrounding religions that female language easily leads to a basic distortion in understanding the nature of God and God's relation to the creation—particularly the tendency to deify nature (see *pantheism* in the glossary). If the Creator is a "goddess," is it not her own body that becomes the universe? Even so, as subsequent history has made painfully clear, insisting on exclusive male images of the Divine is subject to distortions that also can lead to theistic misunderstanding and ungodly injustice for women. Language is power, and problem-free alternatives are elusive.

Coordinate concerns must be honored simultaneously. On the one hand, any shift away from exclusive male language for God should not be paralleled by a shift away from emphasis on the transcendency of God as sovereign over all creation. On the other hand, any retaining of exclusive male language for God should address aggressively the issue of gender-based injustice. While all theological analogies and metaphors for God are to be questioned in the face of the ease of their cultural captivity, there should be no freedom to conceive a new God defined differently than the one revealed in the Bible.[46] This God stands prior to and above creation and is lovingly committed to the well-being of all who suffer and are lost. There is wisdom in the following reflection:

> With respect to the doctrine of the Trinity . . . when we speak about God as "Father," when we speak about the eternal "Son" who comes to us in the man Jesus (who taught us to call his Father "our Father"), and when we speak about the "Spirit" who is the Spirit of the Father and of the Son, we are not talking about the *gender* of God (for God is neither male nor female). We are using analogical language from human experience to talk about the *kind of relationship* that exists between the members of the Trinity and between the triune God and us human beings—a relationship that is like the intimate relationship between parents and their children.[47]

45. Ibid., 25–26.
46. See Thomas C. Oden, *Life in the Spirit,* vol. 3 of *Systematic Theology* (San Francisco: HarperSanFrancisco, 1992), 6–8.
47. Shirley C. Guthrie, *Christian Doctrine,* rev. ed. (Louisville, Ky.: Westminster John Knox Press, 1994), 74.

Chapter 9

Over New Horizons

The LORD waits to be gracious to you; . . . blessed are all those who wait for him.

—Isaiah 30:18

The waiting changes us, schools us, teaches us to know God.[1]
—Maria Boulding, The Coming of God

[God] made darkness his covering around him, his canopy thick clouds dark with water.

—Psalm 18:11

[Jesus Christ] is the image of the invisible God.

—Colossians 1:15

We can find in John Wesley's theology patterns of thought which clearly, although incipiently, lead us to an inclusivist approach to the theology of religions. At one level, this will mean facing the criticism of all inclusivist options, that of interpreting other religions through Christian categories and, therefore, denying their own ultimate claims and metaphysical grounds. This is certainly unavoidable . . . for any theologian seeking to reconcile the particularity of truth revealed through Jesus Christ with the universal possibility of salvation in Jesus Christ.
—Philip R. Meadows, in Wesleyan Theological Journal

*R*ecent generations have seen new emphasis on the category of "hope" as key to the Christian theological vision. They also have seen hope debated and diluted when placed alongside a vigorous pluralism that denies the adequacy

---

1. See the January/February 1987 issue of the journal *Weavings,* which features the theme "Active Waiting."

for all people of the claims of any one religious tradition. Are all faith traditions equally valuable—at least for their own adherents—in characterizing the being and work of "God" and drawing saving benefit from the God they perceive? If so, is there one God by many names or many "gods"? Is there one common hope for humanity, or many hopes, or finally none?

Hope certainly is central to Christian faith. The believer is intended to experience in the present the Spirit of God who is a foretaste of the coming kingdom of God (2 Cor. 1:22). In expecting eventually to be transformed into the likeness of the Christ, the discipleship goal for Christian believers is to seek to be like Christ in the present—on the way to the fuller future (1 John 3:2–3). Hope is not to be a private matter for Christians. Once liberated from fear about one's own future by the assurance of faith, there is granted a freedom to actively care about and creatively minister to the fear and struggles of others. Assurance about tomorrow is to bring power for the living of today.

The recent trends in Christian theology include an elevating of hope both as key to Christian life and as a context for adequately perceiving the being and work of God. Living with a vision of hope fortifies faith, helps in dealing with contemporary religious diversity, and encourages courageous mission in today's world.

Living from the Vision

Traditional Christian theism insists that hoping in God should be done in a biblical context. Looking forward rightly requires being anchored in a looking back faithfully. To really know God requires rightly remembering what God has done. Adequate insight into the Divine comes only by the aid of divine self-revelation, which in the main is narrated in the biblical record. Inevitably, however, the Bible is read in given social contexts and understood in part in relation to these contexts. This introduces diversity inside the Judeo-Christian community—in addition to all that is outside. Today the knowing and hoping of Christians is being done in a global environment, in the dynamic mix of atheism and multiple forms of theism, Christian and otherwise, biblical and otherwise. The God of biblical revelation and classic theological formulation now comes to postmodern Bible readers over the new horizons of the future and through the multiplicity of human perceptions. But God still does come!

As noted in the four short quotations at the beginning of this chapter, Christians are to wait, hope, affirm the centrality of Jesus for true knowledge of God, and be open to the possibility that truth may reach non-Christians, even without their immediate knowledge of the historical Jesus. Traditional Christian theology has insisted that "an idea of God can be allowed to be 'Christian' only if it is subjected to the standard of God's self-disclosure through Jesus Christ, as is made known to us through Scripture."[2] This stance now is critiqued regularly by pluralists who tend to drive a wedge between God and Jesus Christ, opting for a God-focus not tied closely to the necessity of a Christ distinctiveness for Christian theism in the midst of alternative faith systems. Is such a wedge tolerable for a believer wishing to be faithful to biblical revelation? The new theistic frontiers of recent years raise such basic questions.

In this troubled world, the Christian believer often must walk by faith rather than by sight (2 Cor. 5:7). Such faithful walking is to be accompanied by a vision of the coming reign of God and can lead to lives often marked by suffering (1 Cor. 4:8–13; 2 Cor. 4:7–18). Since the love of God reaches toward the whole creation, it is natural for the Christian vision to include a broad sociopolitical dimension. Since the love of God is for all people, the vision of God's coming reign should include the universal possibility of salvation because of the pervasive working of God's Spirit. Since the being of God is beyond human comprehension, the vision should be one of humble hope. The characters in a play are fully developed only when the action is complete. Likewise, in the divine Creator-creation drama, God's self-disclosure is understood fully only when humanity meets its Maker face to face. What the miracle of revelation opens in the meantime is a window through which we glimpse God, although only dimly for now (1 Cor. 13:12).

In a world divided by rampant racism, we are told that God has created another race, a chosen race (1 Pet. 2:9–10). The chosen ones are to function very differently than those who divide on human bases. The new race is to be the united and re-creating body of Christ. It is eschatological because Christ is the head of a new creation, the church, that is called to accept the Spirit's ministry and thus become firstfruits of the coming new order (Rom. 8:23; 2 Cor. 1:22, 5:5; Eph. 1:13–14). The church is to live now in the power of Christ's resurrection (Col. 3:3–4), the dynamic of the coming new day. The community of believers in Christ prepares to live in the coming kingdom through living now by the vision of God's coming reign; the coming reign of God now works in the world by the power of the divine Spirit, who already is introducing that reign and one day will bring it to its fullness. Accordingly, a central concern of the church is to avoid distracting speculations about details of the future and focus instead on faithfulness to God's agenda in the meantime.

2. Alister McGrath, *A Passion for Truth* (Downers Grove, Ill.: InterVarsity Press, 1996), 229.

The present-future relationship is crucial. Embodying in the present the rele-vance of God's coming future is the burden of the New Testament's message and clearly is the church's present mission.

Jesus made clear that the reign of God was at hand in immediate relation to his own appearance. He issued a call to discipleship, made possible by the assurance that the One who is yet coming is the very One already by our side. I have written elsewhere that

> God's Kingdom in its fullest reality and final consummation awaits the sec-ond advent of Christ. That is not yet. In the meantime, as the result of Christ's first advent, the Kingdom now is an inaugurated reality that people are called to enter (Mk. 9:47; Matt. 21:31–32). Recognizing the kingly pres-ence of God in the present time, the Kingdom of God is an invitation for all who will to live in the power of this divine presence, consciously deciding for this reign (Matt. 13:44–46) and doing God's will (Matt. 6:10, 7:21–23).[3]

The God who one day will be all in all is now actively present in the world. Knowing this God who is in Christ through the Spirit is to be enabled to be tomorrow's people today. Unlike cyclical views of history, a Christian eschato-logical perspective allows for and expects *new* things to happen on the way to the final destination. There is the real possibility of actual progress within his-tory toward the intended fullness of the reign of God. To believe in God is to have a hopeful view of the world—history has meaning and goal and there will be something beyond all the evil (primarily there will be *Someone*!). Believers covenant with each other and together with God so that they might be an escha-tological community, God's fellowship of disciples pioneering in the present that which characterizes the coming reign of God. The church is to model in the present that which one day, by God's grace, will appear in its fullness. God's people are thus to be a prophetic even if fragile voice for love, peace, justice, and righteousness in the midst of a very broken world. The world will know God today only as God's people faithfully represent the future, which is God's.

Growing out of the biblical faith and the gross experiences of human suffer-ing and marginalization in recent generations (see chapter 8), there has arisen a fresh focus on hope as a vital dynamic of Christian believing and living. God is the ultimate One of the coming tomorrow who is available as inspiration and enablement for today. After the parade of negatives in recent theology— demythologizing, religionless Christianity, the praise of secularization, the supposed death of God, and so forth—hope seems a welcome attitude of affir-

---

3. Barry L. Callen, *Faithful in the Meantime: A Biblical View of Final Things and Present Responsi-bilities* (Nappanee, Ind.: Evangel Publishing House, 1997), 138.

mation. John Feinberg summarizes: "Since neither heaven nor earth could reveal God, theologians of hope looked to the future."[4] By "heaven" he means the thought of neo-orthodoxy (Karl Barth, etc.) that seemed to lock God out of present history unless God chose to engage it; by "earth" he means the depersonalizing of God by Paul Tillich and others and the loss of confidence in the Bible caused by higher criticism and liberalism generally. These vacuums needed to be filled; thus, there rushed in a new theology of hope.

The Theology of Hope

Early in the twentieth century Albert Schweitzer insisted that Jesus is best understood as an itinerant preacher whose message was fixed on the consummation of history. Jesus was the agent of the *eschaton,* the Christian faith is eschatological, and God is an eschatological reality. God is to be located in the future and eventually will become fully himself (the fullness of his reign). Emphasized here is the power of the future over the present. God is understood as the goal of all things. Recent decades have witnessed many Christian thinkers insisting that eschatology (the doctrine of last things) lies at the heart of Christianity. This view has been coupled with fresh philosophical interest in the phenomenon of hope as a primal human experience.[5] Added to this orientation of Jesus and fresh philosophical interest was the challenge of Marxism and the cries of the world's oppressed people. Where is hope? There must be hope! Jürgen Moltmann announced that the church is to be "like an arrow sent out into the world to point to the future."[6] The Christian hope, in contrast to Marxism, is confident that it is not unrealistically utopian. There can be progress in this present world, but not perfection prior to the final coming of God in the returning Christ. Even so, the good news is that a believer can cope with present human failure without despair by trusting in the *God of hope* (Rom. 15:13), whose full reign is surely coming.

Eschatology has been a playground of Christian speculation, especially for many fundamentalist Christians who use the mass media to tie their "prophetic" readings of the Bible to the headlines of the day. It also has been a subject of derision for many liberals who see in such presumed "prophecy" a simplistic and speculative biblicism leading to world-denying passivity in the face of rampant evil. Often eschatology has been relegated to the realm of

4. John S. Feinberg, *No One Like Him* (Wheaton, Ill.: Crossway Books, 2001), 128.
5. See, for example, Ernst Bloch, *The Principle of Hope*, 3 vols. (Oxford: Blackwell, 1986).
6. Jürgen Moltmann, *Theology of Hope* (London: SCM Press, 1967), 328.

the optional in Christian doctrine, noting that the great ecumenical creeds of Christian history affirm only a second coming of Jesus and subsequent resurrection, judgment, and eternal life (no speculation about end-time dates and events). In line with this modesty and in response to rampant despair of the war-torn twentieth century, the 1970s and 1980s witnessed the fresh emergence of an eschatological emphasis that refused to reduce the subject to detailed predictive prophecy or hopelessly outmoded mythology. In fact, hope became a new theological paradigm, an alternative to both classical Christian theism—featuring an all-controlling and static God—and the newly popular process theology with its much more impotent and developing God who is caught in the present with us.

For the new "theologians of hope," especially the Germans Jürgen Moltmann and Wolfhart Pannenberg,

> God gives human history its own freedom and struggles with it and in it from his own powerful futurity through both the lure of love and powerful prolepsis [e.g., the resurrection of Jesus]. God sends Jesus Christ and the Holy Spirit into the world *from the future* to demonstrate his love and release spiritual forces of anticipation *into the stream of human history*.[7]

Christian eschatology sees present reality in the hands of God and hears God calling into history from its end, saying, "Behold, I make all things new!" Looking ahead, then, should not render the believing church passive in the present; to the contrary, the future (God) comes to the present to release divine power in the midst of the troubled now.

Such Christian eschatology differs from Bultmann's (see chapter 6). He affirmed that, quite disconnected from outward history, any moment can be God's eschatological moment if in it Christ arises with new life in the soul of the believer. But the more recent theologians of hope locate eschatology in the future and then relate it to the present in specific historical terms (e.g., the real resurrection of Jesus). Jürgen Moltmann is clear: "Christianity stands or falls with the reality of the raising of Jesus from the dead by God."[8] This was a historical event that actually happened to Jesus, not merely a spiritual symbol in the experience of believers and a mythological construct to interpret the meaning of the cross.

In 1945 the advancing British captured a young German soldier, beginning Jürgen Moltmann's three years in Allied prisoner-of-war camps. Seeing some

---

7. Roger E. Olson, *The Story of Christian Theology* (Downers Grove, Ill.: InterVarsity Press, 1999), 608–9. Emphasis added.

8. Moltmann, *Theology of Hope*, 165.

Seeing All Anew in the Light of Hope

When I began the "theology of hope," after the "theology of love" in the Middle Ages and the "theology of faith" in the Reformation, I had first thought in terms of hope, its foundation and its future, its experience and its praxis—in other words in terms of an *object* of Christian theology, on which hitherto sufficient light had not yet been cast. . . . In the course of the work, however, hope increasingly became the *subject* of theology for me. I no longer theologized *about* hope, but *from* hope. To think theologically from hope means bringing the whole of theology together in this focus and then seeing it all anew in this light of hope. . . . Not only eschatology—the doctrine of the last things— but all the doctrines of Christian theology, from creation through history to the consummation, then appear in a different light and must be thought through again.

—Jürgen Moltmann, *History and the Triune God*

of his fellow prisoners lose all hope and just die, Moltmann received a Bible from an American chaplain, came to realize that people cannot live without hope, and found his own faith rekindled. Once released, he began theological studies with his own hope for a "more humane Germany" and a "liberated and liberating church of Christ." Sobered by the horrors of war, Moltmann could not be satisfied with any mere "liberal, bourgeois theology."[9] It would have to be a hope-filled theology driven by the historically real cross and resurrection of Jesus. His milestone 1967 book, *Theology of Hope,* launched a reconstruction of central Christian doctrines in light of God's promises for the future and their intended impact on the present. In this book, Moltmann said that God comes to our suffering present through the work of the Holy Spirit, inspiring a hope that re-creates and perseveres. Revelation is essentially *promise* instead of proposition or experience, and salvation is God's historical work being executed in the present from the future. Christian hope is not the individual's avenue for worldly escape; it is the path to realizing God's ultimate design for the real world, both in the present and future. According to the biblical paradigm, one is always on the way from promise to fulfillment.

Moltmann had become convinced that a reorientation toward the future

9. M. Douglas Meeks, *Origins of the Theology of Hope* (Philadelphia: Fortress Press, 1974), xi.

was both biblically warranted and theologically essential. He was active in Marxist-Christian dialogues and influenced by a Marxist colleague, Ernst Bloch, who declared that revolutionary change on behalf of a hoped-for utopia, while yet unrealized, exerts a positive power over the present.[10] Accepting this thesis but rejecting Bloch's Marxist atheism, Moltmann set out to show that Christian hope is the only way to overcome groundless and shallow varieties of hope like that of Bloch's. His goal was a Christian theology that is biblically grounded, eschatologically oriented, and politically responsible. Beginning with the God who has and yet will come in Jesus Christ, the future (God) draws the troubled present forward into new forms of divinely intended reality. The primary value of the Bible, then, is not as a mere recounting of the past, but as a pointing to God's coming reign in ways that enable beginnings of that reign in every present.

Such a vital connection between past revelation and future promise had significant impact on Moltmann's understanding of God. God is not best thought of as "above us" or "in us," but as "ahead of us" in the horizons of the future opened to us in the divine promises. The future is a metaphor of the Divine, a way of viewing the primary mode of God's being.[11] God's existence cannot be proved from examination of the natural world or by existential encounter. Questions of rational proof must remain open and will only be settled later. Here is what is clear. God is the "power of the future" who is pulling present history forward into God's coming new age of peace and justice. God transforms this evil world by drawing it toward the kingdom of glory. Moltmann attempts an interpretation that lies between classic Christian theism and process theology, affirming the God who stands above (transcendence) and the God who also stoops below (immanence). He champions the doctrine of the Trinity, which for him highlights the mutual relationships among the three persons of the Godhead and thus models such relationships between God and the world.

The God who is yet ahead now penetrates the present in order to draw it forward into the gracious and transforming reign of the coming God. History must finally end in God, where it began. Jesus Christ's resurrection is the sign and guarantee of this. Moltmann writes:

10. Ernst Bloch (1885–1977) taught that the idea of God is natural for humans. We strive to progress, to go beyond the present and ourselves, aspiring toward the better future. Philosophy itself begins as an exercise in wonder, a quest of not knowing that dares to move in the direction of the not yet. God, for Bloch, is the human ideal, that which should be and eventually will be, but is not yet. Faith, then, is natural, can be healthy, and by definition is future oriented.

11. Moltmann's German colleague Wolfhart Pannenberg views God as theology's all-inclusive subject. He argues that God's divine status is bound up with God's demonstration of lordship over creation (see his *Theology and the Kingdom of God* [Philadelphia: Westminster Press, 1969], 55–56).

The center has to be *God,* God's kingdom and God's glory. The first three petitions in the Lord's prayer make this clear. What do we really and truly hope for? We hope for the *kingdom of God.* That is first and foremost a hope for God, the hope that God will arrive at his rights in his creation, at his peace in his Sabbath, and at his eternal joy in his image, human beings.[12]

Therein lies the Christian hope. It involves God's tomorrow in a way that does not disassociate hope from present problems and church mission. Moltmann says that "if the Christian hope is reduced to the salvation of the soul in a heaven beyond death, it loses its power to renew life and change the world, and its flame is quenched; it dies away into no more than a Gnostic yearning for redemption from this world's vale of tears."[13]

God, in fact, is to be found and joined in the midst of the vale of human tears. The truth lies in the awkward opposites of the cross and resurrection of Jesus. The first represents destructive godforsakenness and the second the transforming nearness of God. In his death, Jesus identified with the present state of the world in all of its negatives; in his resurrection, Jesus contradicts the cross and becomes the promise for the transformation of reality by the already coming reality of the God of the future. Such a "theology of hope" opens the church simultaneously toward the future of God and the present of the world. The cross was the Father's loving act of solidarity with all the godless and godforsaken. The resurrection was the salvation-offering presence of God now being mediated to the world through the new life of the risen Christ. The cross was an event between the Father and Son and was an atoning gift of suffering. Thus, the Christian understanding of God needs to be Trinitarian (Father-Son-Spirit) and include divine suffering (see *impassibility* in the glossary). The problem of human suffering has been taken up into God's Trinitarian history and therefore offers hope for the eschatological overcoming of all suffering.[14]

Wolfhart Pannenberg essentially agrees with Moltmann's general "hope" perspective. Theology should stress the eschatological goal that draws all history toward God, "the ontological priority of the future," says Pannenberg.

---

12. Jürgen Moltmann, *The Coming God: Christian Eschatology* (Minneapolis: Fortress Press, 1996), xvi.

13. Ibid., xv. George Eldon Ladd agrees: "The Kingdom of God cannot be reduced to the reign of God within the individual soul or modernized in terms of personal existential confrontation or dissipated to an extraworldly dream of blessed immortality. The Kingdom of God means that God is King and acts in history to bring history to a divinely directed goal" (*The Presence of the Future* [Grand Rapids: Eerdmans, 1974], 331).

14. Jürgen Moltmann, in his *The Trinity and the Kingdom* (San Francisco: Harper & Row, 1981), sets forth a strongly social doctrine of the Trinity, one that pictures God as deeply involved in and affected by the world.

The biblical story is a series of God-inspired events suspended between promise and fulfillment. It is the tension-filled drama of the God who is always sovereignly beyond us and yet graciously always with us. The key to understanding the immanent and economic aspects of the Trinity (see glossary) lies in the reciprocal relationship between the divine future and the human present. In fact, says Roger Olson,

> God does not yet fully exist as who he really is and will be—the "all-determining reality." This is because his deity is his rule. Yet, in the final consummation of universal history it will be made clear that God is and always has been the sovereign Lord of history. On the other hand, before and apart from this eschatological denouement God is not yet fully God.[15]

Focus belongs on the great eschatological event, the historical resurrection of Jesus, that is viewed as the prolepsis of God's coming reign when finally God's deity and lordship will be fully visible and no longer challenged as all in all. Writes Carl Braaten, "Christian hope is grounded in the resurrection of Jesus of Nazareth because through it God defined himself as the power of the future beyond the finality of death."[16] God is always "transcendent" in the sense that he does not need the world to be fully God; still, God chooses for the world to be and to go with the world through its troubled history. With biblical help, we discern that the Divine neither abandons fallen creation to its deserved fate nor becomes dependent on it for the divine existence or fulfillment, but allows it to impact him nonetheless. From the human perspective, God is "not yet," since the full realization of the divine lordship is yet to be. But God comes from the divine future to the present, and one day all will move inevitably into that future, with or apart from God.

God's self-revelation must not be lost in mythical abstraction or subjectivism, failing to emphasize its *historical* nature. Pannenberg deviates from the Barth-Bultmann emphases that take faith inward and seek to separate it from reason and public scrutiny. Instead, if Christian theology wants to be influential in today's world, he argues that it must defend its objective claim to truth before the bar of critical reason. Failing to defend the existence of God as the necessary presupposition of all truth and human dignity, much of

---

15. Roger Olson, "Wolfhart Pannenberg's Doctrine of the Trinity," *Scottish Journal of Theology* 43, no. 2 (1990), 204. For a good discussion of this "ontological priority of the future," see Pannenberg's "Appearance as the Arrival of the Future," in his *Theology and the Kingdom of God*, ed. Richard John Neuhaus (Philadelphia: Westminster Press, 1969), 127–43. Traditional Christian theology sees the "becoming" not as some evolution of God's being, but only as an advancing of the realization of God's actual reign in this sinful world.

16. Carl E. Braaten, *The Future of God* (New York: Harper & Row, 1969), 73.

nineteenth-century theology essentially had abandoned the whole idea of God and become increasingly human centered. Pannenberg seeks to reverse this subjectivistic and ultimately atheistic trend. Christian faith is to center in a real God with a real future, the sovereign God who really interacts within humanity's concrete history.

Dealing with Diversity

Humans perceive the nature of the divine interaction with the creation in various ways. It has been difficult enough for the worldwide Christian community to appreciate its own considerable diversity and somehow champion a meaningful unity in the midst of this internal plurality. The ecumenical quest has been a major agenda for many Christian leaders at least since the 1910 milestone missionary conference in Edinburgh, Scotland. One ongoing "roundtable" of ethnic minority Christian theologians has met for years to discover each other and celebrate the richness of their various Christian traditions, what they affirm as a precious rather than a perilous pluralism. They have gone so far as to conclude that "the opposite of a pluralistic church and a pluralistic theology is not simply an exclusivistic church and a rigid theology, but a heretical church and a heretical theology!"[17] The World Council of Churches has been on a similar path. To affirm only part of the truth, or only one way of putting the truth, and think and act as though it were the whole of Christian truth and life for all times and cultures is to render false even what is true.

But the circumstance of diversity today is much more complex and challenging than trying to face constructively the multiplicity of Christian traditions. Humans now are very conscious of living in an external plurality of social and religious communities on one shrinking globe, with travel and communication bringing them into ever closer contact. How should Christians relate to different faith traditions that make their own claims to ultimate reality and refuse to go away in the face of Christian witnessing? Traditionally, Christians have proclaimed a faith based on a "scandal of particularity," the belief that the eternal reality of God is disclosed best and finally in one place, Jesus Christ, not in many places in roughly equal even if very different ways. What about a continuing claim to such uniqueness in a pluralist context? What about the tension seen in Scripture between (1) God's love for *all*

17. Justo L. González, *Out of Every Tribe and Nation: Christian Theology at the Ethnic Roundtable* (Nashville: Abingdon Press, 1992), 25–26.

people and intention that they be redeemed and (2) God's proclaimed incarnation in Jesus, in whom *alone* salvation is said to be available? After all, across human history a large percentage of all persons never heard of Jesus. How then are they to be saved—or have they no opportunity for salvation?

While it surely is appropriate to think in a catholic way about the fullness of the Christian revelation (avoiding the blindness of narrow sectarianism), how far should the breadth of vision go? When does wise inclusion become unacceptable tolerance of what should not be included in the range of Christian wisdom? Denominations regularly resist yielding points of doctrine judged key to their own traditions. Diversity, they insist, does and will not require an eventual uniformity. But now there is the even bigger challenge, a wider field of potential roundtable partners. What about religious traditions other than the Christian one? Is there only one God, although known by many names and explained in various ways? Or are there many "gods"? Or are such questions finally unanswerable? And does it really matter?

In the pluralistic, politically correct, and tolerant environment of today's Western world, normative and exclusive religious claims are increasingly hard to maintain credibly in the public eye. Do morally serious adherents to traditional African religions, virtuous Hindus, and prayerful, peaceful Buddhists really have reference to the same God—and, if not, do they reside outside the orbit of all true salvation potential? Residing outside the saving orbit has been a common claim in Christian church history. Do Jews and Muslims who worship the God of Abraham and seek to follow God's commands as they are able to understand them urgently need to hear the gospel of Jesus Christ, or do they know the true God already?[18] Is Yahweh still Yahweh apart from the person and name of Jesus? Such are some of the pressing theistic questions of our time. It is common to choose the stance of relativism, by which even if there is only one God, each view of God is presumed to be historically conditioned, essentially private, and should be respected along with all the others. Maybe, beneath all of the surface differences, there is only one God and that God is always the one being worshiped—just in a variety of ways and under various names and assumptions.

If such benign plurality is the case, there are vigorous Christian voices arguing to the contrary. Rather than God being "perceived," D. A. Carson thinks that increasingly evangelical Christians today are being "deceived" by the global mix, which really is the "ugly face" of a philosophical pluralism that may be "the most dangerous threat to the gospel since the rise of the gnos-

18. See Marvin Wilson, *Our Father Abraham: Jewish Roots of Christian Faith* (Grand Rapids: Eerdmans, 1989).

tic heresy in the second century."[19] What Carson sees going on is the "gagging of God," a tragic contemporary tendency "to think of God in line with what appears acceptable to the contemporary spirit . . . as if God changes with the cultural mood."[20] Other interpreters view this "ugly face" more kindly. At a minimum, it is clear that recently there has been a cultural shifting that is major and global in scale. It is the general collapse of the Enlightenment idea of universal knowledge. The World Wide Web, for instance, has enabled awareness and information sharing to an extent previously unimagined. Transportation has shrunk the world to a relatively small place. Increasingly, when the concept of God is being considered, there is ready knowledge of how other eyes perceive the Divine. The Carsons of the Christian world view this and its "compromising" temptations with alarm, while others are more relaxed and even enthusiastic about its positive good for all concerned.

Three general approaches are typical, each a way that Christians might understand God-in-Christ in relation to the many other divinity and salvation claims made by the religions of humankind. *Exclusivism* insists that only those can be saved who deliberately place their trust in the Christ of the Bible.[21] *Inclusivism* cautiously opens the door of potential salvation to some people who have placed no conscious faith in Jesus Christ (maybe have not even heard of him), but somehow can be saved through him nonetheless because of divine grace and the universal ministry of God's Spirit.[22] *Pluralism* views all religious options as potentially having the same spiritual value and in themselves offering an equal salvation possibility—regardless of the Jesus Christ connection or lack of it. There is a trend from the first approach to at least the second in the "Quaker Universalist" movement "that regards historic Christ-centered Quakerism as too narrow in a world where we need to join hands with persons of other religious faiths." Quakerism is seen by this radical wing as an appropriate bridge characterized by commitment to "that of God in every one."[23]

Pluralism fits today's cultural mood by championing the postmodern position that no one religious tradition is exclusively true, at least not for those

19. It is important to recall that religious pluralism was as much a fact of life in Paul's day as it is in ours.

20. D. A. Carson, *The Gagging of God: Christianity Confronts Pluralism* (Grand Rapids: Zondervan, 1996), 25.

21. Karl Barth was a leading modern exponent of exclusivism. For him, Jesus Christ is the decisive, unrepeatable, and unsurpassable locus of divine revelation.

22. One might include John Wesley in this category, since his emphasis on "prevenient grace" sees all people as recipients of faith enablement, as part of God's saving quest for redemption of the lost creation (although all will not be saved).

23. Wilmer A. Cooper, *A Living Faith* (Richmond, Ind.: Friends United Press, 1990), 152.

outside it. John Hick argues that all sincere religious persons worship the same reality, except in different ways and under different names. Why the variation of ways and names? Hick says it is because "religious faith is not an isolated aspect of our lives but is closely bound up with human culture and human history, which are in turn bound up with basic geographical, climatic, and economic circumstances."[24] Presumably these varying factors help give rise to the particular ways that God is understood.

Hick sees far more positive than negative in greater awareness and openness to God as variously understood in the complex religious life of humankind. In fact, the more wholistic the view the more there can be "a release from an artificially restricted vision into a greater intellectual honesty and realism and a more mature Christian faith."[25] Such a call to Christian pluralism is supported by the assumption that it is proper to move from *christocentrism* to *theocentrism* (God and not Jesus as the central focus). Jesus Christ thus becomes less than mandatory for salvation since God is the global key and God is not confined to or exhausted by the Jesus revelation. God indeed may have been *in* Christ and *like* Christ, but God is not *limited to* Christ in revealing God or redeeming the world.

But such an affirmation of openness to diversity as the preferred path to spiritual maturity seems to most traditional Christians and Jews to be a denial of the biblical insistence on only one God, with all forms of idolatry to be vigorously rejected. Rather than religious pluralism (the denial that any one religious tradition has a monopoly on truth), the orthodox Hebrew-Christian-Islamic stance has been a religious exclusivism in which only one God is affirmed as real. For Christians who inherited this theism rooted in the Abrahamic heritage, the one and only real God is the one now known best in Jesus Christ. Speaking very exclusively, Jesus said, "I am *the* way, and *the* truth, and *the* life. No one comes to the Father *except through me*" (John 14:6; emphasis added). Peter echoed this particularism by preaching that "there is salvation *in no one else* [other than the risen Christ], for there is no other name under heaven given among mortals by which we must be saved" (Acts 4:12; emphasis added).

Therefore, traditional Christian belief is strongly resistant to any Hick-like homogenizing agenda of religious pluralists that reduces the high Christology at the center of faith in the one true God. Christians understand God to be *in*

24. John Hick, *God Has Many Names* (Philadelphia: Westminster Press, 1982), 51.
25. John Hick, "A Pluralist View," in *More Than One Way? Four Views on Salvation in a Pluralistic World*, ed. Dennis L. Okholm and Timothy R. Phillips (Grand Rapids: Zondervan, 1995), 51. Also see Hick's *An Interpretation of Religion: Human Responses to the Transcendent* (New Haven, Conn.: Yale University Press, 1989).

Jesus Christ and to *be* Christlike, meaning that all other religious perspectives do *not* more or less speak about the same "God." It thus is not acceptable for Christians to smooth the path to interreligious dialogue by agreeing to be God-centered without also being Christ-centered. No wedge is to be driven between the "Christ principle" and the "Jesus event." What makes Christianity distinctive is its particular understanding of God in and through the divine incarnation in the person of Jesus. What Christians classically have meant by "God" is precisely and nothing other than "the Father of our Lord Jesus Christ" (1 Pet. 1:3).

Alister McGrath says clearly that "an idea of God can only be considered 'Christian' if it is subjected to the standard of God's self-disclosure through Jesus Christ, as is made known to us through Scripture."[26] The Lausanne Covenant of 1974 made the general evangelical stance plain:

> We affirm that there is only one Saviour and only one gospel. . . . We recognize that all men have some knowledge of God through his general revelation in nature. But we deny that this can save, for men suppress the truth by their unrighteousness. We also reject as derogatory to Christ and to the gospel every kind of syncretism and dialogue which implies that Christ speaks equally through all religions and ideologies.[27]

It may be the case that, while Christ does not speak "equally," the voice of God in Christ is nonetheless accessible universally and somehow potentially "adequate" even if not equal. There are strong Christian voices today that argue this very possibility.

In recent years Clark H. Pinnock and numerous other Christian theologians have claimed middle ground in the tension between God as known definitively in Jesus and the potential salvation of the many persons not directly aware of God as self-revealed through the incarnation in Jesus. According to these theologians, there is only one God and this God is the one biblically revealed and known best through Jesus Christ. All salvation will be because of and *only* because of the merits of Jesus Christ. But, they nonetheless add, affirming the one God revealed in Jesus Christ does not automatically mean that God's saving grace is restricted to knowledge and acceptance of the

---

26. Alister McGrath, "A Particularist View," in Okholm and Phillips, eds., *More Than One Way?* 169. In his 1996 book, *A Passion for Truth,* McGrath adds, "It is perfectly possible for the Christian to engage in dialogue with non-Christians, whether of a religious persuasion or not, without in any way being committed to the intellectually shallow and paternalist view that 'we're all saying the same thing' . . . Dialogue thus implies respect, not agreement, between parties" (211–12).

27. J. D. Douglas, ed., *Let the Earth Hear His Voice: International Congress on World Evangelization* (Minneapolis: World Wide Publications, 1975), 3–4.

specific Hebrew-Christian tradition in a way that means the unevangelized have no access to truly saving faith.

A key question is this: Would the God who privileges only the properly informed (those who receive clear witness to the historic event of God in Jesus) be the merciful and loving God seen in Jesus? Surely not, concludes Pinnock and others.[28] Does anyone find salvation by a way other than Jesus Christ? No, Christ is the only way. Even so, God wishes salvation for all and intends to have mercy on all (1 Tim. 2:4; Rom. 11:32). God will save all who, on the basis of the "light" they have, respond to God in faith. It is faith in God that is finally crucial (Heb. 11:6), not necessarily hearing and consciously responding to the gospel of Jesus Christ.[29]

So the tension somehow must be maintained among the following critical and interdependent affirmations: (1) God being identified properly and most fully by Jesus; (2) salvation being provided by God through Jesus only; and (3) this salvation being available to all persons—even ones who never hear the name of Jesus in their lifetimes. Abraham was justified by faith without knowing the historic Jesus, and Paul names Abraham as the model believer for us all, even though he never heard the gospel of Christ (Rom. 4:1–25). While we are assured that those who respond in faith to the express preaching of the good news of God in Christ will be saved, we cannot thereby assume that *only* those will be saved. God's revelation, centered in Jesus, is not limited to direct preaching of this good news by Christians. A high Christology that clearly affirms the divinity of Jesus Christ does not need to mean a low level of hope for the unevangelized.

There is a prevenient grace of God that goes before human evangelizing and also goes to the many places where evangelizing never gets. Affirmation of such universal grace is a key teaching of the Wesleyan theological tradition and a natural emphasis of a theology of God's Spirit. The Father God is known in the Son by the ongoing and universal ministry of the Spirit of God. The doctrine of the Trinity, therefore, is crucial to theological balance and wholeness (see chapter 10).[30]

---

28. See Clark H. Pinnock, *A Wideness in God's Mercy: The Finality of Jesus Christ in a World of Religions* (Grand Rapids: Zondervan, 1992); and John Sanders, *No Other Name: An Investigation into the Destiny of the Unevangelized* (Grand Rapids: Eerdmans, 1992). Pinnock speaks of his "hermeneutic of hopefulness," a positive view of the opportunity of salvation being available to all people. While surely a grace-filled optimist, Pinnock is clearly not a pluralist like John Hick.

29. Pinnock, *Wideness in God's Mercy*, 157–63.

30. For extensive studies of the significance and dimensions of the ministry of God's Spirit, see Barry L. Callen, *Authentic Spirituality: Moving beyond Mere Religion* (Grand Rapids: Baker Academic, 2001); and Veli-Matti Kärkkäinen, *Pneumatology: The Holy Spirit in Ecumenical, International, and Contextual Perspective* (Grand Rapids: Baker Academic, 2002).

All salvation is indeed by the sheer grace of the sovereign God. However, John Calvin, Martin Luther, and Roman Catholicism's Second Vatican Council affirm together that valid knowledge of the true God may be gained outside the immediate arena of the Christian tradition and witness.[31] There is redemptive potential in general revelation (see glossary); thus, there are grounds for an evangelical inclusivism that does not sacrifice commitments to biblical authority and high Christology. The Holy Spirit is everywhere active to make God known. The Catholic theologian Karl Rahner, for instance, refers to seriously religious people who do not expressly know about Jesus Christ as "anonymous Christians." While this concept is much debated, there is some truth in it.

The Christian church is called to be the visible expression of what it hopes is also a present although hidden reality outside the visible church—God gracefully at work everywhere on behalf of the salvation of all people. This emphasis on "all people" does not imply that all people in fact will be saved. What is available by God's grace is only the *opportunity* for each person to be saved. The unevangelized can be saved by God through Jesus Christ even when the saving work of Christ is unknown to the grace receiver, at least not known in its historical specifics. John Sanders explains that "the work of Jesus is ontologically but not epistemologically necessary for salvation. No one will be saved without Christ's atonement, but one need not be aware of that work of grace in order to benefit from it."[32]

God and the Future

Christian thinking about God is going over new horizons in the shifting realities of the early twenty-first century. The challenge is to hold fast to essential foundations while adjusting creatively for the sake of effective church mission. For instance, and quite apart from the pressing question of the potential salvation of all people, there now is the urgent concern about the survival or

31. See Carl E. Braaten, "Christ Is God's Final, Not the Only, Revelation," in Braaten, *No Other Gospel! Christianity among the World's Religions* (Minneapolis: Fortress Press, 1992). Also see Miikka Ruokanen, *The Catholic Doctrine of Non-Christian Religions according to the Second Vatican Council* (Leiden: Brill, 1992). According to the Council's "Declaration on the Relationship of the Church to Non-Christian Religions," the Roman Catholic Church "rejects nothing which is true and holy in these religions. She looks with sincere respect upon those ways of conduct and of life, those rules and teachings which, though differing in many particulars from what she holds and sets forth, nevertheless reflect a ray of that Truth which enlightens all men."

32. John Sanders, "Evangelical Response to Salvation outside the Church," *Christian Scholar's Review* 24, no. 1 (1994), 51–52.

at least the well-being of the creation itself. Many theologians are shifting from an anthropocentric (human-centered) to an ecocentric (creation-centered) framework that features the present work of the Spirit of God in relation to all that is. Christianity often has been used to help sanction an exploitative ethic that has allowed science, technology, and human greed to plunder the earth and now space as well. What is the relationship between God's Spirit and the natural world?[33] In what way is our current ecological crisis also a crisis of faith in God? Surely, through the Spirit, God chooses to participate in the destiny of creation—and surely God expects his people to do the same in responsible ways.

The last chapter of Karen Armstrong's best-selling 1993 book, *A History of God,* is titled "Does God Have a Future?" Having surveyed extensively the complex and often conflicted four-thousand-year quest for God by Judaism, Christianity, and Islam, and having reviewed the considerable doubt, despair, and sometimes arrogance of humanity in recent centuries—including even the claim that God has died—Armstrong's concluding question is a natural one. Is the era of the Divine a thing of the past, a fond hope now fading from sight? Maybe so, but apparently not. Faith is persistent and the God question remains, as it always has.

One day in Auschwitz, so the story goes, a group of Jews put God on trial. The evil in this Nazi death camp was so great that all easy answers seemed worse than obscene. The decision was not difficult to reach. God soon was found guilty—either of not being at all, or of not caring enough, or at least of being impotent and thus also a victim of the terrible circumstances. Following the conviction, strangely enough, some of the participating Jews actually returned to their traditional prayers, still hoping and believing in spite of the assumption of God's terrible guilt. There remains a need for faith and reasons for faith, in spite of all questions and circumstances.

Dare we respond today to Armstrong's probing question with a biblical response? Rather than "Does God *have* a future?" biblically informed faith dares to affirm that "God *is* the future!" To be perfectly clear, however, it must be said that the future belongs not to just any "God," not to any idol so easily made and short-lived, but only to the true God known as Father, Son, and Spirit. Thus, the final chapter of this book returns to this ancient claim of God as "Trinity."

33. See the seminal work of Jürgen Moltmann, *God in Creation: A New Theology of Creation and the Spirit of God* (San Francisco: Harper & Row, 1985).

Chapter 10

Still the Great Three-in-One

The doctrine [of the Trinity] has vanished and resurfaced at various times in the history of Christianity. . . . The modern period, with its brass heaven and all-pervasive notion of [human] autonomy has been particularly hostile to Trinitarian conceptions of God. But around the middle of the twentieth century theologians . . . began rediscovering and reappropriating the Trinitarian doctrine.
—*C. Leonard Allen and Danny Gray Swick,*
Participating in God's Life

In order to avoid tritheism, we say that the Trinity is a society of persons united by a common divinity. There is one God, eternal, uncreated, incomprehensible, and there is no other. But God's nature is internally complex and consists of a fellowship of three. It is the essence of God's nature to be relational. This is primordial in God and defines who God is. God is a triadic community, not a single, undifferentiated unity.

—*Clark H. Pinnock,*
Flame of Love: A Theology of the Holy Spirit

"*T*rinity" is a distinctively Christian doctrine, a very particular way of understanding the being and actions of God. The Bible laid the foundations for this understanding (see chapter 3), the classic period oversaw its traditional formulations (see chapter 4), and the centuries to follow have witnessed its fluctuations as a mainstream and much-maligned Christian tenet of faith. While often a source of confusion and controversy, the doctrine of the Trinity nonetheless continues to stand at the heart of the fullness of what Christians mean when they say "God." This doctrine is the product of Christian theological reflection on God's activity in history. The story of Jesus, the center of this history, does not include a dogmatic formula of Trinity as such, but provides its essential foundation. Jesus was aware of being God's Son in a unique sense and was also a unique bearer of the divine Spirit. God was his loving Father, he was the Father's beloved Son, and the Spirit of God was at work in, through, and beyond him. Trinity is the Christian way of capturing the fullness of this divine reality. As the distinctive way of projecting the Christian understanding of God, it has remained across the centuries and cultures in spite of all the criticism.

God as Triadic Community

The Christian doctrine of the Trinity is certainly problematic for Jews and Muslims since, at least on the surface, it appears to violate the basic tenet of their common Abrahamic tradition—God is *one*. Is the singular and "jealous" Yahweh compatible with the "pluralism" of triune thinking? Is the God of Muhammad also the Father of Jesus?[1] I once heard it said that "the world is proof that God is a committee." Well, if not a committee, implying a task-oriented group of "gods," can the God known through biblical revelation somehow be a *singular plurality*? This has been a key question across the centuries of Christian believing.

As Clark Pinnock has stated in the second quotation at the beginning of the chapter, Christians traditionally have affirmed that "God is a triadic community, not a single, undifferentiated unity." The classic Trinitarian teaching of Christians, however, is not intended to suggest that God is only perceived in three modes of the single being (modalism) or is a loose association of isolated divine individuals, a deity composed of three autonomous divine persons. Such suggestions too often have arisen and have been judged unorthodox. The loose association of isolated divine individuals supports both the accusation of polytheism (multiple gods) and a destructive individualism among many Christians rather than highlighting the unity of the one God and the unity among believers envisioned by the New Testament (1 Cor. 12–14). Traditional Christian theologians employ relational terms to particularize the *three* in order to say something about the internal multiplicity of the *One*. The persons of the triune multiplicity "are always in motion, always flowing into one another and giving place to one another, such that it really makes no sense to speak of 'individuals' within God."[2] Father, Son, and Spirit

---

1. See Timothy George, "Is the God of Muhammad the Father of Jesus?" *Christianity Today,* February 4, 2002, 28–35.
2. David S. Cunningham, "The Holy Trinity: The Very Heart of Christian Ministry," *Quarterly Review: A Journal of Theological Resources for Ministry* 22, no. 2 (Summer 2002): 129.

share equally in all essential divine attributes, so that there is only one God (monotheism) but a complex mystery to the divine being (a dynamic and social theism).

For average Christian believers, there is little concern about tritheism being subtly implied when God is spoken of as triune. Surely no one means that there is more than one true God! Even so, there often is a virtual dismissing of Christian Trinitarianism on the ground that it is a misleading enigma, a mathematical problem only understood by professional theologians—and not thought of the same way by all of them. Is it really necessary? It certainly is both inspiring and mystifying for many Christians to sing the great hymn "Holy! Holy! Holy! Lord God Almighty" and finish each verse with the refrain "God in three Persons, blessed Trinity." These hymn lyrics are traditional, uplifting, almost sacred—but what do they really mean?

Spiritual difficulties sometimes have developed in the minds of Christian believers because of a conflict between their images of Jesus and their images of God. The separation of the three persons of the Godhead adversely affects their Christian thought and life. For instance, as Frederic Greeves observes:

> There is often an unrecognized conflict between belief in the Redeemer's goodness and an idea of the indifference (or worse) of the Creator. A belief in the full humanity of the Son of God is uneasily associated with the view that, in God's sight, all that is physical is evil. The Holy Spirit is often depersonalized, thought of as "It" instead of "Him," so that mechanistic and even fatalistic ideas about the Spirit's operations are held alongside trust in the fully personal work of the Father and the Son.[3]

How can one believe in the Trinity without falling into theological confusion and even spiritual dysfunction?

The idea of one God who is said to meet us humans as multiple "persons" may be the least accessible of all Christian teachings. Even so, Christians have long found it necessary to speak of Trinity, not because the matter can be fully fathomed rationally but because such an affirmation has been understood to be central to an adequate expression of the faith of Christians. Trinity refers to what Christians understand about God now that Jesus has come (incarnation) and the Spirit has been poured out (Pentecost). This doctrine is not intended to be an abstract formula designed for its own sake, but a necessary summary way of describing the fullness of the biblical witness of God's love incarnate in Jesus through the Spirit. Christians usually are baptized "in the

---

3. Frederic Greeves, *Theology and the Cure of Souls: An Introduction to Pastoral Theology* (Manhasset, N.Y.: Channel Press, 1962), 59–60.

name of the Father, the Son, and the Holy Spirit." They have been taught to know the Father through the Son in and by the Holy Spirit. Trinitarian thought has been basic. Despite the various concerns related to it, Trinitarianism should remain as the theistic heart of Christianity.

According to the New Testament, God is understood best in light of the divine incarnation in Jesus Christ. Thus, God as biblically pictured, says Donald Bloesch, "is not a monochrome God but a fellowship of persons existing in a dynamic unity. God radiates the splendor not of solitary majesty but of outgoing love."[4] When Christians speak of Trinity, writes Clark Pinnock, the intent is to "express belief in the one God who is not a solitary being but a communion in love characterized by overflowing life. The Trinity is . . . a symbol that points to a three-folded relationality in God. It speaks of shared life at the heart of the universe and establishes mutual relationship as the paradigm for personal and social life."[5] If such a view is necessitated by the very nature of God as biblically revealed, then surely it is to be central and practical for all who believe in the God who is the Father of Jesus Christ.

As highlighted in the quotations heading this chapter, recent decades have seen a renewal of serious attention to Christian Trinitarianism. Rather than being dismissed as a theological enigma or as actual tritheism, which would be a major perversion of the Hebrew heritage of monotheism and an understandable affront to Islam, Trinity has been reaffirmed as the best way of conceiving the one God as this God exists eternally and in relation to the present creation. Much credit for this recent renewal goes to Karl Barth, who begins his massive *Church Dogmatics* with a long discussion of the Trinity. For him this doctrine is at the heart of and not merely a negotiable footnote to any distinctively Christian theology. Barth has not been alone in this judgment, as the centuries of Christian history clearly attest. The ancient Apostles' Creed, first formulated in the late second or early third century and affirmed worldwide to this day, is structured around God as Father, Son, and Spirit. One version of it reads:

> I believe in God, the Father almighty,
>   creator of heaven and earth.
> I believe in Jesus Christ, his only Son, our Lord.
>   He was conceived by the power of the Holy Spirit
>   and born of the Virgin Mary.
>   He suffered under Pontius Pilate,
>   was crucified, died, and was buried.

---

4. Donald G. Bloesch, *God the Almighty* (Downers Grove, Ill.: InterVarsity Press, 1995), 80.
5. Clark H. Pinnock, *Most Moved Mover* (Grand Rapids: Baker Academic, 2001), 30.

He descended to the dead.
On the third day he rose again.
He ascended into heaven,
and is seated at the right hand of the Father.
He will come again to judge the living and the dead.
I believe in the Holy Spirit,
the holy catholic Church,
the communion of saints,
the forgiveness of sins,
the resurrection of the body,
and the life everlasting. Amen.[6]

A working theological consensus about God was reached at the first ecumenical council (in Nicaea, A.D. 325). The post-Nicene Christian teachers generally understood the triune God as having one *ousia* (essence or substance) and being three *hypostases* ("persons"), all equal ontologically (no subordination of any one to the others). Therefore, God the Father always is inseparable from the Son and the Holy Spirit, although the Father should always be distinguished from both. The constant oneness of God is thus to be affirmed in the midst of the appropriate differientiating of Father, Son, and Spirit. God is one by virtue of a common essence, and God is three by virtue of three "persons" within the singular Godhead.

A conflict of judgment remained, however, between the Eastern and Western churches regarding the *filioque* clause ("and from the Son") that the Western church would soon add in relation to the Spirit (see *filioque* in the glossary). The West tended to work from the unity of God and interpreted the relation of the three persons of the Godhead in terms of their mutual fellowship. By some contrast, the Eastern church tended to emphasize the distinct individuality of the three persons of God and then sought to safeguard their unity by stressing the fact that *both* the Son and Spirit derived from the Father, the Father being the principle of unity in the Godhead. Although seeming to be only a minor difference, the Trinity doctrine is so central that this small *filioque* debate has remained a significant issue for centuries (see figure 4).

Christian theologies are sometimes characterized by their degrees of emphasis on one of the three persons of the divine Trinity. Noting the three-part structure of the Apostles' Creed, some theologies can be seen as first article, some second article, and some third article types (particular focus being given to Father, Son, or Spirit). Thomas Aquinas reflects the first (strong "natural" theology of God the creating Father), Martin Luther the second (strong

6. Gerald Bray, *Creeds, Councils, and Christ* (Downers Grove, Ill.: InterVarsity Press, 1984), 204–5.

redemptive theology of the cross of Jesus the saving Son), and John Wesley the third (strong transformative theology of the maintaining Spirit). Each of these emphases is significant, especially when tempered by the strengths of the others. None of them is independently adequate, all being a matter of emphasized focus. There is one God—Father, Son, and Spirit. Christian faith is whole only when informed by the fullest range of God's being and work.

The Enduring Trinitarian Focus

From biblical times, Christian baptism usually has been done in the triple name of Father, Son, and Spirit,[7] with confessions of Christian faith and the meaning of Christian baptism being essentially extended commentaries on the meanings of the divine Trinity. This triune affirmation intends to summarize the core Christian teachings about God. Although the Trinity concept often is said to be only a complicating construct of church theologians, the biblical witness itself appears to call for no less than such an understanding of God. It is, of course, appropriate to be cautious about any premature reading of New Testament teaching into Old Testament writings. Even so, Christian scholars over the centuries have insisted repeatedly that teaching about the triuneness of the one God is at least intimated in the Old Testament[8] and even more overtly suggested in the New Testament.

New Testament writers certainly did not set out to revise Hebrew theism. Jesus, himself a loyal Jew, intended to fulfill and not destroy his beloved religious heritage (Matt. 5:17). What these writers found necessary to do was highlight that they had been encountered savingly by the one Yahweh God in their encounter with Jesus of Nazareth. They declared confidently that Jesus' presence with them was God's own presence. It was more than that Jesus had made God better known to them; it was that God was *in Christ*, reconciling the world to himself (2 Cor. 5:19). This Jesus was nothing less than the Christ-Word of God who had been *with God* in the beginning and *was God* for all time (John 1:1–14). Accordingly, the first Christian communities faced the challenge of articulating the meaning of their direct experience of God in the

---

7. As classically understood, Christian baptism is in the three divine persons who are eternally one, not in the names of three different "gods," or in the name of the one God and two semi-gods, or in three parts or stages of the one God.

8. Thomas C. Oden, *The Living God*, vol. 1 of *Systematic Theology* (Peabody, Mass.: Prince Press, 1998), 189–95. Here he recounts in detail this thesis as set forth by what he calls "major consensual views of influential classical exegetes." Also see John S. Feinberg, *No One Like Him* (Wheaton, Ill.: Crossway Books, 2001), 448ff.

Figure 4
The *Filioque* Debate

The Eastern Approach
to the Trinity

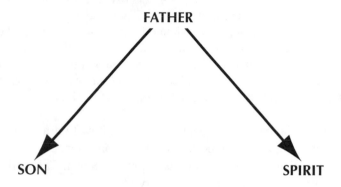

FATHER

SON   **SPIRIT**

The Father "begets" the Son and "breathes" the Spirit. This suggests
the full equality of Son and Spirit in relation to the Father.

- -

The Western Approach
to the Trinity

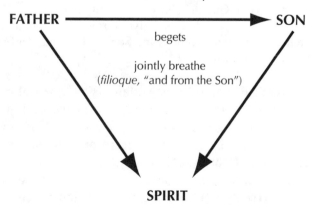

FATHER ⟶ **SON**

begets

jointly breathe
(*filioque*, "and from the Son")

SPIRIT

This dual procession of the Spirit suggests a significance for the
Son with the Father that is not fully shared by the Spirit. As a
corrective, some Western theologians now propose that the Holy
Spirit is "*from* the Father *through* the Son."

historical Jesus and in the continuing presence with them of God by means of
the present Spirit of the resurrected Jesus—all to be done within their strict
monotheism. This was no easy task, but they judged that there was no option.
Thomas Oden describes their situation:

> The earliest Christians were steeped in monotheistic faith, but they had to
> make sense out of this inescapable revelatory event—this living, resur-
> rected presence of the Lord in their midst. They understood Jesus to be not
> a demi-God, not part God, not proximately similar to God, but in the fullest
> sense "true God" (John 17:3; 1 John 5:20; Rev. 3:7). . . . The disciples not
> only experienced the presence of Father and Son, but further experienced a
> powerful impetus of some radically motivating divine Spirit that brought
> the Son to them and enlivened their awareness of the Father.[9]

The problem of the New Testament writers was how to affirm the true deity
of the incarnate man Jesus, who obviously in some sense was distinct from
the Father, and also that of the graciously present Spirit. This had to be done
while maintaining the singularity and unity of God.

What endures to this day as central to orthodox Christian faith is this direct
experience of God who was genuinely in Christ and is still present through
the Spirit. Note Oden's summation:

> The mystery of the triune God is that God is Father, God is Son, and God
> is Spirit, and that God is one. Yet we do not say that there is one Person in
> God, but three Persons, and we do not say that there are three gods, but one
> God. . . . We worship one God in Trinity and Trinity in unity. . . . What the
> Father is to us and gives to us, He is and gives through the Son, in the Holy
> Spirit; no one has the Father except in the Son, and no one confesses the
> Son except in the Holy Spirit.[10]

Also enduring as fundamental to Christian faith is the quest of believers to
become Christlike and to articulate as their witness the central roots and
implications of the experience of worshiping the triune God. In the early
centuries of this theological quest, the concept of "persons" emerged as
believers moved into non-Hebrew settings and sought effective ways to communicate their experience and belief about the self-revealing and ever present
God. Admittedly, the Trinity is a theological formulation rather than explicit
biblical teaching, and its significance lies as much in the theological devia-

9. Oden, *Living God*, 184.
10. Thomas C. Oden, *Life in the Spirit*, vol. 3 of *Systematic Theology* (San Francisco: HarperSan-
Francisco, 1992), 468.

tions it rejects as in the truths it affirms. The considerable reflection and debate that led to its construction and wide adoption was often spurred by threatening heresies.

The result of it all, the formalized Trinity doctrine incorporating three divine "persons," inhabits the world of fragile human analogies.[11] It seeks to set boundaries that protect against distortions of Christian belief. Nonetheless, it is a faithful and fair way of expressing the inexpressible, of stating the rudiments of the true by denying false alternatives, and all without claiming to have fully and finally penetrated, comprehended, and rationally articulated the full mystery of God. Classic Christian theology says that God not only *forms* covenant relationships but *is* a relationship. God, whose nature never changes, is revealed in Jesus Christ as loving and triune—Father, Son, and Holy Spirit. God is a loving community of "persons" so that active love characterizes the inner life of the Divine. God did not have to create the world to experience the fulfillment of loving relationships, since God *is* a dynamic and fulfilled mutuality, with or without the created world.

The Trinity doctrine is theological shorthand for designating the richness of the relational nature and activity of God as known in Jesus through the Spirit. The Gospel of John begins with the amazing affirmation that God had become flesh (1:14). It was not only that God was being *made known* in Christ, but that God *was* in Christ (2 Cor. 5:19), so that Christ was actually God with us, both revealing and being the divine truth. God has never ceased to be truly *other* than all of creation; yet in Jesus, God has come and dwelt with us *as* the flesh that was Jesus of Nazareth. This God-flesh tension (incarnation) lies at the core of Christian belief. Craig Keen puts it this way:

> [T]his Jesus is acutely aware of his *heavenly* Father. It is his Father that he makes known. And yet he looks to his Father as an *Other* who is incomparably free in relation to everything creaturely; an *Other* who cannot be exploited by anyone, however propertied, powerful, prestigious, or pure. . . . This is the oddity of Jesus above all else. He proclaims and he performs and he *is* Immanuel, God with us. Yet God with us is no less God, Wholly Other. In the life and ministry of Jesus, One comes to us who is what we are, who has what we have. But also One comes to us who is in every respect what we are not and cannot be, what we have not and cannot have.[12]

11. One common defense of using the term "person" (a term particularly problematic given today's typical understanding of it) is that it is *sui generis,* and thus not readily reducible to clear definitions and set categories.

12. Craig Keen, "The Transgression of the Integrity of God," *Wesleyan Theological Journal* 36, no. 1 (Spring 2001): 79–80.

Irenaeus long ago may have expressed best the meaning of God's incarnation in Jesus. God became what we are in order that we might become what God is. The incarnation of God in Jesus is the historical event that opens God to human beings and human beings to God.

The earliest Christians, true to their Hebrew heritage, were strong monotheists, but they somehow had to deal with an inescapable revelatory event—the resurrected and living presence of Jesus in their midst. The result was the New Testament witness to a basic Trinitarian consciousness that had taken root in the hearts, thoughts, and direct experiences of the writers. The Trinity concept was no mere abstraction. It arose in the enlivening experience of God's personal presence in the midst of the worshiping community. The faithful were living in Christ, sharing in his resurrection, and praying to the Father through the Son. The Spirit was enabling understanding and implementation of what had happened in Jesus' death and resurrection. Early on, there certainly was in the church no fully developed doctrine of the Holy Trinity, but there was the prevailing awareness of the reality of the Father, Son, and Spirit in Christian experiences, worship, contemplation, and life. When aspects of these were threatened by divergent teachings, a creedal formulation of Trinity became virtually inevitable.

Christian thought soon developed an "economic" Trinitarianism (see glossary). An adequate understanding of God was being built from the unfolding of three acts of the divine drama of human redemption. Steeped in the heritage of Israel, Ignatius, Irenaeus, Tertullian, and others spoke of the covenant-making God from the perspective of the decisive deed of God in Jesus Christ and in the midst of the new era of the Spirit. They saw in the biblical narrative three great acts of the one great God. When Christian church leaders later developed the Apostles' and Nicene Creeds, they found themselves structuring Christian belief affirmations on a triune pattern.[13] The central purpose always has been to affirm the unity and equality in God and simultaneously the distinctive identities of Father, Son, and Spirit.

For almost two millennia now the Christian community has been using Trinity language to bring together the range of its core affirmations about God. As Thomas Oden puts it:

---

13. If Scripture is sufficient for Christian teaching and a Trinity doctrine is crucial, why is the Trinity not fully developed in Scripture itself? Thomas Oden explains: "Classical exegetes observed that it took some time for the proclaiming church to grasp the range of implications of what had happened to it in Jesus Christ under the power of the Spirit. . . . It was only as the church moved further into the Greco-Roman world that it was required to answer highly specialized queries" (*Living God,* 209).

Classical Christian exegetes have viewed the history of salvation as an inclusive threefold movement from beginning to end. . . . This triune history of salvation brings together all the basic issues of Christian theology: creation, redemption, and consummation in and beyond history. . . . The disciples not only experienced the presence of Father and Son, but further experienced a powerful impetus of some radically motivating divine Spirit that brought the Son to them and enlivened their awareness of the Father.[14]

Even with all its inherent difficulties, mystifying complexity, and cultural influence by Greek philosophy ("person" language, for instance), the ancient Trinity doctrine of Christians has survived the centuries.

Beyond mere survival, Trinity teaching has experienced a renewed prominence among Christian theologians in recent decades. The word "person" keeps being used, not because it is adequate to the divine mystery, but because it appears to be the best language available in our feeble attempts to describe God the Father's redemptive work, through God the Son, by God the Spirit. For instance, various early church fathers emphasized that the Son is the one *through whom* the Father works reconciliation, while the Spirit is the one *in whom* the Father's work through the Son occurs. This description of the Divine often was more devotional than speculative. So, for Gregory of Nyssa, *knowing God* is a never-ending and insatiable search and aspiration to become *like God*. In the sermon "On the Trinity," John Wesley said that the words "Trinity" and "person" should not be tests of orthodoxy, even though he used them "without any scruple, because I know of none better." Authentic Christian faith, he said, depends on the testimony of the Holy Spirit when "God the Holy Ghost witnesses that God the Father has accepted [a person] through the merits of God the Son."[15]

Wolfhart Pannenberg has been in the middle of the contemporary debate over the connection between the *immanent* Trinity, or the triune God in God's own eternal essence, and the *economic* Trinity (see glossary), or the triune God as God is perceived in the process of salvation history. For Pannenberg, what can be said about the immanent Trinity necessarily flows from our

---

14. Oden, *Living God*, 182–84. Oden clarifies that "this is not to suggest three chronologically separable modes in God (as in modalism), as if God meets us in disjunctive, successive modes in a progressive sequence, one outdating another. . . . The purpose of triune teaching has been to affirm the equality and unity, and yet the distinguishability of Father, Son, and Spirit" (185).

15. John Wesley, "On the Trinity," in *The Works of John Wesley*, ed. Thomas Jackson (London: Wesleyan Methodist Book Room, 1872), 6:200, 205. Geoffrey Wainwright reports that "Wesley was thoroughly Trinitarian in his understanding of the composition of the Scriptures, in his ways of proceeding with the Scriptures, and in his reading of the content of the Scriptures" ("Wesley's Trinitarian Hermeneutics," *Wesleyan Theological Journal* 36, no. 1 [Spring 2001]: 9).

human understanding derived from the economic Trinity. In other words, the Trinitarian essence of God is derived from the manner in which Father, Son, and Spirit appear to divinely inspired human perception in the life, message, death, and resurrection of Jesus.[16] This approach is said to be doing theology "from below." God is both immanent in the world and transcendent before and beyond it. The transcendence is that of the future over the present. The Spirit is the active energies of the divine essence in relation both to the God of creation and the participation of creation in the divine life (see *energies of God* in the glossary).

Rather than the doctrine of the Trinity being an embarrassment to Christian theology (opening it to the criticism of tritheism and incomprehensibility), it is the crucial key to holding together human understanding of the being of God and the history of divine acts in the world in a way that does not limit God except as God may freely choose out of love to be "limited." Pannenberg does not waiver on monotheism—a foundation that is not negotiable. The "three persons" of the Trinity comprise only one essence, one God; even so, "they cannot be comprehended as merely different modes of being of a single divine Subject, but can only be understood as life-processes of independent centers of activity."[17] Each of the persons relates to the others as *others*. They could not exist separate from each other, having distinctiveness only in the inner-Trinitarian relations. Clark Pinnock highlights this relationality of the divine being as an eternal dance of love. God is one, eternal, uncreated, incomprehensible. God also is a self-contained and yet self-revealing Trinity, "a society of persons united by a common divinity. . . . It is the essence of God's nature to be relational."[18] Explains Frank Macchia, God is not

> pure "rationality" decreeing eternal ideas and causing all things to conform to their fulfillment. God is rather pure "relationality" which seeks to draw all things into the symphony of love that is played eternally within the divine life. The graceless God who forms covenants in order to exact obedience is replaced by the triune God whose very being is an eternal dance of love into which the Spirit of God attempts to bring the entire creation by grace.[19]

16. See Roger E. Olson, "Wolfhart Pannenberg's Doctrine of the Trinity," *Scottish Journal of Theology* 43, no. 2 (1990): 175–206.

17. Wolfhart Pannenberg, *Systematische Theologie* (Göttingen: Vandenhoeck and Ruprecht, 1988), 347. English translation of Pannenberg is by Roger E. Olson.

18. Clark H. Pinnock, *Flame of Love: A Theology of the Holy Spirit* (Downers Grove, Ill.: InterVarsity Press, 1996), 33–35.

19. Frank Macchia, review of Clark Pinnock's *Flame of Love, Journal of Pentecostal Theology* 13 (1998): 34.

Unwillingness to affirm this "social model" of Trinity has troubled Christian theology historically. Defining the Trinity as "three Persons who are subjects of the divine experiences," Pinnock explains that "God's life is thus personal in the fullest sense—it is a life of personal communion. God is constituted by three subjects, each of whom is distinct from the others and is the subject of its own experiences in the unity of one divine life."[20] Deviating from this stance brings theological trouble. For instance, Karl Barth, while making the Trinity central for Christian theology, so elevated unity over diversity that the result was nearly God as one person functioning in three modes (opening the door to the ancient heresy of modalism and to the modern deviation of Unitarianism). Barth has been joined by Karl Rahner, who does not go beyond three "ways of existing" in God. Out of a concern to make Christianity easier for Jews and Muslims to understand and potentially accept, Hans Küng has paid the high price of modalism—affirming the persons of the Trinity as only aspects of a single subject, as three chronologically successive and separable modes in God.

Classical Christian theologians have long judged the modalism approach to theism a heresy. Trinitarianism means more than that God has come and met us humans in a sequence of distinctive manifestations, each outdating the others. Of course, we must never lose sight of God's eternal oneness and unity. The paradoxical intent of Christian Trinitarian thought, however, is to affirm vigorously this oneness and unity of God and also to distinguish Father, Son, and Spirit. This paradox may not always be intellectually comfortable, but it is crucial. When attention to the carefully balanced doctrine of the Trinity declines, history shows that distortions to the Christian understanding of God readily appear. So the doctrine of the Trinity is both proclamation of and protection for the integrity of our human understanding of the whole of Christian theism.

The Practical Significance of Trinitarianism

Reaffirming classic Christian Trinitarianism today is not to be dismissed as merely a stubborn traditionalism. It is recognition that such a view protects Christian theism from a range of common distortions, keeps believers on the fullness of the biblical path, and prevents projections onto God of passing cultural relativities, highly subjective visions, and reductionist accommodation to a prevailing culture. It also has important practical implications.[21] A. W. Tozer

---

20. Pinnock, *Flame of Love*, 35.

21. Augustine is reported to have said that "whoever denies the Trinity is in danger of losing his salvation; whoever tries to understand the Trinity is in danger of losing his mind."

spoke wisely: "A right conception of God is basic, not only to systematic theology, but to practical living as well."[22] Thinking specifically of the Trinity doctrine, Roger Olson adds:

> The whole of the Scripture's witness to who God is and who Jesus Christ and the Holy Spirit are makes no sense at all without the model of Trinity, and all alternative concepts end up doing violence to some essential aspect of revelation, Christian experience, and possibly even reason itself.[23]

While theologians such as Wolfhart Pannenberg reexplore the Trinity doctrine and affirm anew its theological credibility, Catherine LaCugna is especially helpful in reestablishing the doctrine's continuing significance at the level of practical Christian life. The thesis of LaCugna's milestone book *God for Us* is that the Trinity is a *practical* doctrine with crucial consequences for Christian life. The triune life of God by its very nature is a relating and sharing life, so that, instead of belonging to God alone, it comes to be shared with us humans in the face of Christ and in the activity of the Holy Spirit. Thus, Trinity teaching is not restricted to abstract thoughts about the eternal nature of God, but is a recognition and celebration of God's life *with us* and potentially *through us* for others. Trinitarian theology is

> a theology of relationship which explores the mysteries of love, relationship, personhood and communion within the framework of God's self-revelation in the person of Christ and the activity of the Spirit. . . . Jesus Christ, the visible icon of the invisible God, discloses what it means to be fully personal, divine as well as human. The Spirit of God, poured into our hearts as love (Rom. 5:5), gathers us together into the body of Christ, transforming us so that we become by grace what God is by nature, namely, persons in full communion with God and with every creature.[24]

The Trinity doctrine is a way of highlighting the understanding that God's nature is relational, so that we can, by the grace of divine self-giving, participate in God's life because God chooses to participate in ours.

This participation of God in human life has the intent of reestablishing the original purpose of creation, a universal reflection of the divine nature in all that was created. Humans are created to express the "image of God"

---

22. A. W. Tozer, *The Knowledge of the Holy* (New York: Harper & Row, 1961), 6.

23. Roger E. Olson, *The Mosaic of Christian Belief* (Downers Grove, Ill.: InterVarsity Press, 2002), 139.

24. Catherine Mowry LaCugna, *God for Us: The Trinity and Christian Life* (San Francisco: HarperSanFrancisco, 1991), 1.

in their values, attitudes, relationships, and actions. Emil Brunner once wisely observed:

> Human life is characterized as human, not by its attainments in the realm of reason, but by the union of human beings in love. That is the content of human existence, which is in accordance with man's original divine destiny, and is an earthly reflection of the divine nature itself.[25]

The love found at the center of the being and life of the triune God is to characterize the communities of humans. In fact, the essential nature of personhood should consist of mutuality and interdependence, the kind seen in the agape love of God who is a community of love and seeks to enable the duplication of such community among us humans. We can love because God first loved us (1 John 4:19). We are to participate in the divine nature (2 Pet. 1:3–4). Stanley Grenz summarizes: "The triune God desires that human beings be brought together into a corporate whole, a fellowship of reconciliation, which not only reflects God's own eternal reality but actually participates in that reality."[26] There thus arises the significance of the church as central to Christian identity. The personal identity of all people who are "in Christ" is necessarily related to participation in a particular community—"namely, the fellowship of those who live by means of the connection they share to the Jesus story."[27]

Christian thought about God conveys a critical perspective that is foundational for all Christian identity and living. It is a perspective derived from a Trinitarian understanding of God. For instance, Trinity

> wants to redescribe God in the light of the event of Jesus Christ and the outpouring of God's transforming Spirit. It wants to say that God is sovereign, costly love that liberates and renews life. It wants to say that God's love for the world in Christ, now at work by the power of the Spirit, is nothing accidental or capricious or temporary. It wants to say that there is no sinister or even demonic side of God altogether different from what we know in the story of Jesus who befriended the poor and forgave sinners. God *is* self-expending, other-affirming, community-building love.[28]

25. Emil Brunner, *Man in Revolt: A Christian Anthropology*, trans. Olive Wyon (Philadelphia: Westminster Press, 1939), 106.

26. Stanley J. Grenz, *Revisioning Evangelical Theology: A Fresh Agenda for the 21st Century* (Downers Grove, Ill.: InterVarsity Press, 1993), 188.

27. Stanley J. Grenz, *The Social God and the Relational Self: A Trinitarian Theology of the Imago Dei* (Louisville, Ky.: Westminster John Knox Press, 2001), 332.

28. Daniel L. Migliore, *Faith Seeking Understanding* (Grand Rapids: Eerdmans, 1991), 63. Whereas

Such a vision of God yields a vital and very practical implication about the doctrine of sanctification. Since the Spirit proceeds from and is coequal with the Son, we are assured that the work of the Spirit in the life of a believer imparts the benefits of the Father's work in the Son and intends nothing other than to reproduce the character of the Son (the fruit of the Spirit)—who in turn perfectly reflects the character of the Father.

Trinitarian thinking protects from a range of theistic heresies, including the temptation to assign a character and intent to one person of the Godhead over against the other persons (e.g., the sacrifice of Jesus convinced or enabled God the Father to grant forgiveness to sinful humans, as though the Father were unwilling or unable to do so otherwise). One typical way of conceiving the Trinitarian God has encouraged such inappropriate thinking. The Trinity often has been conceived as triangular (see figure 5), easily allowing the thought of a "top" God, the monarchy of the Father, with the Son and Spirit somehow secondary and subservient. This view tends to violate the biblical emphases that there is only one God and that all of God is involved in every- thing that God does. By contrast, there is a more circular model (see figure 5), which has the following advantages:

> Now there is no solitary person separated from the others; no above and below; no first, second, and third in importance; no ruling and controlling and being ruled and controlled; no position of privilege to be maintained over against the others; no question of conflict concerning who is in charge; no possible rivalry or competition between competing individuals; no need to assert independence and authority of one at the expense of the others. Now there is only the fellowship and community of equals who share all that they are and have in their communion with each other, each living with and for the others in mutual openness, self-giving love, and support; each free not *from* but *for* the others.[29]

Trinitarian spirituality helps believers see themselves "not so much as foot soldiers following Divine orders but as active partakers of the Divine

---

the doctrine of the Trinity often has been perceived as picturing an abstract and static-unity God, a unity from which God chooses to initiate contact with the world, many have suggested recently that God's very being is *Being for others.* Thus, God's movement toward creation as Trinity is not a secondary property of a static divine existence, but the very essence of who God is and of what is meant by Trinity. What we dis- cover in the economy of God (God's redemptive actions in creation) reveals God truly. Therefore, the doc- trine of the Trinity is not first about God's stationary being, but instead about the Father's active, self-extending missions in and as Son and Spirit.

29. Shirley C. Guthrie, *Christian Doctrine,* rev. ed. (Louisville, Ky.: Westminster John Knox Press, 1994), 93.

Figure 5
Alternate Conceptions of the Triune God

Model A   **Model B**

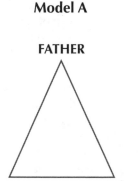

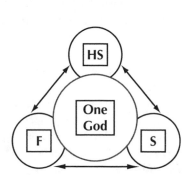

Model A is more hierarchical in nature and lends itself to a strong differentiation among the persons of the Godhead, a "subordinationism" typically with the Father as dominant. Model B highlights more of a nonhierarchical equality, community, and interactivity among the divine persons.

nature."[30] By highlighting divine relationality, the privilege and power of prayer are enhanced.[31] Because each member of the Trinity is fully present in the being and acts of the others, believers should pray to the one God, not to any isolated member of the Trinity—or at least be aware that prayer to one is prayer to all. As Donald Bloesch affirms:

> We do not pray to the Father over the Son or to the Son and Spirit apart from the Father. . . . We pray to the Father in the Son and through the power of

30. C. Leonard Allen and Danny Gray Swick, *Participating in God's Life* (Orange, Calif.: New Leaf Books, 2001), 166.

31. See Gregory A. Boyd, *God of the Possible: A Biblical Introduction to the Open View of God* (Grand Rapids: Baker Books, 2000), 95: "Despite all the pious talk about how God wants and even needs us to pray, many Christians have an understanding of divine sovereignty in which the urgency of prayer simply doesn't make much sense. . . . They believe that God's plans cannot truly be changed; the future is exhaustively settled. . . . The common saying that 'prayer changes us, not God' simply doesn't reflect the purpose or urgency that Scripture gives to petitionary prayer."

the Spirit. We pray to Christ who proceeds from the Father and who is made available to us by the Spirit. We pray to the Spirit through the intercession of Christ and by the grace given to us by the Father. Because of the perichoresis (mutual indwelling), each member of the Trinity is fully present in the being and acts of the others.[32]

It is crucial that Christian believing about God remain Trinitarian in nature. Gilbert Stafford has offered five general reasons for the importance of this.[33] In brief, they are:

1. Trinitarian thought is faithful to the biblical witness that presents God in three persons—Father, Son, and Spirit. To believe thus is to remain biblical.
2. Trinitarian thought upholds the glory of the incarnation. Nothing less than very God of very God dwelt among us in the coming of Jesus of Nazareth. To believe thus is to honor Jesus Christ.
3. Trinitarian thought incorporates the truth that the eternal God is capable of suffering. The death of Jesus is the experience of the Trinitarian God. To believe thus is to know that God truly understands human frailty and loves us dearly.
4. Trinitarian thought confesses the church's experience of the God of the Hebrew Bible, who is both revealed in Jesus and still abiding with us as the Holy Spirit. To believe thus keeps one open to the Spirit's power and present ministry.
5. Trinitarian thought maintains unity with the church's long intellectual history of reflecting on the faith and defending it against ideas about God that are contrary to the biblical revelation. To believe thus is to avoid tempting perversions of theism already known to be such by the church's thoughtful theological past.

C. Leonard Allen and Danny Swick explain how the Trinity doctrine guards against common theological distortions that commonly trouble Christian life. Three examples are (1) "Following the Risen Christ" checks against spiritual elitism and authoritarianism, (2) "In the Power of the Spirit" checks against moralism, legalism, and rationalism, and (3) "To the Glory and Praise of the Father" checks against magic, idolatries, and other domestications of the faith.[34]

Beyond being crucial in these several ways, it is timely to think of God in Trinitarian terms. The philosophical environment today has moved away

---

32. Bloesch, *God the Almighty*, 193.

33. Gilbert W. Stafford, *Theology for Disciples: Systematic Considerations about the Life of Christian Faith* (Anderson, Ind.: Church Ministries Division, Warner Press, 1996), 185–89.

34. Allen and Swick, *Participating in God's Life,* 173–75.

from the older *substantialist* categories of thought in favor of more *relational* categories. The world is now being seen increasingly as a changing organism of interrelated processes. The dynamic, relational, Trinitarian understanding of God serves well the need for a biblically based and intellectually credible witness to our present times.[35] It provides the philosophical resources for handling the "deeply revelation-based ideas like incarnation, suffering, relationality and perfection in change."[36] This does not necessarily imply that Christian theology should adopt process thought in any wholesale way. Such theology, helpful at a variety of points, nonetheless has had difficulty producing a satisfactory account of the Trinity.[37]

Another vital issue for which the Trinity doctrine holds practical potential is that of Christian unity. Jürgen Moltmann's significant book *The Trinity and the Kingdom* is dedicated to overcoming the schism between the Eastern and Western churches that tragically has burdened the Christian faith since 1054. This major split was triggered in significant part by a dispute over a technical aspect of Trinitarian teaching, the inclusion of the *filioque* in the text of the Nicene-Constantinopolitan Creed of 381. According to Moltmann, the insistence on this *filioque* doctrine by Western theologians led to a one-sided Trinitarian doctrine in the West, and thereby hindered the development of a Trinitarian pneumatology. His way of resolving this ancient conflict is to recognize that the *filioque* was an interpretation in a particular setting of theological conflict (when imbalance comes easily) and to propose the following new text for the creed: "The Holy Spirit, who proceeds from the Father of the Son, and who receives his form from the Father and the Son."[38] This preserves the Spirit's full divinity and also relates the Spirit appropriately to the Father and the Son. It suggests a way of resolving a key theological issue that has kept Christians of the West and East deeply divided.

A balanced perspective is crucial on this controversial issue of *filioque*. Both West and East have preserved something crucial about the doctrine of God. Clark Pinnock argues that the "and from the Son" addition to the creed by the West can threaten our understanding of the Spirit's universality, suggesting

---

35. Gregory A. Boyd, *Trinity and Process* (New York: Peter Lang, 1992), 1–11.

36. Pinnock, *Most Moved Mover*, 119.

37. See Samuel M. Powell, "A Trinitarian Alternative to Process Theism," *Thy Nature and Thy Name Is Love,* ed. Bryan Stone and Thomas Oord (Nashville: Kingswood Books, 2001), 143–67. John B. Cobb Jr. has attempted a correlation of the Trinitarian persons of God with process theism's thought, saying that the Father represents God in all aspects, the Son represents God's primordial nature, and the Spirit God's consequent nature (*Christ in a Pluralistic Age* [Philadelphia: Westminster Press, 1975], 261–62).

38. Jürgen Moltmann, *The Trinity and the Kingdom: The Doctrine of God* (San Francisco: Harper & Row, 1981), 187.

that "Spirit is not the gift of the Father to creation universally, but a gift confined to the sphere of the Son and even of the church, [and thus] promotes Christomonism."[39] On the other hand, the *filioque* phrase plays the positive role of making clear that Jesus is the criterion for discerning the Spirit of God at work in the world (there are *other* spirits).

Beyond the issue of church unity is the understanding of the church itself and its role in Christian life. The God who is community (Trinity) seeks to create communities of love. The goal of the theology of Stanley Grenz, for instance, is to recognize community as the integrative motif of Christian theology and thus to consider the Christian faith within the context of God's central program for creation, which is the establishment of communities of love.[40] The God who is plurality-in-unity is the God who establishes as the ideal for humankind persons-in-community. God intends that we reflect the divine nature in our lives and relationships.

Christians worship the God who not only created all things, but saves and walks with us humans through all circumstances. God can enter into fellowship with humans because God is himself a fellowship of love as Father, Son, and Spirit. God is not self-enclosed, a detached dispenser of fixed decisions, but is outgoing, relational, redemptive, communal, the eternal and self-sacrificing lover, the pilgrim God who sets us on our journey and goes with us all the way. He is the God of the whole Bible, the Yahweh of the ancient Hebrews, and the Father both revealed in Jesus Christ and poured out at Pentecost as the Spirit of the Christ. God is *one,* and God is three-in-one, mysteriously and wonderfully so. The Trinity doctrine embraces and exemplifies the grand story of human salvation—the God of creation, redemption, and ultimate consummation, all together, all one God.

The Father is the ground of all being, the Son is the Father's expressed Word of saving love, and the Spirit is the ongoing presence who guides into all truth as it is in Jesus Christ. The Spirit also aids we who believe to appropriate this truth in our lives. To confess that God is triune is to acknowledge (1) that the eternal life of God is a personal life of relationship, (2) that God exists in community and seeks covenant community with the creation, and (3) that the life of God is rightly characterized as self-giving love that empowers others for new life in community with each other and with God. Who God is and how believers relate and pray are deeply intertwined. In fact, as Gerrit Scott Dawson writes:

---

39. Pinnock, *Flame of Love*, 196.
40. Stanley J. Grenz, *Theology for the Community of God* (Nashville: Broadman & Holman, 1994).

The grammar of prayer is the Triune life of God. Even as the divine Persons flow in and out of one another in perfect love, so identifying the role of each in our prayers always leads to the sense that the work of one Person is tumbling into another in an endless circle of love. . . . The Spirit is not only the bond of love between Father and Son but also the bond of union between us and Christ Jesus. In the Spirit we are taken into the very life of God. Our prayer in the Spirit through the Son to the Father is nothing less than a dynamic participation in the Triune God of love.[41]

Benediction

In the concluding paragraph of her 1955 book *Foundations of Christian Knowledge*, Georgia Harkness offered this wisdom:

When we have finished our theologizing, we shall not understand all mysteries. We are but human pilgrims following the pathways of knowledge, and to the end of the earthly way we shall still "know in part." Yet our faith in Jesus Christ our Lord can give us the *assurance* of things hoped for, the *conviction* of things not seen. And is not that, after all, the object of the quest?[42]

The God who knows us fully is known by us feebly—at best. Even so, in Jesus Christ we are dependably guided, inspired, and transformed. We do not journey aimlessly or alone. We are not yet home, but we are already on the way—shepherded by none other than "the Way," Jesus, with the enabling guidance of the Spirit of the Christ.

Trinity language is a frail but necessary way of pointing to the God known in Christ by the Spirit. We have not *comprehended* God, but by the grace of God's Spirit we are helped to *apprehend* adequately and find new life in Christ and with each other. This is enough. For now, continuing use of the following prayer from the Anglican tradition is appropriate:

Almighty God, Father of all mercies, we, Thine unworthy servants, do give thee most humble and hearty thanks for all thy goodness and loving-kindness to us. . . . We bless Thee for our creation, preservation, and all the blessings of this life; but above all, for Thine inestimable love in the

---

41. Gerrit Scott Dawson, "Prayer in the Triune Life," *Weavings,* May/June 2002, 19. Dawson's work reflects that in Scottish theologian James Torrance's *Worship, Community, and the Triune God of Grace* (Downers Grove, Ill.: InterVarsity Press, 1996).

42. Georgia Harkness, *Foundations of Christian Knowledge* (Nashville: Abingdon Press, 1955), 153.

redemption of the world by our Lord Jesus Christ; for the means of grace, and for the hope of glory [i.e., the presence and work of the Holy Spirit in the church]. . . . [May we] show forth thy praise, not only with our lips, but in our lives, by giving up ourselves to Thy service, and by walking before Thee in holiness and righteousness all our days; through Jesus Christ our Lord, to whom, with Thee [Father] and the Holy Ghost, be all honor and glory, world without end. *Amen*.[43]

The Christian doctrine of the Trinity involves no polytheism, which would be an association of three independent deities. Neither is there any pantheism, an overemphasis on immanence, or any deism, an overemphasis on transcendence that presumes God's current detachment from creation's troubled life. God the Father is truly "other" than creation, while at the same time the Father, as Son and Spirit, chooses to be redemptively involved in the creation. What we have is a coinherence of the persons constituting the one God who is the "Source, Guide, and Goal of all that is—to him be glory for ever!" (Rom. 11:36, New English Bible). An ancient prayer of the church gathers the whole range of Christian theology, centered in the triune God: "Glory be to the Father, and to the Son, and to the Holy Ghost; as it was in the beginning, is now and ever shall be, world without end. Amen!"

Seeking to know God should lead to a necessary exercise of human humility in the face of the divine mystery. Even so, because of God's self-revelation, we have begun to really know. Yes, God finally stands above all human concepts and philosophical constructs; nonetheless, we now know that in the beginning, as Genesis 1 reports, there was God in the sovereign act of creating. Revelation 22:20 pictures the end at which God is in the act of inviting all who wish to take the water of life as a gift. The God who *was* remains the God who *will be*. In the meantime, through the sanctifying and sustaining ministry of the Spirit, now graciously active among us all, we have this promise: "The grace of the Lord Jesus [will] be with all the saints" (Rev. 22:21). Therefore, with the New Testament writer, "I commend you to God and to the message of his grace, a message that is able to build you up and to give you the inheritance among all who are sanctified" (Acts 20:32). With the hymnist, I gladly sing:

Alleluia! Alleluia!
Hearts to heaven and voices raise;
Alleluia! Alleluia!

43. The General Thanksgiving from the Daily Service in *The Book of Common Prayer* (1549, 1662, 1928, etc.).

Glory be to God on high;
Alleluia to the Savior
Who has won the victory;
Alleluia to the Spirit,
Fount of love and sanctity;
Alleluia! Alleluia!
To the Triune Majesty.[44]

Those first disciples wanted Jesus to tell them how best to pray. He began his ideal prayer with a strong God-centeredness: "Our Father in heaven, hallowed be your name" (Matt. 6:9). Those who are disciples of Jesus should now look to God, affirm God, and pray for divine guidance. Appropriate descriptive metaphors for God are greatness, mightiness, guidance, and bread. The related prayer hymn begins:

Guide me, O Thou great Jehovah, Pilgrim through this barren land;
I am weak, but Thou art mighty—Hold me with Thy powerful hand:
Bread of heaven, Bread of heaven,
Feed me 'til I want no more, Feed me 'til I want no more.[45]

44. Verse three of Christopher Wordsworth, "Alleluia! Alleluia!"
45. Verse one of William Williams and John Hughes, "Guide Me, O Thou Great Jehovah."

Glossary

agnosticism/atheism. The stance that humans do not or cannot have adequate grounds for affirming or denying the existence of God is agnosticism (does not know, *a-gnosis*). To admit any place for mystery within Christian theology is to confess some level of agnosticism. The stance of atheism goes further by actively denying that the God of biblical revelation exists at all (knows that God is not, *a-theism*). Arthur Schopenhauer (1788–1860) believed that there is no Absolute, no God, no Spirit at work in the world. There is nothing but the brute and instinctive will to live. With no God to save us, we humans can gain a measure of serenity only though art, music, and a discipline of renunciation and compassion.

Biblical writers were concerned primarily with polytheism and idolatry. "Their central problem was not *whether* God is, but rather *who* God is (Gen. 28:10–22; Ps. 20:1ff; Isa. 9:6), that is, What is the character of God?"[1] Early Christians were sometimes called atheists for refusing to venerate the popular civic or imperial deities. William Montague says of Christian faith in God that "it is the acceptance neither of a primitive absurdity nor of a sophisticated truism, but of a momentous possibility—the possibility namely that what is highest in spirit is also deepest in nature, that the ideal and the real are at least to some extent identified, not merely evanescently in our own lives but enduringly in the universe itself."[2] Sometimes atheists are reacting negatively only to the concept of God known to them. Thus, Clark Pinnock remarks, "Atheism is, in part, an unpaid bill of the church which has too often presented God as an alienating substance, remote and unsympathetic, and who exists at

---

1. Thomas Oden, *The Living God,* vol. 1 of *Systematic Theology* (Peabody, Mass.: Prince Press, 1998), 41.
2. William Pepperell Montague, *Belief Unbound: A Promethean Religion for the Modern World* (New Haven, Conn.: Yale University Press, 1931), 6.

humanity's expense. . . . Atheists have not been told about the God of the gospel who loves us freely, wants a relationship with us and wants to empower us, not foster our weakness."[3]

"Practical atheists" can be said to be those nominal Christian believers who regularly occupy pews in church but who (1) become distracted by pursuits into which they would rather not have God intrude or (2) bend God into presumed support of their personal preferences or causes—thus re-creating God in their own images. However, wisdom begins with reverence for God (Prov. 1:7), not with denying, sentimentalizing, or seeking to use God for private ends. The atheism addressed in Psalm 14 has little to do with sheer disbelief and much to do with sheer disobedience. See also **theism.**

anthropomorphism. A figure of speech by which human physical characteristics are attributed to God for the sake of illustration and communication (e.g., the "finger" of God). Anthropomorphism helps make an otherwise abstract truth about God more concrete. God can be described by way of analogy, but not literally or directly. Says Donald Bloesch, "We do not begin our analogical depictions of God by examining human attributes and experiences, but we begin with God's self-revelation and then seek to find reflections of God's being and workings in our experiences. This is the way not of an analogy of being (*analogia entis*), in which we begin with created being and then proceed to the uncreated, but of an analogy of faith (*analogia fidei*), in which we begin with an acknowledgment of God's self-revelation in the Jesus Christ of history."[4]

apatheia. God viewed as serene and self-sufficient, perfect and unchanging, beyond being disturbed by time or emotion. See also **impassibility.**

apophatic theology. *Apophatic* is Greek for "silent and proceeding by negation and denial." Applied to Christian theism, this term highlights the notion that all theology ought to have a key element of silence, paradox, and restraint in order to emphasize the ineffability and mystery of God. God's perfection means that he is unlike anything created, including anything that human language can describe. Thus, God can be truly described only by *what he is not*. Theology should recognize that positive descriptions of God are inherently limited, since God does not fit into normal categories of human language and thought. Thus, apophatic theology is often called "negative" theology (*via negativa*). God is infinite (not finite), immutable (not changing), and so forth.

---

3. Clark H. Pinnock, *Most Moved Mover* (Grand Rapids: Baker Academic, 2001), 2.
4. Donald G. Bloesch, *God the Almighty* (Downers Grove, Ill.: InterVarsity Press, 1995), 50.

This approach suggests that God is known positively through spiritual experience more than rational expressions. This is of key importance in the Eastern Orthodox tradition, which exhibits skepticism about Western rationalism and fosters a positive appreciation for divine mystery. The great mysteries of the faith are judged matters of *adoration* more than *analysis*. Evagrius Pontius speaks of apophatic prayer as a laying aside of thoughts and reaching out toward the eternal Truth that lies beyond all human words and thoughts. It is a waiting quietly on God (Ps. 46:10). In his *Life of Moses*, Gregory insisted that "the true vision and the knowledge of what we seek consists precisely in *not* seeing, in an awareness that our goal transcends all knowledge and is everywhere cut off from us by the darkness of incomprehensibility." See also **energies of God.**

arguments for God's existence. Rather than arguing for God's existence, the Bible just begins with "In the beginning, God . . ." (Gen. 1:1)—presuming that only a fool thinks otherwise (Ps. 14:1). God was before there was any human questioning about God. Classical Christian teaching usually has affirmed that rational arguments can *confirm* but do not *produce* faith in the existence of the biblically revealed God. Even so, Elton Trueblood concludes the following about arguments for the existence of God: "The sophisticated believer knows very well that he *could* be wrong, because there is no incontrovertible evidence, but the path of wisdom is to watch for converging lines. A cable is far stronger than a single wire."[5] Thus, Trueblood outlines what he sees as the encouraging convergences or cumulative effect of evidence for the existence of God derived from scientific, moral, aesthetic, historical, and religious experience and knowledge. Thomas Oden cautions, however, that the "most urgent and demanding question for Christian teaching is not whether 'a God of some kind' exists, but rather whether this incomparably good and powerful and caring source and end of all things, who meets us in Israel and in Jesus Christ, truly *is* as revealed in Scripture."[6]

Christians often have used logic in attempts to establish rationally the existence of God. Thomas Aquinas set forth five rational arguments pointing this way: (1) the argument from *motion*—all things in motion need a mover, and there must be something unmoved that begins other things moving (God, then, is the "Unmoved Mover"); (2) the argument from *cosmology*—all effects must have causes, thus God is the "Uncaused Cause"; (3) the argument from *contingency*—all things exist in dependence on something else, thus there must be something that is absolutely independent of prior cause, namely,

---

5. David Elton Trueblood, *Philosophy of Religion* (New York: Harper & Row, 1957), 76.
6. Oden, *Living God*, 134.

God; (4) the argument from *perfection*—there appears to be an increasing degree of perfection among things; therefore, there must exist a being who is the height of perfection, God, toward whom all things mature; and (5) the argument from *teleology*—there is an observable design in the world and thus there must be an intelligent designer, God, who is the "Master Architect." There also is the argument from *morals*—since humans seek the highest good, logically presupposed is the existence of God who is the lawgiver who will judge and reward the moral striving of humans. Immanuel Kant and C. S. Lewis have set forth versions of this argument.

aseity. Derived from the Latin *a se,* "from oneself," this is the commonly affirmed attribute of divine self-existence. God, in God's inmost self, is entirely independent of the cosmos. God is not dependent on anything for existence, but has eternally existed without any external or prior cause. God exists necessarily, with no need of help from the creation (Acts 17:23–25). Says Donald Bloesch, "[T]he living God is not bound by any necessity save that of his love, which is the core of his nature. He does not need to create the world in order to overcome his supposed loneliness, for he is a community of persons within himself and derives the satisfaction of intimate fellowship from within himself as a Trinity of persons. . . . The only reason for the creation is that he wills to share his love, but he is under no compulsion to do so."[7] Even so, God is free to make himself dependent on those whom he has created—not for continuing divine existence, of course, but for the accomplishment of the divine will. See also **free-will theism; Trinity.**

atheism. See agnosticism/atheism.

attributes of God. Attributes are characteristics or qualities that are thought to appropriately describe God's being and essence. Often they have been grouped into *incommunicable* and *communicable* categories—that is, those uniquely belonging to the Divine and not shared with the creation (infinite, omnipotent, etc.) and those potentially shared by humans (righteous, holy, loving, etc.). Allan Coppedge groups the divine attributes into the categories of absolute, relative, and moral.[8] The first are those that belong to God apart from creation, the second those that arise out of the relationships between Creator and creation, and the third those that specifically relate to God's direction over creatures given the capacity to make their own moral decisions. Scripture highlights two moral qualities on which the character of God

7. Bloesch, *God the Almighty,* 44.
8. Allan Coppedge, *Portraits of God: A Biblical Theology of Holiness* (Downers Grove, Ill.: InterVarsity Press, 2001), 88.

hinges. They are *holiness* and *love* (Ps. 93:5; Hos. 11:1–9; John 17:11–26). These primary divine qualities must be related closely to each other if one is to rightly behold the character of God.

There is a doctrine of simplicity which insists that, although we speak of various characteristics or attributes of God, in fact God has none of them, is not composed of parts, but is an indivisible unity. See also **aseity; energies of God; holiness; immutability; impassibility; omnipotence; omnipresence; omniscience.**

compatibilist view of divine foreknowledge and human freedom. Affirming divine omniscience (all-knowingness) raises the perplexity of its relation to human freedom. What of the apparent dilemma in stating that God foreknows the use of human free will, yet this divine foreknowledge does not determine the course of events? One perspective, common in classical Christian teaching, is that human free will is consistent (compatible) with God's sovereign prerogative to determine or will all things that are to happen. Human freedom is real but limited; God's freedom is unlimited. Divine providence is consistent with voluntary human choice. Augustine affirmed human freedom and denied that God's foreknowledge of the future is a causal condition of sin and evil—which humans elect. Origen taught that what God foreknows is precisely the acts of free will. Classical theists (Augustine, Anselm, Thomas Aquinas) taught that there is no contradiction in claiming both that a future free act of a human is determined by God and that the individual involved retains the capacity to do otherwise. Thus, infallible and comprehensive divine foreknowledge and human free choice are compatible concepts. The paradox is that God does all and we humans do all, but our efforts are entirely dependent on God working in and through us (Phil. 2:12–13). Christianity is not divine determinism, but it is "a divine foreordination that respects rather than annuls human freedom."[9] Process theology tries to resolve this apparent dilemma by viewing God as experiencing temporality, giving up the view of God's full control of history. Millard Erickson argues that the real conflict is between divine foreknowledge and an incompatibilist or libertarian view of human freedom.[10] See also **foreknowledge; free-will theism; incompatibilist view; omniscience.**

cosmological argument for God existence. See **arguments for God's existence.**

---

9. Bloesch, *God the Almighty,* 115.
10. Millard J. Erickson, *God the Father Almighty: A Contemporary Exploration of the Divine Attributes* (Grand Rapids: Baker Books, 1998), 89.

creator. God is the creator of all that exists (except evil), and this creation was accomplished *ex nihilo* ("out of nothing") by divine fiat: "You are worthy, our Lord and God, to receive glory and honor and power, for you created all things, and by your will they existed and were created" (Rev. 4:11). Creation is seen biblically as a wholly free act of a sovereign God who would be God had there been no creation. All things are created for and directed toward Jesus Christ, who is the heir of all things and through whom all things were originally created (Heb. 1:2; Eph. 1:10). By contrast, in process theology, creation is thought of as ongoing, with God directing an evolutionary process and being the cosmic memory that (who) gathers into the Divine all of value and by persuasion draws the world to ever higher possibilities. God is continuously creating and in this way continuously actualizing himself.

creeds. There have been numerous formal statements of Christian belief, or creeds, produced by individuals and church bodies over the centuries. The word "creed" is from the Latin *credo,* "I believe." Typically creeds center on the doctrine of God and the belief implications of this doctrine for a range of other subjects. The ancient and "classic" creeds widely recognized by the Christian community are organized around a Trinitarian concept of God (see **Trinity**). They are:

> *The Apostles' Creed.* By tradition this creed is attributed to the original apostles. Its present form is not found before the sixth or seventh century, but probably it goes back to an ancient Roman baptismal creed of the second century.
> *The Nicene Creed.* Formulated at the Council of Nicaea in 325, this creed was completed at the Council of Constantinople in 381. It defined the relation between Father, Son, and Holy Spirit.
> *The Chalcedonian Creed.* Formulated in 451, this creed formalized the classic Christian view of the "two natures" of Christ, that is, the relation between the humanity and deity of Jesus.

Creeds often have been developed in times of controversy. For example, the Nicene and Chalcedonian Creeds were responding to heated controversy concerning aspects of the doctrine of God. The Westminster Confession of 1646 deals with issues of the Puritan conflict. The Barmen Declaration of 1934 confesses the lordship of Christ in the political and economic sphere, protesting against the modern heresies of nationalism and racism.

deification. God has given us precious promises "so that through them [we] may participate in the divine nature" (2 Pet. 1:4). It is sometimes said that the purpose of life is to become a sharer in the nature of God. This is the meaning of *deification*. It refers to the mystery, purpose, and outcome of the Christian's mystical experience with God. The essence of Christianity is affirmed as the descent of God in order to enable the ascent of humans to union with divinity—not to become part of God's essence, of course, but to share in the divine life and energies. This is a strong emphasis of Eastern Orthodoxy and appears reflected in Galatians 2:20: "[I]t is no longer I who live, but it is Christ who lives in me." John Wesley combined a pessimism about fallen human nature and an optimism about divine grace that resulted in a firm anchoring in justification by faith alone while also focusing on sanctification or attaining the mystic's vision of perfect union (communion) with God in love, or a restoration of the divine image within human life. The ultimate goal of salvation and the reason for the divine incarnation in Jesus was to bring humans to the same status as the *humanity* of Jesus Christ, the same humanity that Adam once had. Adam, prior to the fall, bore the image of the Divine and shared in God's glory in a real although creaturely way. Christ restored this potential and so was our spiritual pioneer back to God. See also **image of God**.

deism. Deism champions a rational approach to religion, highlighting the philosophy and science of the Enlightenment, grounding belief in a natural harmony found with right reason, and elevating human reason and natural religion over faith and special revelation. Deism usually denies the deity of Jesus and the doctrine of the Trinity. God is the First Cause, required by the demands of intellectual cogency, but is not an active factor in day-by-day life. God created and then has left the creation to operate on its own within the structures of creation (i.e., the laws of nature). This view often is illustrated by the analogy of a watchmaker who designs a sophisticated timepiece and then leaves it to run on its own momentum. The cosmos now is a closed system, with its Creator choosing to stand outside. This view tends to deny direct providential control of events and miraculous divine interventions into human affairs. It was characteristic of a group of English writers during the seventeenth century (John Toland, Anthony Collins, Matthew Tindal) and influential among some early American leaders (Thomas Paine, Benjamin Franklin, Thomas Jefferson). Various schools of contemporary Christian theism (i.e., free-will and process) actively refute the tendency of deism to distance God from the current life of the fallen creation. See also **free-will theism.**

economic Trinity. Refers to God as manifested in God's redemptive involvement with the creation. God is one rather than three, but became understood as threefold in his dealings with creation. Who God is can be known in the outworking (economy) of the plan of human salvation. In the biblical narrative, God functions redemptively as Father, Son, and Spirit.

Thus, the members of the Trinity are observed and known by means of the revealing economy of salvation. An objection to this view of the Divine is that it makes God dependent on the divine relationships with the creation. It can tend to confuse an unfolding divine purpose with a supposed unfolding divine being. See **energies of God**; *filioque*; **immanent Trinity**.

energies of God. The Greek *energeiai* (energies) is sometimes employed to refer to God's activities in the world. These activities enable humans to glimpse something of the nature and will of the Divine. This concept intends to distinguish between the human conception of God gained from observation or experience and the ineffable and incomprehensible reality of God that always lies beyond human observation and experience. Basil used Philo's distinction between God's essence (*ousia*) and his activities (*energeiai*) in the world. Therefore, we know God by his operations, but we cannot successfully undertake the impossible task of comprehending the divine essence. This focus on the divine energies became a keynote of theology in the Eastern churches. See also **attributes of God**.

existence of God. See **agnosticism/atheism**; **arguments for God's existence**.

filioque. The concept of *filioque* ("and from the Son") is a Western insertion (Council of Toledo, 589) into the classic Christian creed (Nicene-Constantinopolitan, 381) related to the Holy Spirit. The insertion was strongly opposed by the Eastern church and played a key role in the major division of the church into East and West in 1054. *Filioque* means that there is a double procession of the Spirit, who is said to proceed from the Father *and the Son*. Western theologians have insisted that the Spirit should not be conceived without an essential relationship to the Son. The Eastern churches have preferred the single procession (from the Father only), since this seems to better secure the unity of God. The Father is the sole source of all divinity, so two sources within one Godhead are confusing at best. One alternative now proposed is "from the Father *through* [not *from*] the Son." There is consensus that the Spirit proceeds from the Father and that there is an intimate relationship between Son and Spirit; the task is to affirm this necessary relationship without subordinating Spirit to Son. Jürgen Moltmann suggests this wording: "The Holy Spirit, who proceeds from the Father of the Son, and who receives his form from the Father and the Son."[11] The goal is somehow to affirm that the Spirit proceeds from the one being of the triune God, so that the whole

---

11. Jürgen Moltmann, *The Trinity and the Kingdom: The Doctrine of God* (San Francisco: Harper & Row, 1981), 187.

being of God (Father, Son, and Spirit) belongs in eternal and equal communion, each divine "person" with the others. See also **economic Trinity; immanent Trinity; Trinity;** and **figure 4** in the text.

foreknowledge. God often is said to be aware in every moment of all that ever was, is, or shall be. Since God is not bound by any of the limitations of space and time as are humans, no restriction should be placed on God's knowledge. Prophecy (in the sense of God's predicting future events) is an important part of the biblical record. Depending on one's theological tradition, however, this view is either in mild or massive tension with the concept of human freedom, and may be seen as involving a divine determinism; if God is fully aware in advance of all things and fully capable of controlling all things, predestination appears the result. Does God foreknow the future human use of free will, yet without determining that use? If God knows all things without reference to time, does God then determine all things, and can human freedom have any real meaning? Thomas Oden concludes, "If God knows what I later will do, does that take away my freedom? Although it may at first seem so, the consensus of classical Christian teaching is to answer no. Human freedom remains freedom, significantly self-determining, even if divinely foreknown."[12] It is precisely the acts of free will that God foreknows.

Gregory Boyd asks, "If God foreknew that Adolf Hitler would send six million Jews to their death, why did he go ahead and create a man like that? . . . If God is eternally certain that various individuals will end up being eternally damned, why does he go ahead and create them?"[13] Affirming a particular understanding of the future as including both settled certainties and unsettled possibilities, Boyd explains that the "open" view believes that God does know the future perfectly in reference to its certainties, but not in reference to its possibilities. One certainty is that eventually all things will be brought into subjection to Jesus Christ in the consummation of the creation's history. In the meantime, the possibilities are affected by human choices, so that there is nothing for God to know until the choices are made (Boyd, 16). In contrast, some theologians claim for God a "middle" knowledge that affirms for God the knowledge of all choices that humans will and even could make in all conceivable circumstances.

free-will theism. A contemporary group of evangelical theologians and philosophers views God as the transcendent Creator who grants humans sig-

---

12. Oden, *Living God,* 73.
13. Gregory A. Boyd, *God of the Possible: A Biblical Introduction to the Open View of God* (Grand Rapids: Baker Books, 2000), 10.

nificant freedom to cooperate with or work against God's will for them and the creation in general. God enters into dynamic relationships with humans, who respond to God's gracious initiatives as they will—and God responds to these responses. God takes "risks" by being open to humans in this way, but is endlessly resourceful and competent to finally work successfully toward ultimate divine goals. God chooses not to control everything that happens, but works within a dynamic environment that allows humans to participate with God in bringing the future into being. This view of God is understood to be truly biblical and most satisfying pastorally and devotionally.

According to Thomas Oden's reading of the classical tradition of Christian thought, "God allows and invites the personal freedom and self-determination of other wills within the history that God has enabled and created, and to which God is responsive within the framework of time."[14] Concludes David Basinger, "Since free-will theists believe that God has chosen to create a world in which humans have been granted the power to exercise pervasive, morally significant freedom of choice (and thus action) and that God cannot unilaterally ensure that humans exercising free choice will make the decisions he would have them make (and thus act as he would have them act), freewill theists conclude that God does not exercise unilateral control over many important aspects of what occurs in our earthly realm."[15] Norman Geisler and Wayne House are critical of free-will theism, calling it "neo-theism" and charging that it "capitulates to process theology, which seriously undermines historic Christianity."[16] See also **compatibilist vew; process.**

general revelation. God is knowable, at least in part, by a divine self-revelation that is "general" because (1) it is available equally to all and (2) it provides basic but not specific awareness of God's nature and will. Psalm 19 reports that "the heavens are telling the glory of God," so all people can and should know at least that God exists and is awesome. God has never left himself without a witness (Acts 14:17). While specific knowledge of God comes through Jesus Christ, the creation itself conveys something of God's presence and purposes. Thomas Aquinas (1224–1274) taught that human reason can know that there is transcendent reality, but cannot—apart from divine revelation—know what or who it is. Emil Brunner (1889–1965) diverged from Karl Barth (1886–1968) on the issue of "natural" revelation. Brunner

---

14. Oden, *Living God,* 94.
15. David Basinger, *The Case for Freewill Theism: A Philosophical Assessment* (Downers Grove, Ill.: InterVarsity Press, 1996), 36.
16. Norman L. Geisler and H. Wayne House, *The Battle for God: Responding to the Challenge of Neotheism* (Grand Rapids: Kregel Publications, 2001), 64.

said that there is a certain even if very limited knowledge of God available from creation, especially from the "orders of creation" such as the family. See also **deism; special revelation.**

glory of God. In the Bible, "glory" (Greek: *doxa*) refers to the ineffable majesty and shining splendor of God made evident in God's mighty works in the history of the creation. It is what humans can apprehend of the presence of God. The Son radiates God's glory (Heb. 1:3) in a way similar to God's earlier tabernacling presence in Israel (Heb. 9:2). God is the Father of glory (Eph. 1:17), and Jesus Christ is the Lord of glory (1 Cor. 2:8; 2 Cor. 4:4). The glory of God, who dwells in light unapproachable (1 Tim. 6:16), shone about the shepherds when Christ's birth was announced. The disciples saw God's glory in the earthly Jesus (John 1:14), and Paul said that the "hope of glory" lies in the indwelling Christ (Col. 1:27). It is in the face of Jesus Christ that the light of the knowledge of the glory of God shines in human hearts with creative power (2 Cor. 4:6). The church is never itself to be the object of glorification in this world, but can and should reflect the glory of God by being salt and light to the world (Matt. 5:13–16). "What is the chief end of man?" asks the Westminster Shorter Catechism (1647–1648). The answer: "Man's chief end is to glorify God and to enjoy him for ever." So believers may glorify God by a kind of reflection as they are changed into his likeness "from glory into glory" (2 Cor. 3:18).

holiness. Holiness, necessarily seen together with love, is the quintessential attribute of God. Its central meaning is separateness from all that is evil, unclean, and ordinary, therefore transcending all that belongs to the finiteness of this passing world. The Hebrew prophets often protested against reducing holiness to mere ceremonies (1 Sam. 15:22; Ps. 40:6–8; Hos. 6:6), insisting that God is opposed to all idolatry and injustice (moral and ethical dimensions of holiness). Just as God is holy, so the people of God are to be holy (1 Pet. 1:15–16). Again, holiness is necessarily coupled with love. The God who is majestic purity (holiness) is also the God who is gracefully outgoing to the sinner (love). The separate One who does not tolerate evil is also the incarnate One who comes to the sinner to redeem. Balance is crucial. In John Calvin's theology, God's sovereignty and majesty are much more prominent than God's love. For Karl Barth, God's holiness is ultimately in the service of God's love, which emanates from the depths of God's being. Says Donald Bloesch, "God's love and holiness constitute the inner nature of the living God. These two perfections coalesce in such a way that we may speak of the holy love of God . . . and of his merciful holiness. In the depth of God's love is revealed the beauty of his holiness. In the glory of his holiness is revealed the breadth of his love."[17] In Jesus Christ we approach the best understanding of the unity of God's holiness and mercy, the inseparability of God's intolerance of evil and yet his great love for the sinner.

Holy Spirit. The phrase "Holy Spirit" was used by the rabbis, often interchangeably with *shekinah* (from the Hebrew *shakan,* "to pitch one's tent"). The Spirit is God's presence on earth and active power in the present. This is a way of distinguishing the God we experience and know immediately from the utterly transcendent divinity who forever eludes us. The Spirit is the Hebrew *ruach* and the Greek *pneuma,* the presence, breath, and working of God. The Spirit is a mystery, like the wind, whose movements are too complex and hidden to predict or control (John 3:8). In Christianity, the Spirit is the third "person" of the Trinity. It is the Spirit who bears testimony in the present age to the Father and the Son. See also *homoiousios/homoousios.*

homoiousios/homoousios. The Greek *homoousios* literally means "made of the same stuff or substance." This controversial term was used by Athanasius and others to claim that Jesus was of the same nature (*ousia*) as God the Father and was himself to be thought of as genuinely divine as well as human. Thus, God was incarnate in Jesus to the point that knowing Jesus is actually contacting the essence of the Divine. Salvation of fallen humanity depends on the Son of God *being* God and not merely a great creature "like God." By subtle but significant contrast, *homoiousios* means "of a similar substance" or a "like being" (more the view of Arius) instead of the same substance or being. The difference between *homoousios* and *homoiousios* is that the former (which became the orthodox view) says that the Son *is* God and the latter says that the Son is *like* God. See also **Holy Spirit; incarnation; Trinity.**

idolatry. Human beings appear to need meaning in their lives. If God fails to be that satisfying perspective, then the intolerable vacuum is filled otherwise. The focus of idolatry is the worship of a human or humanly made object, value, or idea instead of the transcendent God. The common use of "icons" by Eastern Christians or statues by Roman Christians highlights the delicate and difficult distinction needed between an artistic aid to worship and an intolerable diversion from worship of God alone. The iconoclastic controversy from 725 to 842 that vigorously debated these matters. Should art be used to teach the faith, glorify God, and enhance worship, or should it be resisted as fostering the exact opposite? For Eastern Orthodox Christians, icons (pictures of Jesus and the saints) are seen as "windows into heaven," points of contact

17. Bloesch, *God the Almighty,* 141.

to aid in prayer and devotion, potential conveyors of the divine presence and energies. Other Christians, such as Quakers, judge such things as potentially dangerous distractions from focus on the true and unseen God. See also **energies of God.**

image of God (*imago Dei*). Biblically speaking, humans are created in the image of God (Gen. 1:26–27; 1 Cor. 11:7; Col. 1:15; Rom. 8:29; etc.). Humans are unique because we are God's creation and are capable of reflecting the divine being (or at least embodying something of some of the divine attributes). Jesus Christ, and by extension those in Christ, are bearers of the image of God. See also **deification.**

immanence. God is said to be present in, close to, and involved with the ongoing processes of creation. God is "not far from each one of us," for in God "we live and move and have our being" (Acts 17:27–28). This divine presence and involvement, however, do not mean that God is exhausted by creation or ceases to be divine in any way—as opposed to pantheism, which views God and the world as so intermingled as to be one, God being only the "soul" or animating principle of the world. A proper balance between the immanence and transcendence of God is vital, but often has not been maintained well. As Stanley Grenz and Roger Olson have made clear, "[T]wentieth-century theology illustrates how a lopsided emphasis on one or the other eventually engenders an opposing movement that, in its attempt to redress the imbalance, actually moves too far in the opposite direction."[18] See also **panentheism; pantheism; transcendence.**

immanent (essential) Trinity. The focus on the immanent or essential Trinity is human searching for knowledge of God's internal life and the relationships inherent among the three persons of the Trinity. This focus strives to express who God is apart from God's relationships with the creation. Father, Son, and Spirit are differentiated and affirmed to be real and true within the eternal being of God apart from the immediate biblical story of human salvation. God is a triune being prior to and independent of the creation. God may be experienced as triune because of a threefold manner of divine revelation, but the meaning of this revelation is also who God is intrinsically and eternally. See also **economic Trinity.** For caution about whether there can be any possible knowledge of the essence of God, see **apophatic theology.**

18. Stanley J. Grenz and Roger E. Olson, *20th Century Theology: God and the World in a Transitional Age* (Downers Grove, Ill.: InterVarsity Press, 1992), 12.

immutability. God's perfection calls for belief in a total divine unchange-ability. God does not experience development or change. God nature is "sim-ple" (totally integrated and consistent), with the divine nature, goals, plans, and ways of acting not subject to alteration. Since God is the being charac-terized by a series of perfections, any change from perfection is necessarily to lessen God—thus, there is and can be no change. This view was common-place among the early church fathers and doctors of the medieval church (Augustine, Anselm, Thomas Aquinas, etc.). Scripture clearly stresses the divine reliability, the constancy of God's purpose, and the trustworthiness of the divine nature. God remains consistent with his own nature and is "the same yesterday, today, and forever" (Heb. 13:8). There is no change in the essence of God's nature and will.

But does immutability imply divine unresponsiveness, or only constancy of covenant intent? Many Christian theologians have affirmed the former, while today many others (see **free-will theism**) argue to the contrary that the concept of a fully static God derives more from Greek philosophy than from biblical teaching. They distinguish between God's unchanging character and will and God's ability and willingness to change divine strategies and actions in response to changing humans and their decisions and circumstances. Psalm 102:26–27 and Hebrews 1:11–12 are concerned with the eternity and incorruptibility of God and should not be used to endorse the Greek idea of God's total unchangeability. Karl Barth sets forth a "holy mutability," mean-ing that God "is above all ages. But above them as their Lord . . . and there-fore as the One who—as Master and in His own way—partakes in their alteration, so that there is something corresponding to that alteration in His own essence. . . . God certainly is immutable, but as the immutable He is the living God and he possesses a mobility and elasticity which is no less divine than His perseverance."[19]

impassibility (*apatheia*). The Greek *apatheia* pointed ancient Greek philosophers and many early Christian theologians toward an emphasis on divine impassibility, serenity, and invulnerability. God's perfection was said to render the Divine invulnerable to suffering. God is not affected by tempo-ral circumstances, particularly by the experience of suffering. It is not that God is impassive and unfeeling, but that creatures cannot on their own will inflict God with pain, suffering, or distress. God may choose pain (e.g., the cross of Jesus), but is never the hapless victim and certainly is not at the mercy of the creation. What God suffered on the cross of Jesus was the suffering of

---

19. Karl Barth, *Church Dogmatics* II/2 (New York: Charles Scribner's Sons, 1957), 496.

the humanness of God *the Son,* not God *the Father*—who is above suffering. The divine nature itself is pure joy, shielded by definition from suffering. God's joy is eternal, not subject to any involuntary pain. "To affirm that God suffered on the cross or that Jesus suffered in His divine nature on the cross, is contrary to virtually every orthodox theologian from the earliest times through the Reformation."[20]

Influencing many contemporary theologians, Alfred North Whitehead hated the old Greek idea of *apatheia,* judging it almost blasphemous in its presentation of God as remote, selfish, and always unaffected by the creation (see **apatheia; patripassianism**). Some theologians (see **free-will theism**) now argue that the traditional concept of divine impassibility derives more from Greek philosophy than from biblical teaching; thus it should not stand without considerable modification.[21] The biblical view suggests that God's love brings a voluntary divine vulnerability to the suffering of the creation. Gregory of Nyssa countered the Hellenistic conception of a monarchial and remote deity as follows: "God's transcendent power is not so much displayed in the vastness of the heavens, or the luster of the stars, or the orderly arrangement of the universe or his perpetual oversight of it, as in his condescension to our weak nature."[22] Adds Donald Bloesch, "Suffering is not inherent in God, but God freely wills to enter into our suffering so that it can be overcome."[23]

incarnation. The classic Christian teaching on the mystery of God's incarnation (enfleshment) comes from the Council of Bishops that met at Chalcedon in 451. They affirmed "one and the same Son, our Lord Jesus Christ, at once complete in Godhead and complete in manhood, truly God and truly man . . . of one substance [*homoousios*] with the Father." Thus, Jesus is the second "person" of the Trinity.

The Greek word *logos* means "reason" or "word," and God's *Logos* was identified by Christian theologians with the "Wisdom" of God spoken of in the Jewish Scriptures, and the "Word" mentioned in the prologue of John's Gospel. The Greek *sophia* (wisdom) may be thought of as the personification of God's divine plan as presented in the Bible, with its fullest expression in God's incarnation in Jesus of Nazareth. See also **economic Trinity; immanent Trinity; Holy Spirit;** *homoiousios/homoousios.*

incompatibilist view of divine foreknowledge and human freedom. The theory that human free will is not consistent (i.e., is incompatible) with

20. Geisler and House, *Battle for God,* 181.
21. D. M. Baillie, *God Was in Christ* (New York: Charles Scribner's Sons, 1948), 198.
22. Gregory of Nyssa, *An Address on Religious Instruction.*
23. Bloesch, *God the Almighty,* 95.

God's sovereign prerogative to determine or will all things that are to happen. Divine determinism is inconsistent with voluntary human choice. "Providence" is the mysterious hand of God at work in all the phenomena of nature and history. God works by a divine grace that invites believing humans to be covenant partners in building the future that God intends. The Bible is said to affirm a "libertarian" freedom for humans, that is, the freedom to choose a course of action without prior divine determination. God always is present, but does not always exercise full control. Freedom for humans to choose is granted and real, including choices against God's known will. See also **compatibilist view.**

monotheism. Monotheism is belief in one God instead of multiple gods (polytheism). The three major monotheistic faith traditions are Judaism, Christianity, and Islam. The Bible excludes any metaphysical dualism. At times, monotheism has appeared to be in awkward tension with the Christian view of Trinitarianism.

moral argument for God's existence. See **arguments for God's existence.**

mysticism. Mysticism is the personal, experiential, contemplative quest for knowledge of and relationship with God by means of direct, nonabstract encounter or union with God. The Greek word *mystikos* refers to the "mystery" of God's love now made accessible in Jesus Christ. People are called to belong to the "fellowship of the mystery" (Eph. 3:9). John of the Cross (1542–1591) spoke of the mystic's triple way of purgation, illumination, and union. If rationalism tends to reduce God to the axioms of logic, mysticism tends to reduce God to an absolute mystery before which (whom) humans can only stand in wonder. For mystics, God can be spoken about only in metaphors and similes. While God can and should be experienced, God nonetheless remains essentially unknowable. For pure mysticism, God is more hidden than revealed. Christian mystics speak of the test of authentic relationship with God being the resulting fruit of the Spirit in one's life. John Wesley was both attracted to and repelled by aspects of the teachings of the Christian mystics.[24]

omnipotence. God has the unlimited ability to do whatever is consistent with the divine being, character, and plan for creation (God cannot deny himself, 2 Tim. 2:13). No power has any other source than God (Ps. 59:11–16; Rom. 13:1; Heb. 6:5). There is nothing too hard for God to do (Jer. 32:17); everything is possible with God (Matt. 19:26). The Nicene and Apostles' Creeds begin by

---

24. Robert Tuttle Jr., *Mysticism in the Wesleyan Tradition* (Grand Rapids: Francis Asbury Press, 1989).

affirming, "I believe in God, the Father *Almighty*." Divine power may be thought of as coercive or persuasive in its nature and typical exercise, with the latter option highlighted through the self-giving love made known on the cross (Col. 2:14–15). In the classical tradition of Christian theology, omnipotence came to be conceived in terms of self-expansion and control instead of self-emptying or self-limitation. Jürgen Moltmann has countered this tradition, reinterpreting the nature of divine power as suffering love rather than irresistible causality (appearing more in line with Isa. 53). Similarly, Wolfhart Pannenberg views divine power as the creative love that opens new possibilities of life and hope for the future of fallen humanity. Feminist theologians call for conceiving divine power as tender care and not domination and control. Biblically speaking, God's power is not capricious, but expresses the divine will that is determined by the holiness, love, and righteousness of God (Isa. 5:16). Says Gabriel Fackre, "In the ancient world, the Oriental potentate furnished the model of omnipotence, and God became the one who by fiat and force exercises immediate sway. . . . But the God of the biblical narrative is the God who is neither an autocratic regent nor a take-charge sheriff. This creator gives the world the space and time it needs to be what it will be. God does not normally act upon it by force or fiat but by vulnerable love."[25]

omnipresence. God is present everywhere in creation at the same time—or one might better say that all things are simultaneously present to God. No location lies beyond the cognition and care of God. God's way of being present with the creation is omnipresent, absolute. Says Proverbs 15:3, "The eyes of the LORD are in every place, keeping watch on the evil and the good." Implied is the sovereign dominion of God over all space. Martin Luther sought to safeguard the mystery that God both infinitely transcends creation and actively relates to every part of creation. God's presence fills all (Jer. 23:24), but all is not to be equated with God's being—which would verge on pantheism. See also **pantheism.**

omniscience. God knows all things without qualification. God's understanding is immeasurable (Ps. 147:4–5), including full awareness of the end from the beginning. Paul exclaimed, "O the depth of the riches and wisdom and knowledge of God! How unsearchable are his judgments and how inscrutable his ways!" (Rom. 11:33). "Before him no creature is hidden, but all are naked and laid bare to the eyes of the one to whom we must render an account" (Heb. 4:13). Daniel Day Williams held that God's knowledge "does not encompass all the specific aspects of future free decisions . . .[but]

25. Gabriel Fackre, *The Christian Story*, rev. ed. (Grand Rapids: Eerdmans, 1984), 258–59.

includes knowledge of all possible outcomes."[26] Jesus is said to be the wisdom of God (Luke 11:49). The book of Revelation calls wisdom an attribute of God (7:12) and of the exalted Christ (5:12). Believers can participate in divine wisdom through the outpouring of the Holy Spirit. To be omniscient, God need not know the future in complete detail (which would render human freedom largely illusory). See also **foreknowledge.**

"open" theism. See **free-will theism.**

panentheism. This Greek compound word means "everything (exists) in God." However, God is more than the universe (distinguishing it from *pantheism,* in which God and the universe are identical). It understands the world to be in an ontological relationship with God, somewhat analogous to God's incarnation in Jesus Christ (truly human, truly divine). This view of God allows both the theistic stance that God is distinct from the world and the pantheistic stance that God is inclusive of the world. God is both distinct and contingent, other than and enmeshed in, permeating and yet greater than creation.

Alfred North Whitehead and Charles Hartshorne developed slightly differing versions of panentheism that became the philosophical basis of process theology. John B. Cobb Jr. has seen the world, especially humankind, as cocreators with God and thus contributors to God's own life—so that God cannot be conceived apart from the world. "Open" theists such as Clark Pinnock use aspects of such process thought in careful coordination with biblical teaching. Richard Rice says that "dipolar theism shows clearly that God is not totally subject to the vicissitudes of change. True, in one pole of the divine reality, God changes constantly in response to events in the creaturely world. But in the other pole, God is utterly unchanging. Indeed, in this aspect of his being God is absolute, necessary, and immutable. This is the pole that individuates or identifies God."[27] Jürgen Moltmann's thought may be characterized as panentheism (God is *in* all) as opposed to pantheism (God *is* all) and atheism (God is *dissolved* in the all).

pantheism. Greek for "everything is God" (*pan,* "all"; *theos,* "God"). Carrying divine immanence as a high priority, pantheism identifies God with the creation, affirming that there is a unity of all reality. That unity is divine "theism"; however, with God as only the "soul" or animating principle of the world and the world as the "body" of God, there is thought to be no existence

26. Daniel Day Williams, *The Spirit and the Forms of Love* (New York: Harper & Row, 1968), 128.
27. John B. Cobb Jr., and Clark H. Pinnock, eds., *Searching for an Adequate God: A Dialogue between Process and Free Will Theists* (Grand Rapids: Eerdmans, 2000), 178.

of God apart from the world. While for traditional Christian theism God minus the world equals God, for pantheism God minus the world leaves nothing. Various religious traditions such as Hinduism tend to view reality in pantheistic ways. Pantheists are often mystical (see **mysticism**) and recognize little or no Creator-creation distinction. Pantheism is an opposite of deism. See also **deism; panentheism.**

patripassianism. This ancient teaching, finally judged heretical, is that God the Father was so identical with Jesus Christ that God died when Christ was crucified and died. Toward the end of the second century, Praxeas taught that the Godhead was emptied into the person of Christ without remainder. God came down into the Virgin's womb and was born as the Son. When the Son suffered, the Father suffered. When the Son died, the Father "died"—although the Father raised himself from the tomb to live on with us as the Spirit. A more recent and extreme form of this line of thought is that of theologian Thomas J. J. Altizer, who asserted in the 1960s that God died when Christ died on the cross. This was God's act of self-emptying and self-annihilation. There was no resurrection, said Altizer, so "radical" believers today are freed of the traditional conception of God as an almighty Creator reigning in transcendental glory. Replacing such a God is the secular presence of the Christ. What actually happened, according to Altizer, is that in the "death" God changed himself from his preincarnate form, becoming a secular presence for good among us instead of being the older remote, transcendent, impassible, self-sufficient being of classic theological thought. While this ancient heresy and modern radicalism are both wide of the biblical mark, the suffering of the Son should be linked closely to the experience and even the nature of the Father. Clark Pinnock writes, "The Father suffers the death of his Son and the Spirit feels both the Father's pain and the Son's self-surrender. . . . The kenosis of Christ is often mentioned, how he humbled himself and became a slave, but this self-emptying was what he had seen his kenotic Father do."[28]

process. This term suggests that reality is not static actuality but a course of becoming in which everyone and everything is intimately and dynamically interrelated. The contemporary movement of Christian process theology is philosophically and religiously opposed to much that has been meant by "God" in the Christian tradition. Reflective of the philosophy of Alfred North Whitehead, process thought especially rejects the notions that God is a cosmic moralist, the unchanging and passionless absolute, the all-controlling power who is male and sanctions the status quo. It sees itself recovering key

28. Pinnock, *Most Moved Mover,* 58.

biblical themes by emphasizing creative-responsive love as the basic character of God. Process theology teaches a "dipolar theism." God is said to have two poles or aspects, one an independent and unchanging abstract essence and the other a concrete actuality that is temporal, relative, dependent, and constantly changing. In the second pole God is "finite," with divine knowledge deriving from developments and the divine emotional state changing as God rejoices with our rejoicings and suffers with our sufferings. God works always lovingly and for the good, using persuasion and not a coercion that violates human freedom. To the degree that we humans allow God to do so, God makes all things new. This school of thought has been very influential in recent Christian theology and brings balance back to various theological assertions about God common in the classic Christian tradition. Even so, many insist that it is an overreaction that finally winds up with a dramatically limited God not adequately reflective of the biblical revelation. See also **foreknowledge; free-will theism.**

sovereignty. Sovereignty refers to the biblical concept of God's absolute and supreme rule and authority over the creation in its entirety. God precedes and supersedes all of creation. Sovereignty as a category is especially emphasized in the Augustinian-Calvinist tradition. It is argued that, without at any stage violating human freedom, God acts and accomplishes everything intended, and exactly as intended. God's sovereignty overrules human disobedience and satanic obstruction. Another Christian tradition insists that sovereignty is not synonymous with "all-controlling." The sovereign God is free to function as his nature and will direct, including a loving nature that chooses to grant meaningful freedom to humans—a freedom with which God must contend when it is misused. Only this style of sovereignty is said to make love possible between Creator and creature. See also **free-will theism.**

special revelation. Beyond "general" revelation, God has chosen to be self-revealed in very specific ways, first to Israel and more fully in the incarnation in Jesus Christ and its New Testament interpretation. Karl Barth denied the reality of revelation outside of Jesus Christ. Thomas Aquinas disagreed, although admitting that little beyond God's existence can be known philosophically. Special revelation is necessary. See also **general revelation.**

subordinationism. Within the three persons of the Trinity there is a vital interdependence, such as the Son in relation to the Father and the Spirit in relation to the Father and Son. Differences of function among the divine persons of the Godhead may be said to involve the voluntary subordination of one to the others. Sometimes, however, teachings about such "subordination" has extended to the degree that they have been judged heresies, perversions of the basic Christian concept of God. All subordinationisms that strip full divinity from any person of the Trinity become unacceptable alternatives to orthodox Trinitarianism. Typically such alternatives affirm the "Father" as fully God and then subordinate the Son and/or the Spirit beneath the Father, arguing that they are divine in some sense while also being lesser beings than the Father. The two basic forms of unacceptable subordinationism are adoptionism and Arianism. See also *filioque.*

teleological argument for God's existence. See **arguments for God's existence.**

theism. Any worldview anchored in the belief that there is a God and that God is the foundational reality that informs all other reality. Judaism, Christianity, and Islam together affirm monotheism (one God). Given classic Christian thought, God is the Creator who is distinct from the creation (*contra* **pantheism**) but also constantly active in the creation (*contra* **deism**) and therefore is worthy of worship. See also **agnosticism/atheism; deism; monotheism; pantheism.**

theodicy. Combining the subjects of God (*theos*) and justice (*dike*), theodicy is the attempt to relate constructively belief in God and the problem of evil in the world. Theodicies attempt explanations and defenses of God as simultaneously loving, just, and all-powerful in spite of evil's reality. How can God be glorious and worthy of praise in the face of dramatic appearances of evil that seem to argue strongly to the contrary? Many Jews, for instance, lost faith in God after the Holocaust. How could this have happened if God truly is God, being both loving and omnipotent? Writers such as Clark Williamson insist that Christians today can do responsible theology only as they deal with a terrible evil like anti-Semitism. On the line is the credibility of a sovereign God who presumably is good, just, and able to stop evil. If God is all of these, then theodicy seeks to explain and even justify the present reality of evil.

theology. This word names the pursuit of wisdom (*logos*) concerning God (*theos*). Theology moves back and forth between two poles, the eternal truth of its foundation and the temporal situation in which this eternal truth must be received and communicated.[29] Theology typically "tries to strike up a conversation between the Christian scriptures and tradition on the one hand and

---

29. Paul Tillich, *Systematic Theology,* vol. 1 (Chicago: University of Chicago Press, 1951), 3.

the context in which we live on the other."[30] It is "reflecting on and articulating the God-centered life and beliefs that Christians share as followers of Jesus Christ, and it is done in order that God may be glorified in all Christians are and do."[31]

theophany. A manifestation of God to humans is a theophany. God wishes to be known and chooses to appear. The problem revolves around the divine assertion "God is spirit" (John 4:24) so that no person has ever seen God (John 1:18). But Genesis 32:30 reports that "I have seen God face to face." The Old Testament reports various manifestations of God in some empirical form. In the Christian calendar there is the season of Epiphany (the manifestation or appearance), often highlighting the baptism of Jesus and his first miracle at Cana—events by which Jesus emerged from his youthful obscurity to carry on a ministry that brought God to humanity.

transcendence. This word is from the Latin for "go beyond." God is related to the creation as the Transcendent One, self-sufficient, having being apart from the world. God is other than the world and comes to it from beyond it. "God is in heaven and you are on earth," writes the Preacher (Eccl. 5:2). The Lord is "seated on a throne, high and exalted" (Isa. 6:1). Such affirmations do not mean that God is not present and involved in the creation, only that God is prior to, more than, and goes beyond the creation.

A proper balance between the transcendence and immanence of God is vital. As Stanley Grenz and Roger Olson have made clear, "[T]wentieth-century theology illustrates how a lopsided emphasis on one or the other eventually engenders an opposing movement that, in its attempt to redress the imbalance, actually moves too far in the opposite direction."[32] Process theology is open to the charge of overstressing God's immanence to the unjustified detriment of transcendence, so that God is pictured as struggling in an evolving cosmos, with even the Divine somehow being finite and also evolving. Allan Coppedge (*Portraits of God*) elaborates on eight central roles of God as biblically revealed, with four placing accent on God's transcendence (Creator, King, Judge, and Redeemer) and four on God's immanence (Personal Revealer, Priest, Shepherd, and Father). All eight together provide a holistic picture of God. See also **immanence.**

30. Clark M. Williamson, *Way of Blessing, Way of Life: A Christian Theology* (St. Louis: Chalice Press, 1999), 3.

31. Stanley J. Grenz and Roger E. Olson, *Who Needs Theology? An Invitation to the Study of God* (Downers Grove, Ill.: InterVarsity Press, 1996), 49.

32. Grenz and Olson, *20th Century Theology,* 12.

Trinity. Trinity is the distinctive Christian understanding of God as triune in both essence and activity. The one divine nature is a unity of three distinguishable "persons"—Father, Son, and Spirit. God the Father is self-revealed in Jesus the Son, and poured out in the Spirit, who is the Spirit of Jesus sent by the Father (see *filioque*). Within the complex unity of the one divine being are three personal centers of identity that eternally interpenetrate, relate in mutual love, and cooperate in all of God's actions. The New Testament presents human salvation as the joint work of the three persons (e.g., Rom. 3; 1 Cor. 12:3–6; 2 Cor. 13:14; Eph. 1; 2 Thess. 2:13–14; Rev. 1:4–5). The classic Trinity doctrine emerged from the two church councils of the fourth century, resulting in the Nicene Creed. God is said there to be three persons (*hypostases*) and one substance (*ousia*). See also **economic Trinity; Holy Spirit; immanent Trinity; subordinationism.**

Yahweh. The name of God in Israel was Yahweh. By the third century before the birth of Jesus, Jews no longer pronounced this holy name. When Moses asked for Yahweh's name and credentials, God replied with a pun, saying, "I AM WHO I AM" or "I WILL BE WHO I WILL BE" is my name (*ehyeh asher ehyeh*, Exod. 3:14). This is a Hebrew idiom conveying a deliberate distance and vagueness and also a comforting assurance. It might be translated "Never mind who I am!" or "I shall be who I shall be, which will be more than adequate for anything you will need!" There was to be no abstract comprehension of the divine being and certainly no manipulation of the divine as pagans hoped to do when they recited the names of their gods. Yahweh is the mysterious and unconditioned One, who will be as he chooses and who promises to be with his people and increasingly known by them in the course of their faithfulness in the drama of unfolding history.

Figures

Insets

Index